IFIP Advances in Information and Communication Technology

666

Editor-in-Chief

Kai Rannenberg, Goethe University Frankfurt, Germany

Editorial Board Members

IFIP – The International Federation for Information Processing

IFIP was founded in 1960 under the auspices of UNESCO, following the first World Computer Congress held in Paris the previous year. A federation for societies working in information processing, IFIP's aim is two-fold: to support information processing in the countries of its members and to encourage technology transfer to developing nations. As its mission statement clearly states:

> *IFIP is the global non-profit federation of societies of ICT professionals that aims at achieving a worldwide professional and socially responsible development and application of information and communication technologies.*

IFIP is a non-profit-making organization, run almost solely by 2500 volunteers. It operates through a number of technical committees and working groups, which organize events and publications. IFIP's events range from large international open conferences to working conferences and local seminars.

The flagship event is the IFIP World Computer Congress, at which both invited and contributed papers are presented. Contributed papers are rigorously refereed and the rejection rate is high.

As with the Congress, participation in the open conferences is open to all and papers may be invited or submitted. Again, submitted papers are stringently refereed.

The working conferences are structured differently. They are usually run by a working group and attendance is generally smaller and occasionally by invitation only. Their purpose is to create an atmosphere conducive to innovation and development. Refereeing is also rigorous and papers are subjected to extensive group discussion.

Publications arising from IFIP events vary. The papers presented at the IFIP World Computer Congress and at open conferences are published as conference proceedings, while the results of the working conferences are often published as collections of selected and edited papers.

IFIP distinguishes three types of institutional membership: Country Representative Members, Members at Large, and Associate Members. The type of organization that can apply for membership is a wide variety and includes national or international societies of individual computer scientists/ICT professionals, associations or federations of such societies, government institutions/government related organizations, national or international research institutes or consortia, universities, academies of sciences, companies, national or international associations or federations of companies.

More information about this series at https://link.springer.com/bookseries/6102

Jason Staggs · Sujeet Shenoi (Eds.)

Critical Infrastructure Protection XVI

16th IFIP WG 11.10 International Conference, ICCIP 2022
Virtual Event, March 14–15, 2022
Revised Selected Papers

 Springer

Editors
Jason Staggs
University of Tulsa
Tulsa, OK, USA

Sujeet Shenoi
University of Tulsa
Tulsa, OK, USA

ISSN 1868-4238   ISSN 1868-422X (electronic)
IFIP Advances in Information and Communication Technology
ISBN 978-3-031-20139-4   ISBN 978-3-031-20137-0 (eBook)
https://doi.org/10.1007/978-3-031-20137-0

This Springer imprint is published by the registered company Springer Nature Switzerland AG
The registered company address is: Gewerbestrasse 11, 6330 Cham, Switzerland

Contents

Contributing Authors

Irfan Ahmed is an Associate Professor of Computer Science at Virginia Commonwealth University, Richmond, Virginia. His research interests include cyber security, digital forensics, malware, cyber-physical systems and cyber security education.

Muhammad Ahsan is a Ph.D. student in Computer Science at Virginia Commonwealth University, Richmond, Virginia. His research interests include securing cyber-physical systems with a focus on using side channels for monitoring additive manufacturing systems.

Radhika Barua is an Assistant Professor of Mechanical Engineering at Virginia Commonwealth University, Richmond, Virginia. Her research interests include rare-earth-free magnetic alloys, magnetoceramics, low-cost magnetic materials processing, metal additive manufacturing and advanced magnetic material characterization using synchrotron probes.

Alexander Beall is an Electrical Engineer and Researcher at Johns Hopkins University Applied Physics Laboratory, Laurel, Maryland. His research interests include resilient control systems, digital twin technology and critical infrastructure protection.

James Cervini is a Doctor of Engineering student at Johns Hopkins University, Baltimore, Maryland; and a Cyber Security Engineer at Johns Hopkins University Applied Physics Laboratory, Laurel, Maryland. His research interests include operational technology cyber security, virtualization, fog computing and penetration testing.

Samuel Chadwick recently completed his M.S. degree in Computer Engineering at the Air Force Institute of Technology, Wright-Patterson Air Force Base, Ohio. His research interests include computer networking, hardware security and critical infrastructure protection.

Gilbert Clark is a Researcher at the Air Force Research Laboratory, Wright-Patterson Air Force Base, Ohio. His research interests include computer networking, embedded systems security, cyber-physical systems security and critical infrastructure protection.

Matthew Dallmeyer is a Cyber Security Research Engineer at the Air Force Institute of Technology, Wright-Patterson Air Force Base, Ohio. His research interests include computer architecture, side-channel analysis and avionics security.

Joel Dawson is a Cyber Security Researcher in the Energy and Control System Security Group at Oak Ridge National Laboratory, Oak Ridge, Tennessee. His research interests include side-channel analysis, advanced manufacturing security and novel challenges in emerging cyber-physical systems.

James Dean is an Assistant Professor of Computer Engineering at the Air Force Institute of Technology, Wright-Patterson Air Force Base, Ohio. His research interests include, deep learning for side-channel analysis, secure processor architecture and vision-aided navigation.

Noah Diamond recently completed his M.S. degree in Computer Engineering at the Air Force Institute of Technology, Wright-Patterson Air Force Base, Ohio. His research interests include computer networking, hardware security and critical infrastructure protection.

Stephen Dunlap is a Cyber Security Research Engineer at the Air Force Institute of Technology, Wright-Patterson Air Force Base, Ohio. His research interests include embedded systems security, cyber-physical systems security and critical infrastructure protection.

Scott Graham is a Professor of Computer Engineering at the Air Force Institute of Technology, Wright-Patterson Air Force Base, Ohio. His research interests include embedded and communications systems security, vehicle cyber security and critical infrastructure protection.

Janne Hagen is a Special Advisor at the Norwegian Water Resources and Energy Directorate, Oslo, Norway; and an Associate Professor at the Institute for Informatics, University of Oslo, Oslo, Norway. Her research interests include cyber security, critical infrastructure protection and security governance.

Bernhard Hämmerli is a Professor of Information and Network Security at the Norwegian University of Science and Technology, Gjovik, Norway; and a Professor of Information and Cyber Security at Lucerne University of Applied Sciences and Arts, Lucerne, Switzerland. His research interests include cyber security, critical infrastructure and operational technology ranging from the technical to the governance and strategic levels.

Elizabeth Kurkowski is a Cyber Security Engineer at Johns Hopkins University Applied Physics Laboratory, Laurel, Maryland. Her research interests include additive manufacturing security, software reverse engineering, networks and critical infrastructure protection.

Ulf Lindqvist is a Senior Technical Director in the Computer Science Laboratory at SRI International, San Luis Obispo, California. His research interests include cyber security, infrastructure systems, intrusion detection and security for systems that interact with the physical world.

Joseph Maurio is the Chief Scientist of the Critical Infrastructure Protection Group at Johns Hopkins University Applied Physics Laboratory, Laurel, Maryland. His research interests include resilient control systems, digital twin technology and critical infrastructure protection.

Daniel Muller is a Cyber Security Engineer and Researcher at Johns Hopkins University Applied Physics Laboratory, Laurel, Maryland. His research interests include cyber-physical systems security, network security and critical infrastructure protection.

Calvin Muramoto recently completed his M.S. degree in Cyber Operations at the Air Force Institute of Technology, Wright-Patterson Air Force Base, Ohio. His research interests include data analytics, hardware security and critical infrastructure protection.

Tiffany Potok is a Cyber Security Technical Professional in the Embedded Systems Security Group at Oak Ridge National Laboratory, Oak Ridge, Tennessee. Her research interests include network and manufacturing cyber security, and data analysis.

Rob Prins is a Professor of Engineering at James Madison University, Harrisonburg, Virginia. His research interests include mechanical properties of specimens generated by additive manufacturing processes and the application of natural-fiber-reinforced composites in additive manufacturing.

Muhammad Haris Rais is a Ph.D. student in Computer Science at Virginia Commonwealth University, Richmond, Virginia. His research interests include cyber security and digital forensics of industrial control systems and additive manufacturing processes.

Mason Rice is a Distinguished Researcher at Oak Ridge National Laboratory, Oak Ridge, Tennessee. His research interests include cyberphysical systems and critical infrastructure protection.

Aviel Rubin is a Professor of Computer Science and the Technical Director of the Information Security Institute at Johns Hopkins University, Baltimore, Maryland. His research interests include medical device security and applied cryptography.

Tricia Schulz is a Senior Research Scientist and Leader of the Embedded Systems Security Group at Oak Ridge National Laboratory, Oak Ridge, Tennessee. Her research interests include hardware and software vulnerabilities in industrial control systems and embedded devices.

Vaibhav Sharma is a Ph.D. student in Mechanical Engineering at Virginia Commonwealth University, Richmond, Virginia. His research interests include magnetic refrigeration and additive manufacturing technology schemes for processing high-performance magnetic materials.

Sujeet Shenoi is the F.P. Walter Professor of Computer Science and a Professor of Chemical Engineering at the University of Tulsa, Tulsa, Oklahoma. His research interests include critical infrastructure protection, industrial control systems and digital forensics.

Curtis Taylor is a Cyber Security Research Scientist at Oak Ridge National Laboratory, Oak Ridge, Tennessee. His research interests include cyber-physical systems and network and system security related to the electric grid, additive manufacturing, vehicles and industrial control systems.

Laura Tinnel is a Senior Computer Scientist in the Computer Science Laboratory at SRI International, Arlington, Virginia. Her research interests include cyber security architectures and system analysis, adversary and attack modeling, and cyber experimentation and testing.

Oyvind Toftegaard is a Senior Advisor at the Norwegian Energy Regulatory Authority, Oslo, Norway; and a Ph.D. student in Information Security and Communications Technology at the Norwegian University of Science and Technology, Gjovik, Norway. His research interests include cyber security, electric power systems and policy analysis.

Alyxandra Van Stockum recently completed her Ph.D. degree in Computer Science at the University of Tulsa, Tulsa, Oklahoma. Her research interests include additive manufacturing security, threat modeling design and implementation, and penetration testing.

Lanier Watkins is a Principal Cyber Security Research Scientist at Johns Hopkins University Applied Physics Laboratory, Laurel, Maryland. His research interests include assured artificial intelligence, data analytics and Internet of Things security.

Neal Ziring is the Technical Director of the Cybersecurity Directorate at the National Security Agency, Fort Meade, Maryland. His research interests include access control systems, security architecture, IPv6 and cyber resilience.

Preface

The information infrastructure – comprising computers, embedded devices, networks and software systems – is vital to operations in every sector: chemicals, commercial facilities, communications, critical manufacturing, dams, defense industrial base, emergency services, energy, financial services, food and agriculture, government facilities, healthcare and public health, information technology, nuclear reactors, materials and waste, transportation systems, and water and wastewater systems. Global business and industry, governments, indeed society itself, cannot function if major components of the critical information infrastructure are degraded, disabled or destroyed.

This book, *Critical Infrastructure Protection XVI*, is the sixteenth volume in the annual series produced by IFIP Working Group 11.10 on Critical Infrastructure Protection, an active international community of scientists, engineers, practitioners and policy makers dedicated to advancing research, development and implementation efforts related to critical infrastructure protection. The book presents original research results and innovative applications in the area of critical infrastructure protection. Also, it highlights the importance of weaving science, technology and policy in crafting sophisticated, yet practical, solutions that will help secure information, computer and network assets in the various critical infrastructure sectors.

This volume contains eleven selected papers from the Sixteenth Annual IFIP Working Group 11.10 International Conference on Critical Infrastructure Protection, which was held virtually on March 14–15, 2022. The papers were refereed by members of IFIP Working Group 11.10 and other internationally-recognized experts in critical infrastructure protection. The post-conference manuscripts submitted by the authors were rewritten to accommodate the suggestions provided by the conference attendees. The eleven selected papers were subsequently revised by the editors to produce the final chapters published in this volume.

The chapters are organized into five sections: (i) themes and issues; (ii) industrial control systems security; (iii) additive manufacturing systems; (iv) infrastructure device security; and (v) telecommunications systems security. The coverage of topics showcases the richness and vitality of the discipline, and offers promising avenues for future research in critical infrastructure protection.

This book is the result of the combined efforts of several individuals and organizations. In particular, we thank David Balenson for his tireless work on behalf of IFIP Working Group 11.10. We also thank the National Science Foundation, U.S. Department of Homeland Security, National Security Agency and SRI International for their support of IFIP Working Group 11.10 and its activities. Finally, we wish to note that all opinions, findings, conclusions and recommendations in the chapters of this book are those of the authors and do not necessarily reflect the views of their employers or funding agencies.

JASON STAGGS AND SUJEET SHENOI

I

THEMES AND ISSUES

Chapter 1

NATIONAL CYBER RESILIENCE AND ROLES FOR PUBLIC AND PRIVATE SECTOR STAKEHOLDERS

Neal Ziring

Abstract   Modern nations are dependent on cyberspace, specifically, on information technology, data communications, smart mobile devices and other globally-connected and computing-enabled services. The dependence includes government operations, national defense, critical infrastructure and economic prosperity. However, cyberspace is subject to accidental disruptions and malicious attacks from a wide variety of sources. Therefore, to ensure resilient functioning, every nation must possess a resilient cyberspace. This chapter describes a model for large-scale (regional to national) resilience of cyberspace, describes mechanisms for applying the model to improve overall national resilience and identifies key stakeholders for implementing the mechanisms in the United States.

Keywords: Cyber security, public sector, private sector, cyber resilience

1. Introduction

The United States and other modern nations depend on a broad set of critical infrastructures to support their populations. The infrastructures depend on each other in multiple ways, but in the most general sense, they form a web of interdependencies such that a sustained disruption of one infrastructure can degrade or halt operations in other infrastructures [22, 74]. For example, the financial system depends on the power grid – banks cannot operate for long without electricity. Interdependencies in multiple critical infrastructures is a broad subject area. This work assumes that national functions, including other critical infrastructures, depend on the availability and reliability of the cyber infrastructure. Therefore, to minimize disruptions of national functions,

© IFIP International Federation for Information Processing 2022
Published by Springer Nature Switzerland AG 2022
J. Staggs and S. Shenoi (Eds.): Critical Infrastructure Protection XVI, IFIP AICT 666, pp. 3–46, 2022.
https://doi.org/10.1007/978-3-031-20137-0_1

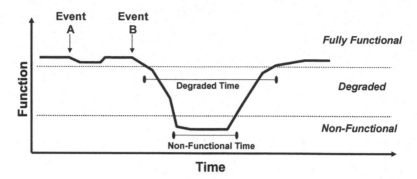

Figure 1. Impact of a disruptive event.

and bolster national security, economic prosperity and societal wellbeing, every nation should ensure that its cyber infrastructure is resilient – resistant to disruptions and attacks and quick to recover.

Resilient cyber infrastructure must be created in a deliberate manner – resilience requires intentional design and focused operation. This chapter defines the properties of a resilient cyber infrastructure, presents a model for achieving resilience at large scales and applies the model at a national scale using the United States as exemplar. Naturally, the operation of any cyber infrastructure depends on other critical infrastructures such as power and transportation. However, the composition and reliability of these infrastructures at a large scale, albeit critical, are outside the scope of this work.

Before considering the properties of resilient cyber infrastructure, it is necessary to select a definition of resilience and a bounded scope for the cyber infrastructure. Resilience is defined in the U.S. national security strategy [33] and other national security documents as "the ability to withstand and recover rapidly from deliberate attacks, accidents, natural disasters, as well as unconventional stresses, shocks and threats." This definition, like others, incorporates two essential elements, the ability to resist degradation and disruption (withstand) and the ability to recover from disruptions that it cannot resist.

One way of measuring the resilience of a service is to characterize the events that impact service functionality and the duration and severity of the impacts. Figure 1 presents the impact of a disruptive event based on the general model presented by Cybenko [21]. The notional service in the figure has a level of functionality that its users expect. Anything above this level is considered to be fully functional. Levels of functionality below the level, but still above some minimum, are considered to be degraded operations. Service below the minimum level is considered to be non-functional.

The service in Figure 1 withstands Event A; there is some impact, but the service remains fully functional. However, the service experiences a serious impact from Event B; it is non-functional for a certain duration and degraded for a longer duration. In practical terms, the resilience of a service is greater when it can withstand more salient events and when the degraded and non-functional durations are shorter.

Cyber infrastructure is a complicated term with no standard definition. The term came into common use after a 2003 report by a U.S. National Science Foundation advisory panel on cyber infrastructure [8]; interestingly, the panel report focused on infrastructure for supporting research.

The U.S. communications infrastructure sector is formally defined by the U.S. Department of Homeland Security (DHS) [22]. However, this sector partially overlaps with cyber infrastructure because the communications sector definition omits the computation, storage, discovery and automated service facets of cyberspace.

Several articles described in the related work section below offer definitions of cyber infrastructure. They are all reasonable, but they lack consistency and detail. They were used as inputs to arrive at the definition used in this work.

In this work, cyber infrastructure is defined as comprising four high-level categories according to the model described in [82]:

- **Physical Support Elements:** These elements include facilities, buildings, cables, antennas, towers, satellites and other physical artifacts that host the cyber infrastructure.

- **Communications Elements:** These elements support the transfer of data between users and infrastructure services, among users and between other elements of the infrastructure. The elements include control systems and overlays that facilitate or manage the communications. Communications elements can be subdivided further in many ways, but in this work, the salient division is between the communications links and the control systems that monitor and manage the links.

- **Computation and Storage Elements:** These elements correspond to the services that support cyberspace users by providing search and retrieval, information management and state update functionality. The category includes three sub-categories:

- Registration, provisioning and discovery services that support the operation of higher-level services.
- Security services, including foundational services that support identification, authentication, access control and integrity.
- Platform services and shared infrastructure elements that provide computational and storage resources to users.

■ **Business and Governance Elements:** These elements correspond to user-level processes that oversee and enable the infrastructure. The elements include economic processes such as billing and financing, regulatory regimes and stakeholder governance.

Detailed lists of technologies and services that comprise the four categories listed above are presented later in this chapter. The resilience analysis described in this work focuses primarily on the communications element and the computation and storage element categories. However, the implementation of resilience improvements would affect all the categories and would require the addition of resilience as a goal in the business and governance element category.

2.   Related Work

This section discusses the literature related to cyber infrastructure threats and cyber infrastructure resilience.

2.1   Cyber Infrastructure Threats

The rich literature on cyber threats and associated security measures dates back to early threats against communications and information systems. Several historical surveys have been published that offer differing views of how threats have been addressed from an information-centric perspective [25] to an emphasis on cryptology [50].

Security threats to computer systems gained attention in the 1960s with the advent of multi-user and time-sharing systems. The early computers were not, typically, connected to each other, and security controls were focused on local threats such as unauthorized data access (confidentiality threat) and interference with shared system functionality (availability threat). A fascinating early example of threats to virtual machine infrastructures covers denial of service and theft of data [58]. Most of the early work was not systematic, focusing on specific threats to, and security features of, specific systems (e.g., Adept-50 system [92]) and on the theoretical foundations of system design (e.g., Saltzer and Schroeder's seminal work [77]). The first systematic treatment was the U.S. Department of Defense's technical evaluation criteria for secure computer systems (TCSEC) proposed in 1979 [64] and codified in 1985 [86]. Despite the emphasis on confidentiality implicit in TCSEC, it defined a rigorous approach to enumerating threat mitigation controls and evaluating their implementation.

The growth of computer networks in the 1980s and early 1990s drew attention to threats against computer networks and their underlying communications. The earliest treatment of threats to large-scale networks such as the Internet was published in 1983 [91].

Modern treatments of cyber infrastructure threats focus on two broad areas, threats to the communications infrastructure from all sources and cyber threats to critical infrastructures in general. A good example of the former is a 2010 survey by Sterbenz et al. [81] on the resilience of communications networks. Threats to critical infrastructure and mitigating them gained national attention in the United States in the mid-1990s, culminating in the creation of the President's Commission on Critical Infrastructure Protection [16]. Emphasis on cyber threats emerged in the early 2000s after Internet worms demonstrated that cyber attacks could cause serious harm to businesses and government [62].

Around the same time, in the late 1990s and early 2000s, the national security community began to focus on risks posed by state and non-state actors that leverage cyber means to advance national aims or conduct large-scale attacks [27, 54, 72]. As evidence of cyber warfare programs emerged over the decade, practical concerns about threats and effective responses gained attention [40].

As cyber infrastructure diversified over the first two decades of the 21st century, considerable research focused on threats and resilience related to cyber infrastructure in general [31] as well as specific infrastructure components. Examples of the latter include the routing infrastructure [14], Domain Name System [7] and transoceanic cables [69]. As companies and governments adopted cloud computing services, researchers noted the broad spectrum of threats to the cloud, including their reliance on other cyber infrastructures [76]. With the emergence of the Internet of Things as a concept in the early 2000s and the proliferation of connected objects starting around 2010, the potential for cyber attacks to affect the physical world has greatly increased. Threat and security research on the Internet of Things has been very active since 2010; recent publications with broad coverage include [1, 12].

2.2 Cyber Infrastructure Resilience

The topic of resilience has been researched for decades and applied to communications and computing systems for nearly as long as the technologies have existed. This review covers work that directly contributes to the analysis and improvement of cyber resilience at a large scale.

Several studies have focused on failures of the Internet and its infrastructure dating back to the first Internet worm [80]. More recent assessments have examined the Internet and its core infrastructures with the intent of characterizing failure modes to inform improvements [30, 93]. The long-term evolution of denial-of-service attacks, from the late 1990s to the present day, has been examined in many ways; a good survey is provided by Mansfield-Devine [59].

General studies of infrastructure resilience have been undertaken by researchers around the world, many of them focus on resilience to natural disasters (see, e.g., [11]). General [9] and cyber-specific [56] models have been proposed for measuring resilience, as well as models for engineering resilient cyber systems [10].

As the reliance of the U.S. military on networks and cyber services increased, national defense analysts became concerned about cyber threats to military operations. This concern led to an in-depth study by the U.S. Defense Science Board that recommended measures for making military operations resilient to advanced cyber threats [26].

The cyber infrastructure has been recognized as a salient aspect of national security and its defense and resilience are vital to the overall national security posture. An exceptional treatment is the coverage of the role of cyberspace in the national security posture of the United Kingdom [19]. Military requirements for cyber capabilities as part of national defense appear consistently in U.S. defense strategy documents since 2005.

3.   Cyber Infrastructure and Threats

Cyber infrastructure is a complex and dynamic fabric comprising multiple technologies and services. This section presents a simple layered model for cyber infrastructure and describes the threats to the large-scale operation of cyber infrastructure organized according to the layered model.

3.1   Cyber Infrastructure Model

A wide variety of technologies, standards, practices and systems underpin the modern cyber infrastructure. The infrastructure components depend on each other in complex ways, but can be envisioned as a set of layers where each layer depends primarily on the layers beneath it.

Figure 2 shows the basic cyber infrastructure layers. Each layer comprises multiple services with complex dependencies. For reasons of space,

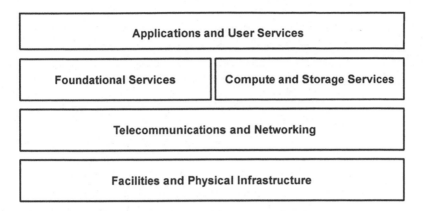

Figure 2. Basic cyber infrastructure layers.

it is not possible to describe all the services in detail; however, references are provided to technical details about the services. Additionally, a large body of mature engineering and operational expertise exists for the bottom facilities and physical infrastructure layer and the top applications and user services layer. Therefore, this chapter focuses on the middle layers, the foundational services, compute and storage services, and telecommunications and networking layers.

The foundational services layer provides the functionality that supports the applications and user services layer. This includes services for discovery, information distribution and security. Table 1 describes the five main elements of the foundational services layer. Interested readers are referred to [5, 6, 29] for details about the foundational services layer.

The compute and storage services layer provides services that host operational systems and services employed by enterprises, which are vital to customers, partners and citizens. In the early days of computing, most enterprises simply purchased computing hardware and operated the equipment in their own facilities. However, public and private enterprises often rely on external service providers for storage, compute, data dissemination, office automation and numerous other services. The dependence on external providers is growing steadily; in 2018, 73% of businesses worldwide hosted some of their applications externally [47]. Table 2 describes the four main elements of the compute and storage services layer.

The telecommunications and networking layer orchestrates the movement of data traffic that supports the upper layers of the cyber infrastructure. Also, it provides connectivity and user-to-user communications services to subscribers, which include enterprises and individuals. Ta-

Table 1. Foundational services layer elements.

Element	Description
Domain Name System	The Domain Name System (DNS) provides translations between hierarchical names (e.g., www.gwu.edu) and network addresses (e.g., 104.17.56.239). Also, it provides look-up for services (e.g., email) to service endpoints [17, 57].
Email	Email services, employing multiple protocols (ESMTP, POP, IMAP) and data formats (MIME, S/MIME), are used for reliable store-and-forward transfer of short messages and files [17, 20].
Web	The World Wide Web (WWW) infrastructure provides services over unsecured (HTTP) and secured (HTTPS) connections that support human and machine interactions [17].
Messaging	Several real-time messaging services are offered in cyberspace for communications between users and as foundational services for distributed applications. This service category is not effectively standardized, but it underlies a range of mobile, web and business applications (distinct from the Short Message Service provided by the telecommunications layer) [32, 49].
Public Key Infrastructure	A public key infrastructure (PKI) provides services for issuing trust artifacts (keys and certificates) and validating them [44].

Table 2. Compute and storage services layer elements.

Element	Description
Utility Compute	Computational services support business, mission and academic applications. The services are offered via diverse delivery models and often support reliability and disaster recovery.
Storage, Backup and Retrieval	Storage services are offered via various models and typically provide long-term storage and retrieval with availability and latency guarantees. The services support reliability and disaster recovery.
Content Delivery	Delivery services support large-scale data dissemination for various purposes. Most software downloads for establishing and maintaining enterprise applications employ these services.
Business Services	Compute and storage providers offer a variety of aggregated and hosted business services that support resource management, logistics, financial transactions and human capital management.

Table 3. Telecommunications and networking layer elements.

Element	Description
Subscriber Connectivity	Telecommunications carriers provide connection services for data and voice at regional, national and international levels. These include direct (cable and fiber) connections and wireless (cellular and other radio frequency) connections [35].
Voice Service	Telecommunications carriers cooperate to offer direct voice service between subscribers as well as various supporting services such as multi-party conferencing and voicemail.
Short Message Service	Telecommunications carriers cooperate to convey text messages and multimedia messages between mobile subscribers, and to transfer to various other services (e.g., email) [83].
Signaling	This global common channel signal control service supports voice and smart message services. Formerly based almost exclusively on the Signaling System 7 (SS7) standard [53], it is migrating to a mix of SS7 and newer standards [73].
Internet Protocol Routing	This global service for conveying Internet Protocol (IP) packets between cooperating telecommunications carriers is designed to be adaptive to changing demand, outages and other factors [45].
Link Switching	Telecommunications carriers depend on various link technologies and protocols to support wide-area network (WAN) connectivity such as optical links [78], multiprotocol label switching [90] and newer software-defined WAN approaches [60].
Time	Networks and services depend on accurate, synchronized time. Two primary synchronization protocols used on the Internet and by telecommunications carriers are the Network Time Protocol (NTP) and Precision Time Protocol (PTP) [51].

ble 3 describes the seven main elements of the telecommunications and networking layer.

The Internet Protocol (IP) routing element is especially important to the resilient operation of the contemporary Internet and other cyberspace services. In the current architecture, major carriers, governments, cloud providers and other large enterprises operate their own IP networks, each of which is an autonomous system. The autonomous systems connect to each other via dedicated gateways, but more often via Internet Exchange Points (IXPs) that connect several carriers and enterprises. Internet exchange points help define the operational topology of cyberspace at the national and international levels [42]. However, the topology is far from uniform. Historically, a small number of highly-connected autonomous system operators (large telecommunications carriers) have underpinned national and global connectedness [34].

Autonomous system operators run Border Gateway Protocol (BGP) installations as cooperative members of the global routing fabric [45]. Participating in global BGP operations enables each autonomous system owner to offer reachability to its users and/or customers as well as to permit transit traffic in accordance with internal link status and business rules. Operated properly, BGP automatically adapts to outages, link failures and other state changes. However, it was not designed to withstand injections of false state information [14].

At the national and global levels, cyberspace depends on the IP routing element. This element depends, in turn, on many individual communications paths that constitute the link switching element. The links may be physical links over fiber optic cable or satellites or they may be overlays controlled by switching protocols such as multiprotocol label switching (MPLS) [90].

3.2   Cyber Infrastructure Threats

Cyber infrastructures face many of the same types of threats as other infrastructures – natural disasters, intentional sabotage, misuse and more. However, unlike most other critical infrastructures, a cyber infrastructure is not tightly bound to geography, in the sense that disruptions in one region may impose impacts much more broadly. Of the cyber infrastructure layers in Figure 2, successively higher layers are increasingly independent of physical location and more dependent on the abstract topology implemented by the other elements that they utilize. The complexity of individual elements and their interrelationships magnifies or spreads the impacts of threats, especially threats against elements in the lower layer that support all the higher layers.

Infrastructure threats can be subdivided along several axes – intentional versus accidental, localized versus wide-area, disruptive versus destructive and more. Special taxonomies have been published for many domains such as Internet security [15] and energy control system operations [36].

The following three axes relevant to impact severity are employed in the treatment of national-level resilience:

- **Intentionality:** This axis covers disruptions caused intentionally by malicious actors and accidents caused unintentionally by non-malicious actors. An implication is that malicious actors may adapt to mitigation and recovery measures.

- **Duration:** This axis covers the durations of disruptive events. A cable cut may be of short duration. A malicious denial-of-service attack may be long lasting. The effects of a serious flood may be extended. A key consideration is whether the events are one-time or recurring.

- **Reversibility:** This axis covers disruptions that can be reversed to a prior state easily to disruptions whose effects are enduring or even permanent. For example, crashing a set of servers is reversible by simply restarting them, but reversing the effects of wiping the servers may not be possible.

Tables 4 through 6 list potential large-scale threats to the infrastructure elements listed in Tables 1 through 3. In particular, Table 4 lists general threats that may be malicious or accidental. Tables 5 and 6 list intentional threats that are typically malicious.

The lists of threats are representative, not comprehensive. The threats are realistic because they have been demonstrated or experienced at a significant scale. National cyber resilience should ensure the ability to absorb these types of threats without serious degradation, and in extreme cases, recover within a timeframe that avoids significant economic, social or national security impacts. Members of the U.S. Defense Science Board [26] have recognized the potential for grave national security and economic impacts from malicious cyber attacks, and advocate increased resilience as a necessary countermeasure.

4.   National-Scale Resilience Model

Economic, social and national security benefits associated with cyberspace accrue from the top layer of Figure 2, the applications and services used by public and private sector enterprises, academia and the general public. When these services are interrupted, cascading impacts ensue, as in the case of natural disasters such as Hurricane Sandy [18].

Therefore, if resistance to disruption and quick recovery in the lower layers can sustain the functionality of the top layer, then the overall cyber infrastructure may be regarded as resilient. A simple metric to consider is the value I_T from [21], the time interval when performance is below minimally acceptable values. In this case, performance denotes the usable operation of services in the top layer, namely, business, government and personal use of cyberspace. For example, if a hospital cannot provide treatment due to inaccessibility of medical records, then a lower value of I_T indicates greater resilience and a value of zero indicates full resilience. Access to medical records is a complex function that is depen-

Table 4.   General threats to cyber infrastructure layers.

Threat	Applicability and Effects
Power Outage	A widespread power outage typically disrupts network services, especially subscriber connectivity across the affected region. If a region has major hubs in the Internet routing topology, impacts spread far beyond the region. *Duration:* Hours to days. *Reversibility:* Reversible.
Cable Cuts	Physical damage to critical data cables can cause regional network disruptions. Multiple cuts could partition national networks. *Duration:* Hours to weeks. *Reversibility:* Reversible.
Routing Failure	Degradation of the global routing process can result in regional or national loss of reachability. Impacts are highly variable. *Duration:* Minutes to hours. *Reversibility:* Reversible.
Internet Exchange Point Loss	Unavailability of an Internet exchange point (IPX) due to physical facility loss. The degraded connectivity impacts multiple carriers with broad service disruptions. *Duration:* Days to months. *Reversibility:* Variable.
Data Loss	Unavailability of large amounts of stored data due to facility failure or malicious deletion. Impacts users and all services that depend on the data. *Duration:* Hours to weeks. *Reversibility:* Variable.
Domain Name System Domain Loss	Unavailability or loss of integrity of a top-level domain (e.g., `.gov` or `.uk`) with impacts to tenants and users. *Duration:* Seconds to hours. *Reversibility:* Reversible.
Supply Chain Compromise	Disruption, service degradation or destruction via the malicious introduction of vulnerabilities in a product or product line. Impacts include regional, national or global loss of connectivity, service or integrity. An example is the 2002 multi-vendor SNMP vulnerability [84]. *Duration:* Unknown. *Reversibility:* Low, reconstitution is required.

dent on the foundational, compute and storage, and telecommunications and networking services described in Section 3.

Several studies of critical infrastructure risk have noted that fragility and vulnerability to cascading failures is a consequence of infrastruc-

Table 5. Intentional threats to cyber infrastructure layers.

Threat	Applicability and Effects
Route Hijacking	Malicious misrouting or non-routing of a range of network addresses. Impacts reachability of services and connectivity. *Duration:* Seconds to hours. *Reversibility:* Reversible.
Congestion Denial of Service	Degradation of service or connectivity imposed by flooding networks or service providers. Impacts all users of affected networks, even users outside the directly-affected area. *Duration:* Seconds to hours. *Reversibility:* Reversible.
Domain Name System Poisoning	Injection of false, misleading or malicious mappings in domains. A large-scale attack can disrupt services, degrade trust in services or support other large-scale malicious activities. *Duration:* Minutes to days. *Reversibility:* Variable.
Domain Name System Denial of Service	Degradation or interruption of DNS services by congestion, route hijacking or other mechanisms. Impacts to tenants and users of the affected domains; usually all the domains hosted by the victim DNS service provider. *Duration:* Minutes to hours. *Reversibility:* Reversible.
Widespread Malware Execution	Operation of disruptive or destructive software on numerous devices in a region, nation or industry verticals. Impacts due to congestion [62] and data destruction [43]. *Duration:* Hours to weeks. *Reversibility:* Variable.
Compute and Storage Denial of Service	Interrupted access to compute and storage services by resource consumption, misauthorization or other non-destructive means. Loss of higher-level business, government and user services. *Duration:* Minutes to days. *Reversibility:* Reversible.
Message System Flooding	Degradation or disruption of enterprise functions and user interactions that depend on the underlying message system. Severe impacts on affected industry verticals. *Duration:* Seconds to hours. *Reversibility:* Reversible.
Public Key Infrastructure Denial of Trust	Loss of ability to trust high-level web, email and application services due to compromises of trust foundations. Disruptions of business functions and user interactions [3]. *Duration:* Days to weeks. *Reversibility:* Difficult, reconstitution is required.

Table 6.   Intentional threats to cyber infrastructure layers (continued).

Threat	Applicability and Effects
Signaling Denial of Service	Interruption or loss of integrity of signaling services that underpin voice and SMS services. Impacts single carriers, multiple carriers or the national network. *Duration:* Seconds to hours. *Reversibility:* Reversible.
Time Desynchrony	Loss of time synchronization in portions of networks degrades services until synchrony is restored. Impacts are varied. *Duration:* Seconds to hours. *Reversibility:* Reversible.

ture complexity [55, 61]. The common feature of the infrastructures cited in these studies is that they grew more complex over time without considering the resistance to attacks or efficient recovery from degraded operations. Studies in the electric energy sector have shown that complex infrastructure need not be fragile if it is engineered and operated for resilience [4].

4.1   Cyber Infrastructure and Resilience

Cyber infrastructure has several features that can help support resilient design and operation:

- Cyber infrastructure is amenable to highly detailed, accurate and responsive instrumentation. Response to adverse conditions requires the detection of these conditions. Cyber infrastructure is well-suited to timely detection.

- Cyber infrastructure is not static. Communications, compute and application services are defined largely by software, which can be updated and improved at a far lower cost than replacing the components. For example, network operators can implement software-defined wide-area networks using existing switch hardware without the capital investment of purchasing new switches [60].

- Cyber infrastructure operation is not bound to physical geography. Several elements of cyber infrastructure can and do function in a geographically-distributed manner. While this aspect of cyber infrastructure allows the impacts of disruptions to extend well beyond an initially-affected facility or region, it also permits distributed resilience – disruption in one region or even one nation

Table 7.   Resilience engineering goals/stages.

MITRE Framework [10] "Goal"	Linkov et al./ NAS [56] "Stage"	High-Level Description
Anticipate	Plan/Prepare	Establish a state of informed preparation for disruptions or attacks, lay foundations and maintain awareness.
Withstand	Absorb	Continue operations through a disruption or attack, limit or minimize impacts, repel attack or isolate its effects.
Recover	Recover	Restore capability and capacity, assess damage and requirements for complete reconstitution.
Evolve	Adapt	Adjust architecture, processes, operations and system configurations to minimize future impacts and facilitate recovery.

can be mitigated to varying degrees by service offerings elsewhere. This is not true of all cyber infrastructure elements. A critical exception is subscriber connectivity, which is typically tied to geography.

These features support flexible implementation of resilience measures, enabling a nation to amortize investments across multiple sectors, regions and infrastructure elements to achieve resilience goals.

4.2   Basic Resilience Model

Two widely-cited sources on resilience engineering are the MITRE cyber resiliency engineering framework [10] and the work of Linkov et al. [56], which define four very similar basic parts, the latter based on previous work by the National Academy of Sciences (NAS). Table 7 describes the resilience engineering goals and stages in the two sources. The remainder of this chapter uses the MITRE terminology, but ideas from both sources are used in the discussion.

It is possible to measure many aspects of resilience based on the four goals in the MITRE framework. The metrics can inform planning and preparation, response during disruptions, priorities for recovery and areas for attention during evolution.

The MITRE resiliency engineering framework [56] is designed for application at enterprise scales, up to very large enterprises such as the

U.S. Department of Defense. At a national scale, additional issues come
into play:

- Planning and preparation for large-scale disruptions or attacks are
  necessarily incomplete. It is not possible to enumerate all possible
  failure modes of complex interdependent systems or the impacts
  of cascading failures on the economy or society [11].

- National-scale cyber infrastructure is built, maintained, operated
  and regulated by multiple stakeholders with different degrees of
  visibility and control. These stakeholders have different motiva-
  tions, but typically have little to no incentive to collaborate to
  improve the overall resilience [19, 55].

- Cyber infrastructure at the national scale is visible to and observable by almost anyone, include threat actors. In enterprise
  contexts, concealing or obscuring the properties of cyber infrastructure is a generally-accepted practice, but at the national scale,
  secrecy cannot be effective. For example, an enterprise can hide
  its internal network architecture, but the top-level topology of the
  Internet is exposed to all participants in the global BGP fabric.

- Planning for resilience and responding during a disruption require
  collating information across multiple infrastructure providers and
  even multiple infrastructures. In the United States and many other
  advanced countries, legal obstacles discourage the sharing of information necessary to craft informed responses [65].

As described in Sections 5 and 6, preparing and planning for national-
scale resilience must take these factors into account.

4.3   Applying Resilience to Cyber Infrastructure

The MITRE framework defines 14 practices that an enterprise can
apply to achieve resilience goals [10]. Some of the practices must be
adapted to apply at the national scale whereas other practices are directly applicable. Tables 8 and 9 list the 14 practices and identify the
goals for which they are effective.

For each of the 11 applicable practices in Tables 8 and 9, national
resilience requires one or more measures to inform investment direction
and readiness estimates.

4.4   Measuring Practices in Cyber Infrastructure

For each of the applicable practices, effective resilience requires viable
measures. Measures suitable at the national scale are proposed based

Table 8. Resilience practices and national scale.

Practice	Application	Remarks
Adaptive Response	Withstand, Recover	Adapting to disruptions and degradation is central to withstanding and recovery. At the national scale, adaptive response can use assets/resources from multiple providers.
Analytic Monitoring	Anticipate, Withstand, Recover, Evolve	All the resilience goals depend on the visibility and cross-provider understanding of the operational state of the cyber infrastructure.
Coordinated Defense	Anticipate, Withstand (Adapted)	Coordinated defense must be adapted to the differing authorities of providers, customers and government stakeholders.
Deception		Deception is impractical to apply at the national scale – multi-party operation of the national cyber infrastructure precludes deceiving other parties.
Diversity	Anticipate, Withstand, Recover, Evolve	Infrastructure providers embody diversity at the national scale, but it is a byproduct of diverse business models and history. Resilience requires diversity to be applied intentionally and with measures of provider independence.
Dynamic Positioning	Anticipate, Withstand, Recover	Anticipation entails pre-identification of assets to mitigate disruptions dynamically. Withstanding and recovery require substitutions of alternative capacity for the impacted services.
Dynamic Representation	Anticipate, Withstand	Requires building and maintaining accurate representations of infrastructure elements and their interactions to identify nascent disruptions and inform response activities.
Non-Persistence		Requires operating various portions of the cyber infrastructure in ephemeral and shifting ways, but this can be impractical at the national scale.
Privilege Restriction	Anticipate, Withstand (Adapted)	Privilege restriction must be adapted to apply at the national scale. Instead of managing entity privileges in enterprises, trust relationships must be managed between enterprises, providers and government authorities.

in part on the metrics described in [56] and its references, especially the detailed work by Allen and Curtis [2].

Table 9. Resilience practices and national scale (continued).

Practice	Application	Remarks
Realignment	Anticipate, Recover, Evolve	Realignment of resources, assets and capacity are central to preparing for disruptions and adapting operations after disruptions. But realignment must be informed by effective monitoring and analysis.
Redundancy	Anticipate, Withstand	Redundancy is the provisioning of additional assets or capacity to prepare for disruptions.
Segmentation	Anticipate, Withstand, Recover	At regional and national scales, segmentation entails preparing and activating mechanisms to isolate disrupted infrastructure segments in order to minimize cascading impacts and manage recovery activities. Intentional segmentation across multiple services and providers is very challenging.
Substantiated Integrity	Anticipate, Withstand, Recover	Substantiated integrity becomes the foundation of trust for cooperative planning, response and, especially, recovery.
Unpredictability		Complexity of multi-party infrastructure offers some degree of unpredictability. Intentionally introducing unpredictability may be impossible to coordinate at the national scale.

Adaptive Response. In the foundational services and compute and storage services layers, measures must include an ability to replace or supplement a degraded service with a redundant asset or a substitute, the delay time after decision that the response becomes usable (latency of effective restoration) and the capacity of the redundant or substitute (service load that the substitute can provide). During the anticipate stage, these measures can be quantified through simple testing and exercises, but they apply during the withstand and recover stages.

In the telecommunications and networking layer, adaptive response includes two types of actions. The first type of actions include the ability to block, throttle or render harmless the specific traffic or transactions that cause the disruption. Measures for this include the breadth of coverage (elements of the infrastructure that are covered by the ability (Table 2)), precision of the response action (how selectively blocking or throttling can be applied), consistency of response (whether all the telecommunications providers apply similar blocking or throttling) and the time delay from decision to effective imposition of the response.

The second type of actions entail the ability to utilize redundant or alternative network capacity to recover from a disruption or destruction. Individual telecommunications carriers possess this ability today, but for national-scale resilience abilities are needed that span the carriers serving each region. The measures include the capacity of redundant assets, coverage that carriers can offer in using the capacity (geographic distribution of the redundancy, especially the identification of locations that lack redundant capacity) and time delay between decision to employ redundant or alternative capacity and effective service recovery.

Analytic Monitoring and Dynamic Representation. The analytic monitoring and dynamic representation practices are separate in the MITRE framework, but need to be planned together in a national-scale resilience effort. A dynamic representation can only be created by monitoring and monitoring at large scales is useful only when processed into an actionable and timely representation. A common, aggregated dynamic representation is a form of shared situational awareness that is identified as important in several large-scale cyber security strategy studies [26, 38].

The analytic monitoring and dynamic representation practices apply to all four resilience stages.

In the foundational services layer, the practices must include fine-grained monitoring and fusion into an actionable representation of service availability and accuracy. However, in this layer, it is especially important that the monitoring include observations of foundational service availability from different national regions and extra-national regions, and comparisons of service-reported data with ground truth samples in order to detect integrity compromises. The measures in this layer include the coverage of elements and service providers, ability to distinguish independent service failures, timeliness of updating the national-scale dynamic representation and accuracy of characterization of service degradation (failure rates, latency, completeness of responses).

In the compute and storage services layer, measures must cover fine-grained monitoring and collation of monitoring data into an accurate high-level picture of service availability and integrity. The measures include the coverage of the monitoring (percentage of provider storage and compute assets monitored), timeliness of updating the national-scale dynamic representation and accuracy of the mapping between monitored assets and overall service posture.

The telecommunications and networking layer must be monitored and represented with exceptional fidelity because all other services and recovery mechanisms depend on the layer. Telecommunications and network carriers already perform a great deal of analytic monitoring, but at this time there is no national-scale effort to build a faithful dynamic representation of network service posture from the data. Creating such a representation is a vital requirement for informing a national-scale resilience effort. The measures in this layer include the independence of the elements comprising the layer, monitoring coverage across carriers, regions and service types (voice, IP traffic, other data traffic, SMS, etc.), timeliness of updating the national-scale dynamic representation and accurate characterization of the capacity of each major asset that provides key services. It does little good to know that an inter-regional link is carrying 5 Gbps of traffic unless the representation also includes the fact that the link capacity is 100 Gbps.

Dynamic representation in all the layers must also have the ability to represent mitigation and recovery response in progress.

Coordinated Defense. Significant research has focused on information sharing for enhancing situational awareness and helping individual defenders coordinate responses; interested readers are referred to [38] for a survey of the literature on situation awareness. Much of the work assumes that coordination is among independent enterprises, each making its own decisions to defend its assets. Such independently-motivated actions that lack common objectives will not achieve resilience at the national scale. Therefore, the coordinated defense practice must have a goal (withstanding and recovering from disruptions and attacks nationally) along with measures of success. The primary measures of success are drawn from shared dynamic representation. Coordination of defensive action depends on mechanisms for selecting coordinated response and recovery actions, and on robust means for disseminating the actions to all parties that can execute them.

In the foundational services and compute and storage services layers, coordinated defense largely involves conventional defensive responses such as blocking, quarantining, segmenting and patching implemented in concert. Measures include the coverage of relevant service providers with the means to accept coordinated action instructions and have agreed to do so, time delay between a response decision and application of the action at covered providers, and breadth of response actions included in the coordinated defense repertoire.

In the telecommunications and networking layer, the same measures apply as in the foundational services layer, but an important additional measure is automation. Some defensive actions can gain broad impacts automatically via global network control systems such as the global BGP routing fabric or the telecommunications signaling system if providers pre-configure trigger mechanisms such as remote triggered BGP black hole filtering [51]. Therefore, a salient measure is the coverage of telecommunications carriers that have pre-configured the mechanisms and have agreed to accept remote coordinated triggers from an authorized source.

Diversity. The MITRE framework and other resiliency engineering strategies identify infrastructure heterogeneity as a means for reducing the impacts of disruptions and attacks. At the national scale, some inherent diversity may be gained from the various providers in the cyber infrastructure layers. However, a diverse set of providers does not guarantee the technological or process diversity needed to reduce impacts. Measures of diversity across different service elements are essential to understand potential impacts; this applies to all service elements and layers. Measures include diversity assessments of several facets of service elements, including service implementation supplier (web server for the web element, mail transfer agent server for the e-mail element and router vendor for the IP routing element), service platform, service protocol and service management system.

Dynamic Positioning and Realignment. Measures for the dynamic positioning and realignment practice must inform the readiness for disruptions and attacks and extent to which dynamic responses to disruptions and attacks can sustain or restore service availability. Note that this practice is different from redundancy because it involves dynamically shifting capacity or realigning assets to ensure a usable or minimally-degraded service profile for a cyber infrastructure layer.

In the foundational services layer, measures include the coverage of service element scope (e.g., extent to which generic compute resources can be enlisted to restore DNS services), capacity of dynamic response as a fraction of the original service capacity, time delay to implement dynamic response and transparency of the dynamically-realigned service compared with the original service.

In the compute and storage services layer, measures include coverage, capacity fraction and time delay as in the case of the foundational services layer. But a measure of prioritization is also needed, specifically, the degree to which dynamically-realigned assets can support the highest priority workloads or stored data during the withstand and recover stages, and the degree to which dynamically-realigned assets can serve the highest priority workloads or stored data.

In the telecommunications and networking layer, the key measures are capacity and latency. Telecommunications providers already manage the dynamic allocation of network resources, so the measure of capacity must reflect the fraction of the resource that can be dynamically repositioned within a particular element (e.g., shifting switched link capacity from a local customer to transit usage) and between elements (e.g., shifting IP routed capacity from customer IP usage to signaling system usage).

Privilege Restriction. For national scale resilience, the privilege restriction practice applies to privileges extended between providers. For many types of cyber disruptions, trust between service providers can help propagate disruptive and malicious effects. For example, disruptive route hijacking can occur in the global BGP fabric partly because autonomous system owners (mostly carriers) have too much trust in route information received from their peers [14]. In all the cyber infrastructure layers, measures of trust relationships are critical to qualifying and improving resilience.

Two key measures are the ability of service providers to authenticate peers with whom they interact and the extent of trust that providers extend to authenticated peers compared with the minimum trust necessary to provide service. During the withstand stage, an important response action for some services is minimizing the trust that service providers have on each other in order to slow or halt the spread of disruptions. Therefore, an important measure for all service providers must be their ability to consistently and positively alter their trust configurations and the time delays involved in accomplishing the alterations.

Redundancy. The redundancy practice is one of the simplest means to support resilience, but it must be measured to quantify the national ability to withstand disruptions and to recover from them. Also, redundancy can be economically inefficient. A redundant asset requires capital investment and maintenance, but may not generate full returns. Therefore, an investment in redundancy must be intentional and directed to yield maximum resilience benefits.

In the foundational services and compute and storage services layers, measures of redundancy include the simple ratio of available capacity to expected normal load and the time delay involved in bringing redundant capacity into service after a decision is made. Also, there must be some measure of the geographic or provider distribution of the redundant capacity. National resilience requires the ability to employ redundant capacity across service providers. For example, if one DNS service provider is disabled by a cyber attack, then another provider must be able to serve the affected domains using its redundant capacity. The time delay for recovering DNS service in such a scenario may be considerable.

In the telecommunications and networking layer, redundancy cannot be measured simply by capacity; instead, it must be characterized geographically and topologically. Simple and general measures for this do not appear to exist. Omer et al. [69] have conducted a deep resilience analysis of a critical portion of the global telecommunications infrastructure. The measures researched in the study should be extensible to the characterization of more general networks.

Note that national resilience requires two types of redundancy to be considered. One is internal redundancy, the measure of available extra capacity within a single provider. The other is external redundancy, the measure of extra capacity accessible by shifting the load to other providers.

Segmentation. Segmentation is the partitioning of a network or service layer into disjoint portions with defined and controlled interfaces between them. It enhances resilience because imposing a limiting interface can halt the spread of disruptive effects. At the national scale, carrier boundaries already constitute the first stratum of segmentation. Within a service layer, large providers should further segment their own portions of the infrastructure to reduce the impacts of disruptions targeted at them or propagated from peers. Effective management of trust relationships also contributes to segmentation during the anticipate stage. In the withstand stage, additional segmentation or subdividing of existing segments can limit impacts and simplify subsequent recovery efforts. Measures for segmentation must include the quantification of segmentation (e.g., number of segments and ratio of largest to smallest segment size) and degree of control imposed between segments. Practices for segmenting services at the enterprise level are available [37]. Some of these practices can be extended to the national scale.

Substantiated Integrity. Substantiated integrity is a subtle but critical practice in resiliency engineering – it is the ability for an infrastructure provider, defensive operator or decision maker to trust that a peer or dependency has not been compromised or co-opted by an attacker such that information or requests from the peer can be used as the basis for action. Few options are available for service layers at the national scale. One exception is the IP routing element for which multiple global-scale trust frameworks are defined but not yet implemented [46].

During the anticipate stage, service providers and carriers must pre-establish trust mechanisms. Two such mechanisms have been used successfully at a large scale:

- Authoritative sources identify and designate sources of authoritative information in advance; these can be individuals or systems. During the withstand and recovery stages, peers accept actionable information or requests only from these trusted sources.

- Cryptographic trust is achieved when peers agree to a mechanism for cryptographically substantiating important information and exchange (in advance) the keys and credentials necessary to support the mechanism.

Taken together, the practices listed above offer a means for service providers, carriers and operators that manage the national cyber infrastructure to prepare for disruptions and attacks, withstand them by reducing their duration and severity, recover from adversity and improve over time.

5.   Implementing the Resilience Model

This section offers recommendations on implementing national-scale resilience through the application of the practices detailed in Section 4. The implementation steps are divided into a cycle of four phases, prepare, implement, exercise or test, and evaluate.

5.1   Phase 1: Prepare

Before attempting to apply the practices, the parties involved must gather information and establish relationships.

Step 1.1: Map Dependencies. Dependencies between infrastructure elements and providers for each element must be mapped. The technical operation of each element imposes certain dependencies as shown in Figure 3. But the technical dependencies are only a rough guide for enumerating the operational dependencies in a national infrastructure.

Mapping operational dependencies requires information from all the involved providers. For some elements, basic dependencies can be approximated from information that is publicly visible, especially DNS and IP routing. However, for all other elements, dependency information is scattered among the providers of the elements. This information must be gathered by surveying the providers and refreshed regularly.

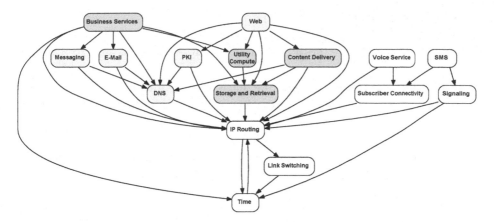

Figure 3. Dependencies between cyber infrastructure elements.

Step 1.2: Assess Key Measures. A critical aspect of preparation is establishing baseline values for critical metrics. In this step, individual providers must assess their infrastructure elements and quantify their postures with respect to each of the practices listed in Section 4. Parties with oversight of infrastructure elements and layers, such as industry sector groups and government agencies, must measure the postures for practices that span multiple providers (e.g., external redundancy and diversity).

Step 1.3: Identify and Build Monitoring and Dynamic Representation Mechanisms. All detection, response and recovery activities depend on the accurate and timely representation of the state of the cyber infrastructure. In this step, responsible parties identify existing monitoring and dynamic representation support, and build new structures where national-scale analysis capacity is lacking.

The monitoring and dynamic representation mechanisms must include data ingestion, processing and delivery of analytic results to automated systems and analysts and decision-makers.

Step 1.4: Identify Key Response and Recovery Tactics. During this step, key stakeholders and service providers enumerate the activities they will employ for particular infrastructure elements and types of disruptions. These include the following practices:

- **Adaptive Response:** Specific response mechanisms are employed to reduce the impacts of disruptions and attacks, including remapping, blackholing, filtering and blacklisting.

- **Coordinated Defense:** Specific defensive measures such as multi-party blocking, redirecting and throttling that providers undertake cooperatively are employed in the event of disruptions and attacks.

- **Dynamic Positioning:** Service loads are shifted between providers or a provider can take on a service burden in support of a disrupted peer.

- **Segmentation:** Additional controlled boundaries between providers or within shared networks are imposed to halt the spread of disruptions.

- **Realignment:** Capacity is realigned from one service to another in order to mitigate a disruption or support recovery.

Step 1.5: Characterize Current Trust Relationships. There are two reasons to enumerate and characterize trust relationships between providers during the prepare phase. First, excessive or unnecessary trust relationships offer malicious actors additional ways to propagate their attacks; these relationships should be minimized as part of the privilege restriction practice. Second, many coordinated defense, realignment and other active responses require trust between participants; all trust relationships that are needed to execute the response and recovery tactics identified in Step 1.4 should be enumerated during this step.

Step 1.6: Identify Mechanisms for Substantiating Integrity. Response and recovery activities, both manual and automated, require that participants are able to trust the information and requests received from service providers and response operators. During this step, mechanisms for establishing and maintaining trust must be selected, characterized and accepted by participants.

5.2   Phase 2: Implement

National resilience stakeholders are responsible for setting up mechanisms and assets for resilience before large-scale disruptions and attacks. This phase includes the major facets of the implementation.

Step 2.1: Establish Response and Recovery Trust Relationships. In this step, infrastructure providers and decision makers set up trust relationships that support the exchange of information for maintaining dynamic representation and coordinating response and recovery activities.

Step 2.2: Initiate Monitoring and Representation. After the trust relationships have been set up, providers can initiate data flows that support the analytic monitoring and dynamic representation practices. Stakeholders responsible for operating the analyses that drive dynamic representation must set up their systems during this step.

Step 2.3: Define Segmentation Boundaries for Response. The segmentation practice can be very effective at bounding the impacts of disruptions and attacks. However, imposing new segmentation requires prior identification of the candidate points at which new interface controls can be placed. During this step, providers in a layer cooperate to identify the candidate points and applicable mechanisms.

Step 2.4: Provision Substantiated Integrity Mechanisms. In this step, providers implement the substantiated integrity practice by provisioning keys, credentials, authoritative sources and other mechanisms defined in Step 1.6. This may include configuring automated systems and protocols, and exchanging lists of designated trusted individuals and their contact information.

Step 2.5: Establish Mechanisms for Key Response and Recovery Tactics. For each of the response and recovery actions identified in Step 1.4, providers pre-provision, document and configure necessary systems and processes for conducting the actions. These include manual processes that must be documented and automated processes that may need to be scripted or installed on operational infrastructure components. This step also includes configuring fail-over and load-shifting mechanisms for utilizing redundant capacity or realigning capacity to service recovery.

Step 2.6: Minimize Trust Relationships. In the last implementation step, providers implement the privilege restriction practice – minimizing external trust relationships to those necessary for normal operations and resilience response.

5.3 Phase 3: Test

This phase is essential to effective response and recovery operations when a national cyber infrastructure is under genuine threat. Testing and exercising responses and recovery actions are a standard part of continuity of operations and disaster recovery readiness [79] and are critical to resilience operations. To facilitate resilience at the national scale, where multiple private and public sector stakeholders must cooperate to respond and recover, conducting exercises is even more important.

Step 3.1: Hold Tabletop Exercises.   As an initial, low-overhead test of response and recovery tactics, key stakeholders should hold simulated manual exercises. These tabletop exercises would not involve real systems or services, but instead rehearse and debug response processes, responsibilities and inter-party relationships. Guidance for running such exercises, albeit in somewhat different contexts, is available from multiple sources [24, 41, 88].

Step 3.2: Test Monitoring and Dynamic Representation.   The stakeholders must test monitoring and dynamic representation facilities to ensure that they deliver accurate and actionable information. In this step, providers collaborate with each other and with decision makers to gain assurance. There are several ways to test monitoring systems, but a simple approach that works at any scale is to perturb service functioning either by taking some capacity out of service or applying an artificial service load, and then check that the dynamic representation accurately tracks the actual service posture.

Step 3.3: Test Response and Recovery Actions Internally.   This step is performed separately and independently by each provider. It involves testing the internal mechanisms for adaptive response, dynamic positioning, segmentation and other practices. This is an essential step because proper functioning of the independent mechanisms must be assured individually before a national response attempts to use many of them in a concerted fashion.

Monitoring individual tests also offers further opportunities to test monitoring and dynamic representation.

Step 3.4: Test Multi-Party Response and Recovery Actions. This step is very complex, but it is a critical aspect of testing. Providers and decision makers cooperate to test the response and recovery tactics identified in Step 1.4. Tests must include the following facets:

- Application of practices at all providers concurrently.

- Selective application of practices (e.g., blocking or throttling at a subset of providers).

- Staged or sequential application of practices.

- Application of practices when subsets of providers are unable to act.

- Application of multiple independent practices concurrently (e.g., shifting loads to redundant capacity while simultaneously throttling attack traffic).

- Ceasing the application of practices (i.e., testing the actions performed after disruptions as part of return to normal operations).

Step 3.5: Hold Large Scale Functional Exercises. After the dynamic representation is shown to be accurate and individual practices have been tested, the final step is to hold simulation exercises using real infrastructure. These exercises should be confined to individual layers initially to reduce the likelihood of unplanned impacts to service users. Guidance for planning such exercises is available from the National Institute of Standards and Technology (NIST) [41].

5.4   Phase 4: Evaluate

In this phase, the findings from Phases 2 and 3 are compiled and used to characterize gaps, issues and improvements.

Step 4.1: Assess Dynamic Representation. This step evaluates the accuracy and timeliness of the infrastructure state shown by the dynamic representation. Missing elements, excessive time lag and desynchrony, and inaccurate analyses are all opportunities for improvement.

Step 4.2: Assess Operation of Response and Recovery Tactics. During Phase 3, service providers test response and recovery mechanisms, first internally and then cooperatively. All the measures listed in Section 4 can be captured, or at least approximated, during the tests. It is especially important to identify situations where practices can be applied and where applications of different practices conflict.

Step 4.3: Assess Responsibilities and Relationships. Because national cyber resilience depends on the cooperation of many parties, the working relationships between the parties are vital to effective response and recovery. In this step, stakeholders must use the findings from exercises and tests to identify missing relationships and areas that lack clear lines of responsibility.

Practical Considerations Implementing national cyber infrastructure resilience will vary across nations. Several considerations affect how resilient operation can be built up and how response and recovery practices can be managed.

First, the centralization and ownership of infrastructure affects implementation. Highly-centralized services present fewer obstacles to new policies and controls, but offer less inherent diversity, redundancy and segmentation. Decentralized services offer the potential for better inherent support of resilience practices, but require reliable distributed control and associated trust relationships to be built. It is productive to compare the centralized approach taken by Estonia after the attacks against its national cyber infrastructure in 2011 [23] with the decentralized approach proposed for Canada's diverse financial sector in 2014 [39].

Ownership models also impact implementation. Private owners of service infrastructure are driven by business motives, including competitiveness, efficiency and fiduciary obligations to shareholders. Public owners may be responsible for public good, but may lack competitive incentives. In the case of multiple service providers under private ownership, competition concerns can prevent the adoption of resilience practices unless obligations are uniform and consistent (i.e., retain a level playing field).

Regulation can be used to impose requirements on certain behaviors and investments, especially for measures that are easy to quantify such as redundant capacity. Economic incentives such as investment credits and tax reductions can also nudge private sector cyber infrastructure providers to implement resilience practices. Incentive strategies have been advocated in various national policy study reports [19, 71]. However, these incentives must be carefully selected to drive resilience practices that need improvement. Also, incentives leave decision making to infrastructure owners on whether or not to implement a resilience practice; some may choose to forego the incentive.

National cyber resilience absolutely requires information sharing and cooperation among the infrastructure providers that serve the nation. In nations with private ownership of cyber infrastructure, the providers are business competitors. Some nations, especially the United States and several European Union members, impose legal barriers to cooperation among competitors [65]. When these legal barriers can be reduced, information sharing can improve, but other challenges remain [52].

Finally, resilient operation at the national scale requires aggregated visibility (dynamic representation practice) as well as coordinated control (adaptive response, realignment, coordinated defense and other practices). The breadth of the cyber infrastructure and the presence of complex dependencies (Figure 3) imply that no single provider has an incentive to accept responsibility for such visibility and control. The role will fall to the government in some way, either directly as in the United

Kingdom [19] or via some form of government coordination and support as in models proposed for the United States [71].

6.   Stakeholders and Roles

The cyber infrastructure of the United States offers excellent opportunities to implement resilience, but legal and economic factors impose substantial challenges.

6.1   Cyber Resilience Government Stakeholders

The first aspect of U.S. national governance that affects cyber infrastructure operation is the number and diversity of government organizations and government-sponsored organizations that share responsibility for cyber issues. Excellent, but security-focused, overviews of this topic appear in the U.S. national plan for cyber incident response [89], in a legal analysis for Congress [75] and in a NATO assessment of the United States as a member [70]. Tables 10 and 11 provide details about the main U.S. Government stakeholders.

In addition to federal authorities, state and territorial governments have regulatory power over some infrastructures in domains, especially subscriber connectivity services.

The key responsibility for cyber infrastructure resilience belongs to the Critical Infrastructure Security Agency, a U.S. Department of Homeland Security entity. However, the telecommunications and information technology sectors, for which CISA is the sector-specific agency, are very large and complex. To foster intra-sector cooperation on cyber matters and to streamline cooperation with the federal government, each sector has an Information Sharing and Analysis Center (ISAC).

- The Communications ISAC is the coordination body responsible for the telecommunications and network infrastructure layer. It is located within CISA as the National Coordinating Center for Communications (NCCC).

- The Information Technology ISAC is the coordination body for the information technology industry, including information technology enterprises and some service providers. Its members cover a portion of the foundational services and compute and storage services layers.

Of the seven service areas in the telecommunications and networking layer, all are represented to a significant degree by the NCCC or an aligned government organization. However, of the nine service areas

Table 10. Main U.S. Government cyber infrastructure stakeholders.

Organization	Description
U.S. Department of Homeland Security (DHS)	Primary responsibility for critical infrastructure protection and cyber incident response with the U.S. Department of Defense, National Security Council Cyber Response Group and sector-specific agencies [66, 68].
Critical Infrastructure Security Agency (CISA)	New agency under DHS (2018) whose responsibilities were located in DHS. Responsible for incident response in federal and critical infrastructure networks. Responsibilities include infrastructure resilience and serving as the sector-specific agency for the telecommunications and information technology sectors [66].
U.S. Department of Defense (DoD)	Responsible for national defense, including defending U.S. territory from foreign threats (Title 10 USC). Several DoD organizations have specific cyber-related authorities. May support any civilian agency in this list under the Defense Support to Civil Authorities Directive [87].
U.S. Cyber Command (USCC)	Unified combatant command under the DoD. Responsible for defending DoD networks and infrastructure, and the national infrastructure when commanded to do so by the U.S. President.
National Security Agency (NSA)	Delegated responsibility for protection and defense of national security systems under National Security Directive 42 [13]. May provide technical support to any federal agency under a Request for Technical Assistance under Executive Order 12333.
National Security Council (NSC)	Maintains oversight of all national security matters, including homeland security and critical infrastructure. Chairs the Cyber Response Group and may convene Cyber Unified Coordination Groups.
Cyber Threat Intelligence Integration Center (CTIIC)	Responsible for providing coordinated intelligence on cyber threats as part of the U.S. Intelligence Community [67].

in the foundational services and compute and storage layers, few are represented by the publicly-disclosed members of the IT-ISAC [48].

To conduct the resilience steps outlined in Section 5, engagement through the IT-ISAC and NCCC are necessary but possibly not suffi-

Table 11. Main U.S. Government cyber infrastructure stakeholders (continued).

Organization	Description
Federal Bureau of Investigation (FBI)	Primary responsibility for investigating and prosecuting cyber crime.
National Cyber Investigative Joint Task Force (NCIJTF)	Established in 2008 as a partnership of 20 federal agencies that cooperate on cyber threat investigations and incident response.
National Institute of Standards and Technology (NIST)	Provides cyber security and cyber risk guidance to the public and private sectors. Under legal authority [67], develops standards to reduce the risk of cyber attacks to critical infrastructure [85]. Also responsible for standards and metrology and supports the global time infrastructure.
Federal Communications Commission (FCC)	Responsible for regulating interstate communications, including portions of the telecommunications and networking layer.

cient. Additional engagement is necessary to ensure participation by the largest providers of the Domain Name System, Web, messaging, public key infrastructure, utility compute, storage, retrieval and backup, and content delivery. Each of these service areas has a different mix of private sector providers:

- **Domain Name System:** Small number of large service providers support multiple top-level domains with the assistance of a large number of registrars. Also includes some major cloud providers.

- **Web:** Large number of service providers of all sizes offering various business models. Also includes most major cloud providers.

- **Messaging:** Most major cloud providers as well as specialist providers in various industry verticals.

- **Public Key Infrastructure:** Small number of major certificate authority providers, including some major cloud providers.

- **Utility Compute:** A few large providers, including most cloud providers, along with an ecosystem of medium-sized and smaller specialty companies.

- **Storage, Retrieval and Backup:** Major cloud providers along with a wide range of specialty providers.

- **Content Delivery:** A few large providers, including most major cloud providers.

The size and variety of the provider space presents challenges to establishing comprehensive analytic monitoring and associated dynamic representations. However, a small number of large cloud providers dominate the U.S. market [28]. Enlisting the cooperation of these dominant private sector companies would provide substantial coverage of the U.S. cyber infrastructure.

6.2   Building Cyber Infrastructure Resilience

The nature of the cyber infrastructure ecosystem and legal and regulatory environments in the United States implies that any campaign to boost resilience would require broad public and private sector cooperation. Each type of entity has different strengths and must assume different roles as described in U.S. Presidential Policy Directive 21 [66] because the resilience of critical infrastructure is a shared responsibility.

The U.S. Federal Government responsibilities include:

- Overall drive and structure of the resilience effort.

- Legal framework for cooperation.

- Economic and regulatory incentives [71].

- Clearinghouse for situational awareness driven by analysis and dynamic representation.

- Intelligence and law enforcement backing for threat warning and deterrence [26].

- Foundations for cross-provider trust relationships.

- Cross-layer and cross-service coordination.

The U.S. infrastructure provider responsibilities include:

- Participation in the resilience engineering and operations campaigns.

- Instrumentation of their own portions of the cyber infrastructure.

- Provisioning and sustaining redundancy.

- Analytic monitoring and timely contributions to the national dynamic representation.

- Cooperation in response and recovery activities.

- Participation in cross-provider trust relationships.

- Engagement in cross-provider redundancy and dynamic repositioning measures.

- Implementation of substantiated integrity measures.

Various U.S. Government agencies, such as the Defense Information Systems Agency (DISA) and NIST, are infrastructure providers. As such, they would be responsible for the same activities as their private sector counterparts.

With the responsibility structure outlined above, the implementation of national cyber resilience in the United States could be achieved in phases, starting with key services on which all the others depend and expanding to the other services. Lessons learned in this phase, especially in Steps 4.1 through 4.3, can be used to guide relevant regulation and investment.

Phase 1. This initial phase should focus on the three telecommunications and networking elements on which all the other cyber infrastructure elements depend, IP routing, link switching and time. The designated sector-specific agencies, especially CISA and FCC, must identify and assemble the service providers with the greatest capacity and largest customer base while also ensuring geographic and sector coverage. NIST should also be involved because it is the ultimate time authority in the United States. After the key providers are assembled, CISA should lead them through the steps described in Section 5, concentrating on applying the resilience practices and testing for the three telecommunications and networking elements.

Phase 2. In Phase 2, the scope of the resilience effort must be expanded to cover all the telecommunications and networking layer elements along with DNS, the foundational services layer element on which most other elements depend. CISA would also lead this phase, but it would engage the DoD because it is the operator of one of the DNS root servers and a top-level DNS domain (.mil).

The scope of this phase is quite broad because it covers eight service elements. As a result, it would not be possible to conduct comprehensive tests of attack and disruption scenarios.

Test and exercise scenarios should be drawn from two sources. Leading service providers should provide disruption scenarios based on historical observations. CTIIC should provide attack scenarios based on intelligence assessments of the capabilities, plans and intentions of hostile entities.

The service providers engaged in Phase 2 would include all the providers engaged in Phase 1, along with other telecommunications and networking providers based on their capacity and coverage of subscriber connectivity, signaling, voice service and SMS elements. Finally, major DNS service operators would need to be engaged. The critical activity in Phase 2 is testing dynamic representation, coordinated defense, adaptive response and other resilience practices that span multiple service elements. An example is mitigating a DNS disruption by coordinating IP routing response actions with participating IP routing providers.

Phase 3. In the final phase, resilience engineering practices must be applied to all the service elements in all three layers. Primary considerations during this phase include the accuracy and completeness of the dynamic representation, effectiveness and timeliness of dynamic repositioning and realignment practices, and efficiency of cooperative industry and government response actions. A critical type of testing to be conducted in Phase 3 is the recovery of high-level services (e.g., from the compute and storage services layer) through actions taken in the lower layers.

7. Conclusions

Modern society depends on cyber infrastructure for economic, social and national security. Recent history has shown that cyber infrastructure disruptions and attacks cannot be ignored. Any nation that wishes to continue to enjoy the benefits of its cyber infrastructure must have the ability to withstand disruptions and attacks, and recover from them. At the national scale, the only way to ensure this ability is to build resilience into the cyber infrastructure and establish trust and cooperative relationships between private sector infrastructure operators and responsible government entities.

This paper has presented several suggestions for improving cyber infrastructure resilience at the national scale. But several open issues will present challenges to achieving a robust implementation. Some of the issues are technical in nature and should be resolved through conventional research. The biggest challenge is applying resilience engineering to a diverse and evolving cyber infrastructure, especially when the components of the infrastructure often cross-national boundaries. However, the reliance and dependence on cyber infrastructure will not permit inaction because the potential impacts of disruptions and attacks to national security, prosperity and societal well-being are just too great.

References

[1] F. Alaba, M. Othman, I. Hashem and F. Alotaibi, Internet of Things security: A survey, *Journal of Network and Computer Applications*, vol. 88, pp. 10–28, 2017.

[2] J. Allen and P. Curtis, Measures for Managing Operational Resilience, Technical Report CMU/SEI-2011-TR-019, Software Engineering Institute, Carnegie Mellon University, Pittsburgh, Pennsylvania, 2011.

[3] B. Amann, R. Sommer, M. Vallentin and S. Hall, No attack necessary: The surprising dynamics of SSL trust relationships, *Proceedings of the Twenty-Ninth Annual Computer Security Applications Conference*, pp. 179–188, 2013.

[4] M. Amin, Challenges in reliability, security, efficiency and resilience of energy infrastructure: Towards a smart self-healing electric power grid, *Proceedings of the IEEE Power and Energy Society General Meeting – Conversion and Delivery of Electrical Energy in the 21st Century*, 2008.

[5] M. Armbrust, A. Fox, R. Griffith, A. Joseph, R. Katz, A. Konwinski, G. Lee, D. Patterson, A. Rabkin, I. Stoica and M. Zaharia, A view of cloud computing, *Communications of the ACM*, vol. 53(4), pp. 50–58, 2010.

[6] M. Assuncao, R. Calheiros, S. Bianchi, M. Netto and R. Buyya. Big data computing and clouds: Trends and future directions, *Journal of Parallel and Distributed Computing*, vol. 79-80, pp. 3–15, 2015.

[7] D. Atkins and R. Austein, Threat Analysis of the Domain Name System (DNS), RFC 3833, 2004.

[8] D. Atkins, K. Droegemeier, S. Feldman, H. Garcia-Molina, M. Klein, D. Messerschmitt, P. Messina, J. Ostriker and M. Wright, Revolutionizing Science and Engineering Through Cyberinfrastructure: Report of the National Science Foundation Blue-Ribbon Advisory Panel on Cyberinfrastructure, Alexandria, Virginia (`www.nsf.gov/cise/sci/reports/atkins.pdf`), 2003.

[9] T. Aven, On some recent definitions and analysis frameworks for risk, vulnerability and resilience, *Risk Analysis*, vol. 31(4), pp. 515–522, 2011.

[10] D. Bodeau and R. Graubart, Cyber Resiliency Engineering Framework, Technical Report MTR110237, MITRE Corporation, Bedford, Massachusetts, 2011.

[11] A. Boin and A. McConnell, Preparing for critical infrastructure breakdowns: The limits of crisis management and the need for resilience, *Journal of Contingencies and Crisis Management*, vol. 15(1), pp. 50–59, 2007.

[12] T. Brooks, *Cyber-Assurance for the Internet of Things*, IEEE Press, Piscataway, New Jersey, 2017.

[13] G. Bush, National Security Directive – National Policy for the Security of National Security Telecommunications and Information Systems, National Security Directive 42, The White House, Washington, DC, July 5, 1990.

[14] K. Butler, T. Farley, P. McDaniel and J. Rexford, A survey of BGP security issues and solutions, *Proceedings of the IEEE*, vol. 98(1), pp. 100–122, 2010.

[15] A. Chakrabarti and G. Manimaran, Internet infrastructure security: A taxonomy, *IEEE Network*, vol. 16(6), pp. 13–21, 2002.

[16] B. Clinton, Executive Order 13010 – Critical infrastructure protection, *Federal Register*, vol. 61(138), pp. 37345–37350, 1996.

[17] D. Comer, *The Internet Book: Everything You Need to Know About Computer Networking and How the Internet Works*, CRC Press, Boca Raton, Florida, 2019.

[18] T. Comes and B. Van de Walle, Measuring disaster resilience: The impact of Hurricane Sandy on critical infrastructure systems, *Proceedings of the Eleventh International ISCRAM Conference*, pp. 190–199, 2014.

[19] P. Cornish, R. Hughes and D. Livingstone, Cyberspace and the National Security of the United Kingdom: Threats and Responses, A Chatham House Report, Chatham House, London, United Kingdom, 2009.

[20] D. Crocker, Internet Mail Architecture, RFC 5598, 2009.

[21] G. Cybenko, Quantifying and measuring cyber resiliency, *Proceedings of SPIE*, vol. 9825, pp. 98250R-1–98250R-6, 2016.

[22] Cyber Security and Infrastructure Security Agency, Critical Infrastructure Sectors, Arlington, Virginia (www.dhs.gov/cisa/criti cal-infrastructure-sectors), 2020.

[23] C. Czosseck, R. Ottis and A. Taliharm, Estonia after the 2007 cyber attacks: Legal, strategic and organizational changes in cyber security, *International Journal of Cyber Warfare and Terrorism*, vol. 1(1), pp. 24–34, 2011.

[24] D. Dausey, J. Buehler and N. Lurie, Designing and conducting tabletop exercises to assess public health preparedness for manmade and naturally-occurring biological threats, *BMC Public Health*, vol. 7, article no. 1, 2007.

[25] K. de Leeuw and Jan Bergstra (Eds.), *The History of Information Security: A Comprehensive Handbook*, Elsevier, Amsterdam, The Netherlands, 2007.

[26] Defense Science Board, Task Force Report: Resilient Military Systems and the Advanced Cyber Threat, U.S. Department of Defense, Washington, DC, 2013.

[27] D. Denning, Activism, hacktivism and cyberterrorism: The Internet as a tool for influencing foreign policy, in *Networks and Netwars: The Future of Terror, Crime and Militancy*, J. Arquilla and D. Ronfeldt (Eds.), RAND Corporation, Santa Monica, California, pp. 239–288, 2001.

[28] L. Dignan, Top cloud providers 2019: AWS, Microsoft Azure, Google Cloud; IBM makes hybrid move; Salesforce dominates SaaS, *ZDNet*, August 15, 2019.

[29] T. Dillon, C. Wu and E. Chang, Cloud computing: Issues and challenges, *Proceedings of the Twenty-Fourth IEEE International Conference on Advanced Information Networking and Applications*, pp. 27–33, 2010.

[30] C. Doerr and F. Kuipers, All quiet on the Internet front? *IEEE Communications*, vol. 52(10), pp. 46–51, 2014.

[31] M. Dunn Cavelty, Critical information infrastructure: Vulnerabilities, threats and responses, *UNIDIR Disarmament Forum*, vol. 2007(3), pp. 15–22, 2007.

[32] M. Elgazzar, Perspectives on M2M protocols, *Proceedings of the Seventh IEEE International Conference on Intelligent Computing and Information Systems*, pp. 501–505, 2015.

[33] Executive Office of the President, National Security Strategy of the United States of America, The White House, Washington, DC, 2017.

[34] M. Faloutsos, P. Faloutsos and C. Faloutsos, On power-law relationships of the Internet topology, *ACM SIGCOMM Computer Communication Review*, vol. 29(4), pp. 251–262, 1999.

[35] Federal Communications Commission, Annual Report and Analysis of Competitive Market Conditions with Respect to Mobile Wireless, Nineteenth Report, Washington, DC, 2016.

[36] T. Fleury, H. Khurana and V. Welch, Towards a taxonomy of attacks against energy control systems, in *Critical Infrastructure Protection II*, M. Papa and S. Shenoi (Eds.), Springer, Boston, Massachusetts, pp. 71–85, 2008.

[37] J. Frahim and A. Raza, A Framework to Protect Data Through Segmentation, Cisco Systems, San Jose, Califormia (`www.cis co.com/c/en/us/about/security-center/framework-segmenta tion.html`), 2019.

[38] U. Franke and J. Brynielsson, Cyber situational awareness – A systematic review of the literature, *Computers and Security*, vol. 46, pp. 18–31, 2014.

[39] H. Gallagher, W. McMahon and R. Morrow, Cyber security: Protecting the resilience of Canada's financial system, *Bank of Canada Financial System Review*, vol. 2014, pp. 47–53, 2014.

[40] K. Geers, The cyber threat to national critical infrastructures: Beyond theory, *Information Security Journal: A Global Perspective*, vol. 18(1), pp. 1–7, 2009.

[41] T. Grance, T. Nolan, K. Burke, R. Dudley, G. White and T. Good, Guide to Test, Training and Exercise Programs for IT Plans and Capabilities, NIST Special Publication SP 800-84, National Institute of Standards and Technology, Gaithersburg, Maryland, 2006.

[42] E. Gregori, A. Improta, L. Lenzini and C. Orsini, The impact of IXPs on the AS-level topology structure of the Internet, *Computer Communications*, vol. 34(1), pp. 68–82, 2011.

[43] J. Hernandez-Castro, E. Cartwright and A. Stepanova, Economic Analysis of Ransomware, arXiv: 1703.06660 (`arxiv.org/pdf/17 03.06660.pdf`), 2017.

[44] R. Housley and T. Polk, *Planning for PKI: Best Practices Guide for Deploying Public Key Infrastructure*, John Wiley and Sons, New York, 2001.

[45] C. Huitema, *Routing in the Internet*, Prentice Hall, Paramus, New Jersey, 1999.

[46] G. Huston, M. Rossi and G. Armitage, Securing BGP – A literature survey, *IEEE Communications Surveys and Tutorials*, vol. 13(2), pp. 199–222, 2011.

[47] IDG Communications, 2018 Cloud Computing Survey, Needham, Massachusetts, 2018.

[48] Information Technology – Information Sharing and Analysis Center, IT-ISAC Membership, Manassas, Virginia (`www.it-isac.org/members`), 2022.

[49] R. Jennings, E. Nahum, D. Olshefski, D. Saha, Z. Shae and C. Waters, A study of Internet instant messaging and chat protocols, *IEEE Network*, vol. 20(4), pp. 16–21, 2006.

[50] D. Kahn, *The Codebreakers: The Comprehensive History of Secret Communication from Ancient Times to the Internet*, Scribner, New York, 1996.

[51] T. King, C. Dietzel, J. Snijders, G. Doering and G. Hankins, BLACKHOLE Community, RFC 7999, 2016.

[52] N. Kshetri, Recent U.S. cybersecurity policy initiatives: Challenges and Implications, *IEEE Computer*, vol. 48(7), pp. 64–69, 2015.

[53] P. Kuhn, C. Pack and R. Skoog, Common channel signaling networks: Past, present, future, *IEEE Journal on Selected Areas in Communications*, vol. 12(3), pp. 383–394, 1994.

[54] J. Lewis, Assessing the Risks of Cyber Terrorism, Cyber War and Other Cyber Threats, Center for Strategic and International Studies, Washington, DC, 2002.

[55] T. Lewis, *Critical Infrastructure Protection in Homeland Security: Defending a Networked Nation*, John Wiley and Sons, Hoboken, New Jersey, 2020.

[56] I. Linkov, D. Eisenberg, K. Plourde, T. Seager, J. Allen and A. Kott, Resilience metrics for cyber systems, *Environment Systems and Decisions*, vol. 33(4), pp. 471–476, 2013.

[57] C. Liu and P. Albitz, *DNS and BIND*, O'Reilly Media, Sebastopol, Califormia, 2006.

[58] S. Madnick and J. Donovan, Application and analysis of the virtual machine approach to information system security and isolation, *Proceedings of the ACM Workshop on Virtual Computer Systems*, pp. 210–224, 1973.

[59] S. Mansfield-Devine, The growth and evolution of DDoS, *Network Security*, vol. 2015(10), pp. 13–20, 2015.

[60] O. Michel and E. Keller, SDN in wide-area networks: A survey, *Proceedings of the Fourth International Conference on Software-Defined Systems*, pp. 37–42, 2017.

[61] J. Miriam and R. Kerber, Critical Homeland Infrastructure Protection, Report of the Defense Science Board Task Force on Critical Infrastructure Protection, U.S. Department of Defense, Washington, DC, 2007.

[62] D. Moore, V. Paxson, S. Savage, C. Shannon, S. Staniford and N. Weaver, The Spread of the Sapphire/Slammer Worm, Center for Applied Internet Data Analysis, University of California San Diego, La Jolla, California, 2003.

[63] T. Neagoe, V. Cristea and L. Banica, NTP versus PTP in computer network clock synchronization, *Proceedings of the IEEE International Symposium on Industrial Electronics*, pp. 317–362, 2006.

[64] G. Nibaldi, Proposed Technical Evaluation Criteria for Trusted Computer Systems, Technical Report M79-225, MITRE Corporation, Bedford, Massachusetts, 1979.

[65] A. Nolan, Cybersecurity and Information Sharing: Legal Challenges and Solutions, CRS Report R43941, Congressional Research Service, Washington, DC, 2015.

[66] B. Obama, Presidential Policy Directive – Critical Infrastructure Security and Resilience, Presidential Policy Directive 21, The White House, Washington, DC, February 12, 2013.

[67] B. Obama, Presidential Memorandum – Establishment of the Cyber Threat Intelligence Integration Center, The White House, Washington, DC, February 25, 2015.

[68] B. Obama, Presidential Policy Directive – United States Cyber Incident Coordination, Presidential Policy Directive 41, The White House, Washington, DC, July 26, 2016.

[69] M. Omer, R. Nilchiani and A. Mostashari, Measuring the resilience of the transoceanic telecommunications cable system, *IEEE Systems Journal*, vol. 3(3), pp. 295–303, 2009.

[70] P. Pernik, J. Wojtkowiak and A. Verschoor-Kirss, National Cyber Security Organization: United States, NATO Cooperative Cyber Defence Centre of Excellence, Tallinn, Estonia, 2016.

[71] President's Commission on Enhancing National Cybersecurity, Report on Securing and Growing the Digital Economy, Executive Office of the President, The White House, Washington, DC, 2016.

[72] A. Rathmell, Cyber-terrorism: The shape of future conflict? *Journal of Financial Crime*, vol. 6(3), pp. 277–283, 1999.

[73] Ribbon Communications, What is Diameter Protocol? Plano, Texas (ribboncommunications.com/company/get-help/glossary/dia meter-protocol), 2019.

[74] S. Rinaldi, J. Peerenboom and T. Kelly, Identifying, understanding and analyzing critical infrastructure interdependencies, *IEEE Control Systems*, vol. 21(6), pp. 11–25, 2001.

[75] J. Rollins and A. Henning, Comprehensive National Cybersecurity Initiative: Legal Authorities and Policy Considerations, CRS Report R40427, Congressional Research Service, Washington, DC, 2009.

[76] F. Sabahi, Cloud computing security threats and responses, *Proceedings of the Third IEEE International Conference on Communication Software and Networks*, pp. 245–249, 2011.

[77] J. Saltzer and M. Schroeder, The protection of information in computer systems, *Proceedings of the IEEE*, vol. 63(9), pp. 1278–1308, 1975.

[78] K. Sivalingam and S. Subramaniam (Eds.), *Optical WDM Networks: Principles and Practice*, Kluwer Academic Publishers, New York, 2000.

[79] S. Snedaker, *Business Continuity and Disaster Recovery Planning for IT Professionals*, Syngress, Waltham, Massachusetts, 2013.

[80] E. Spafford, The Internet Worm incident, *Proceedings of the Second European Software Engineering Conference*, pp. 446–468, 1989.

[81] J. Sterbenz, D. Hutchison, E. Cetinkaya, A. Jabbar, J. Rohrer, M. Scholler and P. Smith, Resilience and survivability in communication networks: Strategies, principles and survey of disciplines, *Computer Networks*, vol. 54(8), pp. 1245–1265, 2010.

[82] C. Stewart, S. Simms, B. Plale, M. Link, D. Hancock and G. Fox, What is cyberinfrastructure? *Proceedings of the Thirty-Eighth Annual ACM SIGUCCS Fall Conference: Navigation and Discovery*, pp. 37–44, 2010.

[83] A. Taylor and J. Vincent, An SMS history, in *Mobile World*, L. Hamill, A. Lasen and D. Diaper (Eds.), Springer, London, United Kingdom, pp. 75–91, 2005.

[84] U.S. Computer Emergency Readiness Team, CERT Advisory CA-2002-03: Multiple vulnerabilities in many implementations of the Simple Network Management Protocol (SNMP), Washington, DC, March 11, 2002.

[85] U.S. Congress, Public Law 113 – 274, Cybersecurity Enhancement Act of 2014, Washington, DC, 2014.

[86] U.S. Department of Defense, Department of Defense Trusted Computer System Evaluation Criteria, Publication DoD 5200.28-STD, Washington, DC, 1985.

[87] U.S. Department of Defense, Defense Support of Civil Authorities (DSCA), Directive 3025.18, Washington, DC, 2010.

[88] U.S. Department of Defense, The Department of Defense Cyber Table Top Guidebook, Version 1.0, Washington, DC, 2018.

[89] U.S. Department of Homeland Security, National Cyber Incident Response Plan, Washington, DC (`www.us-cert.gov/sites/de fault/files/ncirp/National_Cyber_Incident_Response_Plan .pdf`), 2016.

[90] A. Viswanathan, N. Feldman, Z. Wang and R. Callon, Evolution of multiprotocol label switching, *IEEE Communications*, vol. 36(5), pp. 165–173, 1998.

[91] V. Voydock and S. Kent, Security mechanisms in high-level network protocols, *ACM Computing Surveys*, vol. 15(2), pp. 135–171, 1983.

[92] C. Weissman, Security controls in the ADEPT-50 time-sharing system, *Proceedings of the AFIPS Fall Joint Computer Conference*, pp. 119–133, 1969.

[93] J. Wu, Y. Zhang, Z. Mao and K. Shin, Internet routing resilience to failures: Analysis and implications, *Proceedings of the ACM Co-NEXT Conference*, article no. 25, 2007.

Chapter 2

ARE EUROPEAN SECURITY POLICIES READY FOR ADVANCED METERING SYSTEMS WITH CLOUD BACK-ENDS?

Oyvind Toftegaard, Janne Hagen and Bernhard Hämmerli

Abstract   Advanced metering systems deployed in Europe are enablers of distributed power production where prosumers can feed surplus energy into the grid. Successfully managing complex energy systems requires real-time data access, flexible production and rapid demand response. The accompanying need for data storage capacity and processing power has rendered cloud services an attractive option. However, at this time, European cyber security legislation related to advanced metering systems does not reflect the broad usage of cloud technology.

This chapter describes an advanced metering system reference model based on the cloud profiles of five distribution grid operators. It identifies cloud-related gaps in current European Union cyber security legislation applicable to advanced metering systems. The gaps are identified via a holistic mapping of security principles from prominent cloud security frameworks to existing European Union legislation. A novel, advanced metering system security policy framework that covers all the identified cloud security gaps is specified. The security policy framework is an important first step towards cloud-ready security legislation for advanced metering systems. Authorities overseeing cyber security and energy resources can employ the policy framework as a starting point for a broad debate among the various stakeholders to institute cloud-ready security policies for advanced metering systems.

Keywords: Advanced metering systems, cloud, security policies, legislation

1.   Introduction

The European Union (EU) Green Deal requires a shift from coal-based power production to renewable sources such as wind and solar energy [12]. Electricity production by wind farms and solar panels is

© IFIP International Federation for Information Processing 2022
Published by Springer Nature Switzerland AG 2022
J. Staggs and S. Shenoi (Eds.): Critical Infrastructure Protection XVI, IFIP AICT 666, pp. 47–69, 2022.
https://doi.org/10.1007/978-3-031-20137-0_2

highly dependent on climate and weather conditions – wind turbines operate in certain wind speed ranges and solar irradiance is seasonal and latitude dependent. Long-term planning and short-term adaptation to balance supply and demand from weather predictions are challenging. Meanwhile, consumption patterns are changing and the introduction of induction stoves and proliferation of electric vehicles are expected to drive the maximum consumption peaks higher.

The European power grid, which is maintained and operated by transmission and distribution grid operators, must continuously balance production and consumption. When power production is less than demand, smart computing systems manage the demand response to achieve system balance. Digital technology, sensors, cloud services, big data analytics and optimization algorithms are cornerstones for managing demand. The introduction of 3G mobile broadband in 2001 and 4G in 2011 made rapid data transfer more available and affordable [36]. The introduction of Amazon Web Services in 2006 and Microsoft Azure in 2008 made cloud services available to the masses. The shift to advanced metering system (AMS) architectures with cloud-based back-ends is a natural consequence of these technological developments. Fast mobile broadband enables large amounts of data to be collected from smart meters at customer premises for billing and data analytics. Cloud services are attractive because they provide high availability and scalability of data storage, and processing power. Costs can be reduced by customizing cloud resources to accommodate individual smart meter systems.

Smart meters incorporating onboard circuit breakers are common in the European Union [1]. Millions of new, computer-controlled circuit breakers have been introduced across the European energy system. The European power grid, like the Internet, crosses national borders and grid balancing is coordinated in multi-state synchronous areas. As a result, an incident in one member state can impact the grid in other member states. In 2003, cross-border cascading effects originating in France and Switzerland resulted in the loss of power to about 56 million Italians [27]. In 2006, more than 15 million households lost power supply due to cascading effects across Germany, France, Italy, Belgium, Spain and Portugal [40]. Proper security regimes and resilient power infrastructure are needed to reduce the risk of cross-border impacts such as cascading blackouts.

Several policies have been developed to advance cross-border cyber security harmonization. Examples are the information security components in the ISO 27000 series of standards [24] and the European Union cyber security guidelines published by the European Union Agency for Cybersecurity (ENISA) [20, 21]. An important difference between legislated policies (regulations) and standards or guidelines is that regulations are compulsory. During the past decade, the European Union has issued several regulations [15–19] covering security requirements that are applicable to advanced metering systems [9]. However, developing and approving regulations are time consuming, and there is always the risk that legislated requirements will become obsolete or even counterproductive [23]. Therefore, when large numbers of European grid operators are procuring cloud-based advanced metering systems, national authorities should ensure that security regulations adequately cover cloud operations.

This chapter assesses whether the European security legislation applicable to advanced metering systems reflects the broad usage of cloud technology. An advanced metering system reference model is presented to guide the scope of the assessment. Gaps in cloud-related European Union legislation are identified by mapping security principles from prominent cloud security frameworks against regulatory requirements. Finally, a novel, cloud-secure policy framework for advanced metering systems that covers the cloud security gaps is articulated.

2. Background

This section describes the evolution of advanced metering systems and discusses European Union legislation related to cyber security.

2.1 Advanced Metering System Evolution

Modern advanced metering systems are complex systems of systems that connect distributed smart meters with centralized applications via two-way metering. These systems have been enabled by tremendous technological advancements over the decades.

The first electromechanical meters had analog displays [33]. Electricity consumption data was read manually by consumers and communicated by mail or orally to power grid operators. Automatic meter reading (AMR) was introduced in 1962 [37]. The deployed systems enabled grid operators to collect information using handheld data collectors or via landline telephone networks. The meters that supported automated readings incorporated solid-state metering components and digital displays. However, the cost effectiveness of automatic meter reading systems was questioned [8]. In 1999, it was demonstrated that advanced metering infrastructures (AMIs) with two-way data communications could reduce costs [8]. Soon after, grid operators across Europe began to invest heavily in advanced metering infrastructures.

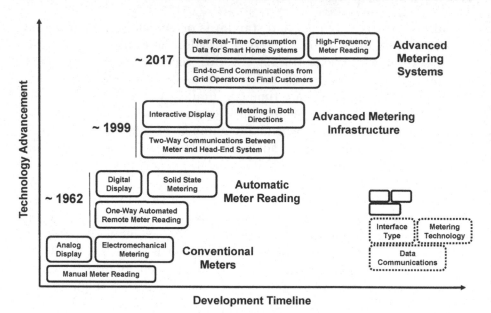

Figure 1. Electricity metering system evolution in the European Union [3, 10, 15].

Advanced metering infrastructures were upgraded further with more sophisticated meters with interactive displays and two-way metering. The upgrades provided customers with information about their electricity consumption and enabled them to participate in energy markets by selling excess energy produced by solar panels.

In recent years, ecosystems of advanced metering system applications have been built around advanced metering infrastructure backbones. The upgrades include meter readings with high frequency and end-to-end communications between grid operators and consumers. The frequent meter readings provide detailed consumption profiles that benefit operators and customers. Home energy management systems and electric vehicle charging stations can combine the consumption data with power price and grid tariff information to schedule and optimize electricity usage. End-to-end data streams from grid operators to consumers enable operators to customize the data content transmitted to consumers and rapidly adapt to load changes.

Figure 1 shows the advances in electricity metering technology in three prominent areas, interface type, metering technology and data communications. It is a modified version of a figure in [3] in that it describes the evolution of electricity metering systems in Europe and limits the content to interface type, metering technology and data communications.

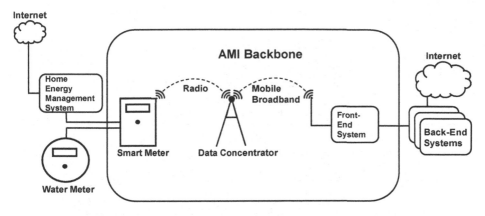

Figure 2. Advanced metering system applications.

In the future, increasing numbers of advanced metering system applications are expected to be built around advanced metering infrastructure backbones. These systems include customer management systems, grid information systems and consumer apps such as those used for home energy management. Other systems that are gaining popularity include integration services that enable related technologies, such as water meters, to communicate using advanced metering infrastructure backbones. Figure 2 shows advanced applications for consumer price schemes and water meter reading built around an advanced metering infrastructure backbone.

Cloud services are being leveraged to address the data processing needs in current and future advanced metering system deployments. The trend involves smart meters with cloud-based back-ends [29, 38]. As the complexity of advanced metering systems grows, security and privacy will become increasingly important. Clearly, it is necessary to institute cloud security standards and related policies governing cyber security.

2.2 European Union Cyber Security Legislation

Figure 3 shows a timeline covering technological advancements, cyber security concerns and European Union security legislation. The cyber security concerns and related legislation are mapped to the three steps in electricity metering technology advancement, automatic meter reading, advanced metering infrastructures and advanced metering systems. The figure shows how legislation has developed in relation to technological advancements to address emerging cyber security concerns.

In 1995, the European Union Data Protection Directive [14] came into force to protect the privacy of citizens in member states. Despite the

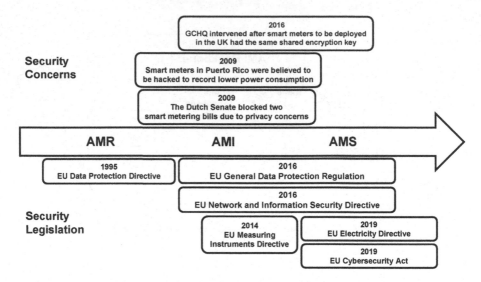

Figure 3. Technology, cyber security concerns and legislation timeline.

privacy protections provided by the legislation, the Dutch population expressed considerable skepticism when the decision was made to install smart meters compulsorily. In 2009, the Dutch Senate blocked two proposed smart metering bills due to privacy concerns [7]. In 2016, the European Union Data Protection Directive was replaced with the European Union General Data Protection Regulation (GDPR) [16]. GDPR updated the security and privacy requirements, and tackled privacy challenges related to technological development.

In 2009, smart meters in Puerto Rico were reported to have been hacked, possibly causing an annual loss of 400 million dollars [39]. The attacks supposedly adjusted the settings that recorded power consumption. In 2014, the European Union issued the Measuring Instruments Directive (MID) [15], which provided specific rules governing data integrity related to electricity measurements by smart meters.

The European Union Network and Information Security (NIS) Directive [17] published in 2016 introduced minimum cyber security requirements for operators of essential services. Because power grid operation is an essential service, grid operators were subject to the cyber security requirements imposed by the directive. The same year, the UK Government Communications Headquarters (GCHQ) intervened to change the nationwide smart meter design, where all smart meters had the same encryption key [34]. Without the intervention, a malicious actor who cracked or otherwise obtained a smart meter key could have gained access to all the smart meters in the country.

The European Union Electricity Directive [19] published in 2019 contains the first compulsory rules on security and privacy that are exclusive to smart metering systems. The high-level rules state that smart metering security "shall comply with relevant Union security rules" with "due regard of the best available techniques for ensuring the highest level of cyber security protection while bearing in mind the costs and the principle of proportionality." The Electricity Directive also states that the "privacy of final customers and the protection of their data shall comply with relevant Union data protection and privacy rules."

In 2019, the European Union also passed the Cybersecurity Act [18], which covers a voluntary program for the security certification of products, processes and services. The certification program targets products such as smart meters [11]; however, progress has been limited because the program in voluntary.

3.   Research Methodology Overview

The comparative study of cloud security frameworks and European Union legislation with security requirements applicable to advanced metering systems was conducted by applying an exploratory research design comprising three phases.

The objective of the first phase was to understand how applications built on the advanced metering infrastructure backbone are transferred to the cloud. A qualitative analysis was performed that categorized cloud-based advanced metering system applications such as head-end systems (HESs), meter data management systems (MDMSs) and customer information systems. The categorization was based on the advanced metering system architectures deployed by five Norwegian grid operators. The architectural descriptions were collected by the Norwegian Water Resources and Energy Directorate during advanced metering system supervision activities conducted in 2017 and 2018. The categorization led to the specification of an advanced metering system as a service (AMSaaS) reference model covering advanced metering systems with cloud-based back-ends.

The objective of the second phase was to identify cloud-related security gaps in European Union legislation that are applicable to advanced metering systems. A qualitative approach was employed that mapped European Union legislation related to advanced metering system security against security principles from three cloud security frameworks, the Cloud Security Alliance (CSA) Egregious 11 [5], the International

Organization for Standardization (ISO) Cloud Services Standard (ISO 27017) [26] and the UK National Cyber Security Centre (NCSC) Cloud Security Principles [30].

Five European Union legislative constructs were considered, Measuring Instruments Directive (MID), General Data Protection Regulation (GDPR), Network and Information Security (NIS) Directive, Cybersecurity Act and Electricity Directive. The five constructs were selected after a thorough review of European Union legislation because they contain security requirements applicable to advanced metering systems.

The effort sought to create a holistic overview of prominent cloud security principles and map the principles to the legislative constructs while noting whether or not the principles are covered by the constructs. The three cloud security frameworks were selected because of their distinctive features and relevance to cloud security. The CSA framework was specified to reduce the risk of the most prominent cloud threats. The ISO framework was designed to complement requirements in the ISO Code of Practice for Information Security Controls (ISO 27002) Standard [25] that was created to support the implementation of the ISO Information Security Management System (ISO 27001) Standard [24]. The NCSC framework was designed to provide general cloud security guidance for various organizations.

Next, the mapping of the security principles from the cloud security frameworks to the European Union legislative constructs was placed in relevant categories specified in the National Institute of Standards and Technology Cybersecurity Framework (NIST CSF) [31]. NIST CSF is a widely-used cyber security standard that has contributed to the creation of several cyber security frameworks [2, 32]. The use of the NIST CSF categories provided an excellent functional overview that rendered the subsequent analysis more efficient.

The objective of the third phase was to close the identified cloud related security gaps and provide a first step towards cloud-ready security legislation applicable to advanced metering systems. Therefore, a cloud-ready European advanced metering system security policy framework was created based on the NIST CSF categories and a policy hierarchy model. The mapping of security principles from the cloud security frameworks and the scope of the AMSaaS reference model were used to select relevant NIST CSF categories. The advanced metering system security policy framework was subsequently created to cover all the cloud security principles relevant to the AMSaaS reference model that were found to be missing in the European Union legislative constructs during the gap analysis.

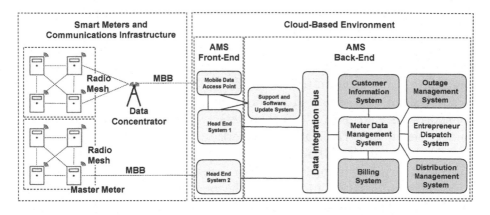

Figure 4. AMSaaS reference model for AMSs with cloud-based back-ends.

4. Reference Model

Traditional advanced metering system models comprise smart meters, a communications system and a centralized head-end system. Modern advanced metering system back-ends have applications that support a variety of automated functions such as electricity billing, distribution management and entrepreneur dispatching [4]. Cloud services are now being used to support these functions. Little attention has focused on advanced metering system back-ends; as a result, the paradigm shift to the cloud by the back-end systems has been largely ignored.

Figure 4 shows the advanced metering system as a service (AMSaaS) reference model created to capture the architectures of advanced metering systems with cloud-based back-ends. As mentioned above, the reference model is derived from the advanced metering system architectures of five Norwegian grid operators. Details about these architectures are not available to the public. However, access was obtained for this research because it was conducted in cooperation with the Norwegian Water Resources and Energy Directorate.

The AMSaaS reference model was designed by identifying advanced-metering-related systems in the five architectures that were "in the cloud," meaning that the systems were located at remote servers not operated by the grid operators. The identified in-the-cloud systems included one grid operator mobile data access point, two grid operator head-end systems, two grid operator meter data management systems, three grid operator integration services for external and internal systems (data integration bus in Figure 4), one grid operator support and software update system, and two grid operator entrepreneur dispatch systems. These systems are highlighted in light gray in Figure 4. The boxes in dark gray are legacy systems that the grid operators operate in their premises. The legacy systems are included to render the reference model more holistic and because legacy systems are prominent candidates for migration to the cloud.

Analysis of the advanced metering architectures revealed that data concentrators and master smart meters are commonly used to connect smart meters in a radio mesh network with the head-end system via mobile broadband (MBB). After reaching the head-end system, the advanced metering system data is often transferred to a meter data management system that functions as the master data repository. When more than one head-end system is in use, a data integration bus may be employed to ease data transfer from the head-end systems to the meter data management system. Other back-end systems, such as entrepreneur dispatch systems, billing systems, distribution management systems, customer information systems and outage management systems, may access relevant data from the meter data management system. These back-end exemplars are relatively immature. Several back-end systems (see, e.g., [28, 35, 41]) may be procured or deployed as cloud applications in the future.

5.   Framework to Legislation Mapping

The security principles in the three prominent cloud security frameworks mentioned above were mapped to the five European Union legislative constructs applicable to advanced metering systems, Measuring Instruments Directive (MID), General Data Protection Regulation (GDPR), Network and Information Security (NIS) Directive, Cybersecurity Act and Electricity Directive. The three cloud security frameworks are described in the following paragraphs.

The Cloud Security Alliance (CSA) Egregious 11 [5], published in 2019, describes the 11 most pressing cloud security threats. The framework specifies measures for mitigating the threats. However, the measures are highly technical and stem from a more comprehensive CSA standard [6]. To maintain the policy-level focus, it was decided to work with the 11 threats and not consider the detailed technical measures in the CSA standard.

ISO 27017, the International Organization for Standardization (ISO) Cloud Services Standard [26], was published in 2015. Like the CSA's Egregious 11 framework, the ISO 27017 standard adopts a detailed technical approach. The standard provides additional guidance on the implementation of measures in the ISO 27002 standard, with a focus on cloud provision and usage. To maintain the cloud focus, only the seven cloud-specific principles in ISO 27017 were considered in the mapping. To ease the mapping process, it was decided to adopt a high-level version of the seven ISO 27017 principles published by the German Federal Office for Information Security [22].

The UK National Cyber Security Centre (NCSC) Cloud Security Principles [30], published in 2018, comprises two frameworks. One framework targets board members whereas the other framework targets technical personnel. The first framework was employed in the mapping because it is at a high level that matches the European legislative constructs. The NCSC cloud security principles enable organizations to assess whether or not cloud services are secure enough to handle their data.

The National Institute of Standards and Technology Cybersecurity Framework (NIST CSF) [31] was employed to categorize the cloud security principles in the three frameworks. Only the NIST CSF categories relevant to the cloud framework principles were considered. As mentioned above, the main reason for introducing the NIST CSF categories was to facilitate the creation of a policy framework.

Tables 1, 2 and 3 show the mappings between the cloud security principles in the frameworks and the European Union legislative constructs. Note that the NIST CSF categories (left-most column of the three tables) are used for categorization only. As a result, multiple security principles may fall in a given NIST CSF category.

Analysis of Tables 1, 2 and 3 reveals that seven cloud security principles are mapped to the Cybersecurity Act whereas only three principles are mapped to GDPR, two to MID and one each to the NIS and Electricity Directives. However, since the Cybersecurity Act focuses on a voluntary certification scheme, the seven principles mapped to the construct would not be compulsory. Therefore, the cloud readiness of the compulsory cyber security principles mapped to the European Union legislative constructs are considered to be lower than the overall analysis results because the analysis includes compulsory as well as voluntary principles.

It is important to note that there are only two NIST CSF categories for which where all three cloud security frameworks have coverage. The two categories, maintenance and continuous security monitoring, have the highest consensus regarding their importance. The maintenance category includes operational security such as system patching, checking new configurations for vulnerabilities and hardening where necessary. The continuous security monitoring category includes usage visibility such as collecting audit logs and monitoring security.

Table 1. Mapping of cloud security principles from frameworks to EU legislation applicable to AMSs.

NIST CSF Category	CSA EE Principles	ISO 27017 Principles	NCSC CSP Principles	EU Legislation Principles
Asset Management		Deletion and removal of cloud service customer assets	Asset protection and resilience	Cloud security is not covered
Governance	Cloud security architecture and strategy	Roles and responsibilities in cloud environments	Governance framework	Cloud security is not covered
Supply Chain Risk Management	Strong control plane		Supply chain security	Cloud security is not covered
Identity Management, Authentication and Access Control	Identity, credential, access and key management	Segregation in virtual computing environments	Secure user management	Cyb. Act Art. 51(b) (Access rights and authorization)
			User separation	Cloud security is not covered
			Identity and authentication	Cyb. Act Art. 51(b) (Access rights and authorization)
	Account hijacking protection			Cloud security is not covered

Table 2. Mapping of cloud security principles from frameworks to EU legislation applicable to AMSs (continued).

NIST CSF Category	CSA EE Principles	ISO 27017 Principles	NCSC CSP Principles	EU Legislation Principles
Awareness and Training	Insider threat security		Personnel security	Cloud security is not covered
			Secure use of services	Cloud security is not covered
Data Security	Data breach prevention and handling		Data-in-transit protection	GDPR Art. 5, 1.(f) (Data protection) Cyb. Act Art. 51(a-b) (Lifecycle data protection) MID H1, 4.3b and Annex I: High level of integrity protection and security
	Secure configuration and change control	Physical and virtual network alignment		Cyb. Act Art. 51(i) (Security by default and by design)
			Secure development	Cyb. Act Art. 51(i) (Security by default and by design)
	Metastructure and applistructure failure prevention			GDPR Art. 32, 1(d) (Testing and evaluation of technical and organizational measures)
Information Protection Processes/ Procedures		Operational security for administrators	Secure service administration	Cloud security is not covered
	Data breach prevention and handling			NIS Art. 14, 2. (Incident prevention and handling) NIS Art. 14, 4. (Significance of incident determination) Cyb. Act Art. 51(d) (Known dependency and vulnerability identification and documentation)

Table 3.   Mapping of cloud security principles from frameworks to EU legislation applicable to AMSs (continued).

NIST CSF Category	CSA EE Principles	ISO 27017 Principles	NCSC CSP Principles	EU Legislation Principles
Maintenance	Secure configuration and change control	Virtual machine hardening	Operational security	Cyb. Act Art. 51(g,j) (Vulnerability and update management)
Protective Technology	Interface security		External interface protection	Cloud security is not covered
Continuous Security Monitoring	Cloud usage visibility	Cloud service monitoring by cloud service customers	Auditing information for users	Cyb. Act Art. 51(e-f) (Access and activity recording)
	Abuse and nefarious use of cloud service prevention			MID Annex I point 8.2 (Evidence of intervention)
				Cloud security is not covered
Communication	Data breach prevention and handling			El. Dir. Art. 14, 3. (Notification of cyber events with significant impacts to authorities) GDPR Art. 33 (Notification of personal data breaches to supervisory authorities) GDPR Art. 34 (Communication of personal data breaches to the data subjects)

The analysis exposes 11 cloud security gaps in the cloud security principles covered by the European Union legislative constructs. The gaps are identified in Tables 1, 2 and 3 using the annotation "Cloud security is not covered." Gaps occur in eight of the 11 NIST CSF categories. It is suggested that, because the NIST CSF categories are common starting points for cyber security policies [2, 32], authorities should use the eight categories with gaps as starting points to strengthen legislation based on the key cloud security principles.

6. Cloud-Secure AMS Policy Framework

This section describes the novel, cloud-secure European advanced metering system security policy framework that draws from three prominent cloud security frameworks. Principles from the three cloud security frameworks were mapped to the NIST CSF categories and existing European Union security legislation applicable to advanced metering systems. The mapping facilitated the identification of relevant cloud security policies from the NIST CSF categories and the evaluation of the cloud-security readiness of European Union legislation.

Figure 5 shows the proposed cloud-secure European advanced metering system security policy framework. The security policies in the dark gray boxes are not covered by current European Union legislation. The security policies in the light gray boxes are partially covered by European Union legislation. The security policies in the unshaded boxes are covered completely by European Union legislation. It is important to note that the term "coverage" considers only the security principles that are related to the AMSaaS model. As a result, European Union legislation requiring, for example, national authorities to conduct asset management or governance of general national concerns are considered to be out of scope.

Figure 5 shows the most prominent security policies for advanced metering systems with cloud-based back-ends. The security policy framework has three organizational layers of protection for defense in depth, strategic, tactical and operational. The strategic layer contains high-level cyber security policies that are connected to strategic business goals; awareness and training is included on this layer due to its influence on corporate culture. The tactical layer covers security and privacy administration functions with a focus on streamlining processes. The operational layer covers day-to-day cyber security activities and hands-on procedures.

Table 4 lists the cloud security principles, organized according to the three organizational layers and NIST categories, that must be covered

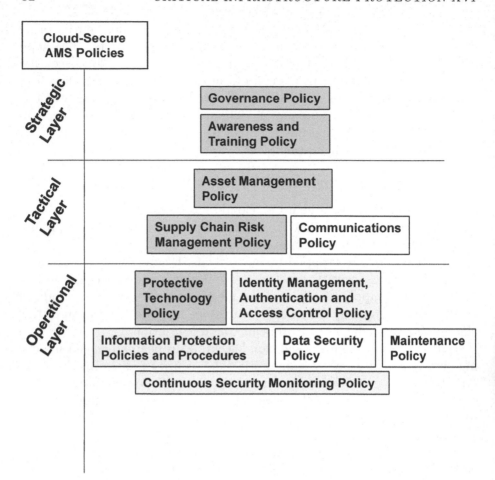

Figure 5.   Cloud-secure European AMS security policy framework.

to close the cloud security gaps identified in Section 5. These principles should be used as supplementary requirements in future European Union legislation to address cloud security in advanced metering systems.

The security principles in the Cybersecurity Act only pertain to voluntary certification programs. Therefore, authorities in member states that do not have certification programs would need to add these principles in the advanced metering system security policy framework shown in Figure 5. Of course, since the principles from the Cybersecurity Act are not compulsory, the question arises why they are included in the analysis and not treated as gaps. The reason is that this work focuses on policy readiness. Perhaps, future European Union legislation will mandate the missing security principles and also make the voluntary security principles compulsory.

Table 4. Cloud security principles to be incorporated as supplementary requirements.

Layer	Policy	Legislation	Supplementary Requirements
Strategic	Governance	No	Governance framework that also establishes roles and responsibilities for cloud service providers
	Awareness and Training	No	Personnel education covering insider threats, screening of personnel and secure use of cloud services
Tactical	Asset Management	No	Asset protection and resilience program covering cloud security architecture and cloud strategy emphasizing asset disposal
	Supply Chain Risk Management	No	Supply chain risk management program covering strong control plane principles
Operational	Protective Technology	No	Documentation of interface and API protection
	Identity Management, Authentication and Access Control	Partial	Identity, credential, access and key management program protecting against account hijacking and covering segregation and separation
	Information Protection Processes/ Procedures	Partial	Operational security procedures for administrators covering secure service administration
	Continuous Security Monitoring	Partial	Systematic audit logging routines for identifying abuse and nefarious use of cloud services

The policy framework is a first step towards cloud-ready security legislation applicable to advanced metering systems in the European Union. The policy framework is specified at a high level and serves as a preliminary proposal at this time. However, it can be further developed and refined with feedback from the various stakeholders, which would enhance the possibility of implementation. A well-composed set of cloud security requirements may be the primary motivation for grid operators to acquire the knowledge and competence needed to fully manage the security of outsourced advanced metering systems in the cloud.

7.   Conclusions

Advanced metering applications that operate with cloud resources or even reside in the cloud are being built around advanced metering infrastructure backbones, drawing new cloud-related cyber security risks. These risks must be managed by grid operators and authorities may need to mandate appropriate security principles to manage the risks. This research has demonstrated that existing European Union legislation applicable to advanced metering systems has gaps related to cloud security. The gaps were identified by mapping security principles in prominent cloud security frameworks to relevant European legislation while noting whether or not the principles are covered by the individual legislative constructs. The mapping and subsequent analysis focused on existing legislative coverage and lack thereof, not on the adequacy of the legislation in addressing the security principles for which there is already full or partial coverage.

A novel, cloud-secure European advanced metering system security policy framework is specified to assist authorities in addressing the identified gaps. This policy framework is an important first step towards creating cloud-ready security legislation that applies to advanced metering systems. Authorities overseeing cyber security and energy can employ the policy framework as a starting point for a broad debate among the various stakeholders to institute cloud-ready security policies for advanced metering systems. The next steps are to discuss the policy framework in industry seminars at the member state levels and pass the knowledge gained to European organizations such as the Council of European Energy Regulators (CEER) and the European Union Agency for the Cooperation of Energy Regulators (ACER). In fact, ACER is currently contributing to new legislation for the European energy sector called the Network Code on Cybersecurity [13]. Considerable efforts will be required on the part of all the stakeholders, industry groups, consumers and authorities, to articulate, and eventually legislate, a holistic European advanced metering system security policy framework. But this must be done because the migration of electric power management and distribution functionality to the cloud significantly elevates the threats to critical infrastructure as well as personal privacy.

A potential limitation of the research is that elements of security principles may have been lost during the consolidation phase. This is because, in some instances, there were no clear or matching levels of aggregation between the NIST CSF categories, cloud security frameworks and European Union legislative constructs. Another limitation is that the focus on cloud security principles ignored other important principles such as security testing, backup and restoration. These and other missing principles should be incorporated in a holistic security policy framework.

One aspect of future research is to assess how European Union security policies cover fully-managed advanced metering systems. Advanced metering system suppliers have begun to offer complete AM-SaaS solutions, including complete advanced metering ecosystems that incorporate leased smart meters and communications networks, and diverse cloud-based advanced metering applications. Consequently, cloud-outsourcing of advanced metering systems will have a much larger physical scope and induce increased risks related to vendor lock-in, lack of transparency and supply chains.

Acknowledgements

This research was supported by the Norwegian Energy Regulatory Authority in the Norwegian Water Resources and Energy Directorate. The authors wish to thank Ph.D. candidate Jenny Sjastad Hagen of the University of Bergen and the Bjerknes Center for Climate Research for her critical reading and language vetting. The authors also wish to thank Ms. Guro Grotterud of the Norwegian Energy Regulatory Authority for providing valuable comments during the preparation of this chapter.

References

[1] C. Alaton and F. Tounquet, Benchmarking Smart Metering Deployment in the EU-28, Final Report, Directorate-General for Energy, European Commission, Brussels, Belgium, 2019.

[2] Australian Cyber Security Centre, Cyber Security Principles, Canberra, Australia (`www.cyber.gov.au/acsc/view-all-content/gu idance/cyber-security-principles`), 2022.

[3] D. Avancini, J. Rodrigues, S. Martins, R. Rabelo, J. Al-Muhtadi and P. Solic, Energy meter evolution in smart grids: A review, *Journal of Cleaner Production*, vol. 217, pp. 702–715, 2019.

[4] R. Bago and M. Campos, Smart meters for improved energy demand management: The Nordic experience, in *Eco-Friendly Innovation in Electricity Transmission and Distribution Networks*, J. Bessede (Ed.), Woodhead Publishing, Sawston, United Kingdom, pp. 339–361, 2015.

[5] Cloud Security Alliance, Top Threats to Cloud Computing – The Egregious 11, Seattle, Washington (`cloudsecurityalliance.org`

`/artifacts/top-threats-to-cloud-computing-egregious-ele ven`), August 6, 2019.

[6] Cloud Security Alliance, Cloud Controls Matrix (CCM), Seattle, Washington (`cloudsecurityalliance.org/research/cloud-con trols-matrix`), 2022.

[7] C. Cuijpers and B. Koops, Smart metering and privacy in Europe: Lessons from the Dutch case, in *European Data Protection: Coming of Age*, S. Gutwirth, R. Leenes, P. de Hert and Y. Poullet (Eds.), Springer, Dordrecht, The Netherlands, pp. 269–293, 2013.

[8] EME Analys, Introduction of AMI Systems in Sweden and Europe (in Swedish), Stockholm, Sweden (`docplayer.se/9943 18-Inforandet-av-ams-system-i-sverige-och-europa.html`), 2007.

[9] S. Eskeland, Temporal anonymity in the AMS scenario without TTPs, *Proceedings of the Twelfth European Conference on Software Architecture: Companion Proceedings*, article no. 57, 2018.

[10] European Commission, 2012/148/EU: Commission Recommendation of 9 March 2012 on Preparations for the Roll-Out of Smart Metering Systems, Document 32012H0148, Brussels, Belgium, 2012.

[11] European Commission, Proposal for a Regulation of the European Parliament and of the Council on ENISA, the "EU Cybersecurity Agency" and Repealing Regulation (EU) 526/2013, and on Information and Communication Technology Cybersecurity Certification ("Cybersecurity Act"), COM/2017/0477 Final, Document 52017PC0477, Brussels, Belgium, 2017.

[12] European Commission, Communication from the Commission to the European Parliament, the European Council, the Council, the European Economic and Social Committee and the Committee of the Regions – The European Green Deal, COM/2019/640 Final, Document 52019DC0640, Brussels, Belgium, 2019.

[13] European Network of Transmission System Operators for Electricity, ENTSO-E and the EU DSO Entity submit the network code on cybersecurity for ACER review, News Release, Brussels, Belgium (`www.entsoe.eu/news/2022/01/14/entso-e-and-the-eu-dso-entity-submit-the-network-code-on-cybersecu rity-for-acer-review`), January 14, 2022.

[14] European Parliament and the Council of the European Union, Directive 95/46/EC of the European Parliament and of the Council of 24 October 1995 on the Protection of Individuals with Regard to the Processing of Personal Data and on the Free Movement of Such Data, Document 31995L0046, Brussels, Belgium, 1995.

[15] European Parliament and the Council of the European Union, Directive 2014/32/EU of the European Parliament and the Council of 26 February 2014 on the Harmonization of the Laws of the Member States Relating to Making Available on the Market of Measuring Instruments, Document 32014L0032, Brussels, Belgium, 2014.

[16] European Parliament and the Council of the European Union, Regulation (EU) 2016/679 of the European Parliament and of the Council of 27 April 2016 on the Protection of Natural Persons with Regard to the Processing of Personal Data and on the Free Movement of Such Data, and Repealing Directive 95/46/EC (General Data Protection Regulation), Document 32016R0679, Brussels, Belgium, 2016.

[17] European Parliament and the Council of the European Union, Directive (EU) 2016/1148 of the European Parliament and of the Council of 6 July 2016 Concerning Measures for a High Common Level of Security of Network and Information Systems Across the Union, Document 32016L1148, Brussels, Belgium, 2016.

[18] European Parliament and the Council of the European Union, Regulation (EU) 2019/881 of the European Parliament and of the Council of 17 April 2019 on ENISA (the European Union Agency for Cybersecurity) and on Information and Communications Technology Cybersecurity Certification and Repealing Regulation (EU) No. 526/2013 (Cybersecurity Act), Document 32019R0881, Brussels, Belgium, 2019.

[19] European Parliament and the Council of the European Union, Directive (EU) 2019/944 of the European Parliament and of the Council of 5 June 2019 on Common Rules for the Internal Market for Electricity and Amending Directive 2012/27/EU, Document 32019L0944, Brussels, Belgium, 2019.

[20] European Union Agency for Network and Information Security, ENISA Smart Grid Security: Recommendations for Europe and Member States, Heraklion, Greece, 2012.

[21] European Union Agency for Network and Information Security, Smart Grid Threat Landscape and Good Practice Guide, Heraklion, Greece, 2013.

[22] Federal Office for Information Security, Mapping from the BSI Cloud Computing Compliance Controls Catalog (C5) to ISO/IEC 27017, Bonn, Germany, 2018.

[23] M. Fenwick, W. Kaal and E. Vermeulen, Regulation tomorrow: What happens when technology is faster than the law? *American University Business Law Review*, vol. 6(3), pp. 561–594, 2017.

[24] International Organization for Standardization and International Electrotechnical Commission, ISO/IEC 27001:2013 Information Technology – Security Techniques – Information Security Management Systems – Requirements Standard, Geneva, Switzerland, 2013.

[25] International Organization for Standardization and International Electrotechnical Commission, ISO/IEC 27002:2013 Information Technology – Security Techniques – Code of Practice for Information Security Controls Standard, Geneva, Switzerland, 2013.

[26] International Organization for Standardization and International Electrotechnical Commission, ISO/IEC 27015:2015 Information Technology – Security Techniques – Code of Practice for Information Security Controls Based on ISO/IEC 27002 for Cloud Services Standard, Geneva, Switzerland, 2015.

[27] C. Johnson, Analyzing the causes of the Italian and Swiss blackout, 28th September 2003, *Proceedings of the Twelfth Australian Workshop on Safety-Critical Systems and Software and Safety-Related Programmable Systems*, pp. 21–30, 2007.

[28] Kamstrup, OMNIGRID – The digital substation, Skanderborg, Denmark (www.kamstrup.com/en-en/electricity-solutions/smart-electricity-meters/omnigrid), 2022.

[29] Kamstrup, Services and training for electricity utilities, Skanderborg, Denmark (www.kamstrup.com/en-en/electricity-solutions/services), 2022.

[30] National Cyber Security Centre, Cloud Security Guidance, London, United Kingdom (www.ncsc.gov.uk/collection/cloud/the-cloud-security-principles), 2018.

[31] National Institute of Standards and Technology, Framework for Improving Critical Infrastructure Cybersecurity, Version 1.1, Gaithersburg, Maryland (nvlpubs.nist.gov/nistpubs/CSWP/NIST.CSWP.04162018.pdf), 2018.

[32] Norwegian National Security Authority, The National Security Authority's Basic Principles for ICT Security (in Norwegian), Oslo, Norway (nsm.no/getfile.php/133747-1592917276/Demo/Dokumenter/Veiledere/nsm_grunnprinsipper_for_ikt-2018.pdf), 2018.

[33] C. Osaretin, Smart Meter and Energy Management in an Integrated Power System (www.researchgate.net/publication/305043932_Smart_Meter_and_Energy_Management_In_An_Integrated_Power_System), 2016.

[34] Power Engineering International, Intervention saves 11bn-pound UK smart meter system from potential mass hack, Maarssen, The Netherlands, March 18, 2016.

[35] H. Saele, K. Ingebrigtsen and M. Istad, Advanced Netering and Management Systems of the Future (in Norwegian), Report No. 34/2019, Norwegian Water Resources and Energy Directorate, Oslo, Norway (`publikasjoner.nve.no/rapport/2019/rapport2019_34.pdf`), 2019.

[36] S. Sahoo, M. Hota and K. Barik, 5G networks, a new look into the future: Beyond all generation networks, *American Journal of Systems and Software*, vol. 2(4), pp. 108–112, 2014.

[37] H. Shahinzadeh and A. Hasanalizadeh-Khosroshahi, Implementation of smart metering systems: Challenges and solutions, *TELKOMNIKA Indonesian Journal of Electrical Engineering*, vol. 12(7), pp. 5104–5109, 2014.

[38] Siemens, Cloud-based apps and services for advanced metering infrastructure (AMI), Munich, Germany (`new.siemens.com/global/en/products/energy/energy-automation-and-smart-grid/managed-services.html`), 2022.

[39] Smart Energy International, Puerto Rico smart meters believed to have been hacked – and such hacks likely to spread, Cape Town, South Africa, April 11, 2012.

[40] Union for the Coordination of Transmission of Electricity, Final Report: System Disturbance on 4 November 2006, Brussels, Belgium (`eepublicdownloads.entsoe.eu/clean-documents/pre2015/pu2015/publications/ce/otherreports/Final-Report-20070130.pdf`), 2007.

[41] U.S. Department of Energy, Advanced Metering Infrastructure and Customer Systems: Results from the Smart Grid Investment Grant Program, Washington, DC (`www.energy.gov/sites/prod/files/2016/12/f34/AMI%20Summary%20Report_09-26-16.pdf`), 2016.

II

INDUSTRIAL CONTROL
SYSTEMS SECURITY

Chapter 3

IMPORTANCE OF CYBER SECURITY ANALYSIS IN THE OPERATIONAL TECHNOLOGY SYSTEM LIFECYCLE

Laura Tinnel and Ulf Lindqvist

Abstract   This research focuses on the importance of cyber security analysis in the operational technology system lifecycle. Specifically, cyber security issues are analyzed when using information technology workstations to manage modern safety instruments that are critical components of safety instrumented systems. Attack paths and security controls in real-world industrial control safety system architectures typically used in the oil and gas sector are examined to determine whether a safety-instrumented-system-mediated architecture could provide better protection against unauthorized and malicious safety instrument configuration changes than a multiplexer-mediated architecture. The determination leveraged crafted assessment questions that were answered using standard cyber security assessment methods.

The research reveals that recurring vulnerabilities exist in all safety systems due to design issues in safety instruments, the Highway Addressable Remote Transducer protocol, third-party device management software and safety instrument management solutions. Additionally, device-native hardware write protection provides the best defense followed by safety instrumented system write protection. When using safety instrumented system security controls, a safety-instrumented-system-mediated architecture can protect against unauthorized device reconfigurations better than a multiplexer-mediated architecture. The key insight is that cyber security analyses commonly used in information technology systems must be adapted and used in the lifecycles of operational technology systems such as industrial control systems and safety instrumented systems to manage the safety risks induced by cyber attacks.

Keywords: Industrial control systems, safety instrumented systems, cyber security

© IFIP International Federation for Information Processing 2022
Published by Springer Nature Switzerland AG 2022
J. Staggs and S. Shenoi (Eds.): Critical Infrastructure Protection XVI, IFIP AICT 666, pp. 73–101, 2022.
https://doi.org/10.1007/978-3-031-20137-0_3

1. Introduction

Industrial control systems (ICSs) operate critical physical processes in manufacturing and industrial facilities, but they do not manage process risk adequately. Safety instrumented systems (SISs) independently monitor process operations and take corrective actions to bring industrial control systems back to their defined safe states when predetermined hazardous processing conditions arise [15]. Catastrophic events can occur when safety instrumented systems do not perform their functions properly, as in the case of a 2005 Texas refinery explosion and fire that killed 15 people and injured 180 [19]. The real-world consequences of such failures depend entirely on the operational context. Safety instrumented systems are used in chemical and petrochemical processing, water and wastewater treatment, power generation in nuclear reactors and elsewhere, so the consequences can be far-reaching.

Safety instrumented systems rely on safety instruments (devices) that provide inputs (e.g., pressure and temperature) required to detect hazardous process states and take corrective actions (e.g., close a valve). Attacks against safety instrumented systems can prevent corrective actions or force process shutdowns. An attack could, for example, change the safe limits on a pressure sensor that could cause the safety instrumented system to fail to take the appropriate action. Nation-state actors have already targeted safety instrumented systems [10], so attackers are well aware of the importance of these systems. More recently, malware described as a "Swiss Army Knife for hacking control systems" was discovered and found to hijack and embed malicious commands in control system communications [8]. Attacking safety instrumented systems would be an easy way to cause physical harm.

Modern safety instruments provide "smart" features such as valve partial stroke testing and advanced diagnostics. They are typically connected to a safety instrumented system using direct cabling and communicate via analog signals. Smart data is superimposed over analog communications using the Highway Addressable Remote Transducer (HART) protocol [5], the industry standard for safety instrument communications. HART enables safety systems to monitor and modify safety instrument device configurations and states.

HART implements three command types for reading device state and updating function parameters, universal, common and device-specific. All HART devices are required to implement the universal command set. Devices may implement common commands (used by many device types and vendors) and device-specific commands to support unique features.

Operators configure HART devices using HART-based handheld devices. Alternatively, they may use information-technology-based instrument management systems (IMSs) or asset management systems (AMSs) that communicate with devices via serial connections using HART, or over an Internet Protocol (IP) network using HART and HART-IP, or a proprietary vendor protocol. In the first case, packets flow through a serially-connected HART multiplexer (MUX). In the second case, packets flow from an IMS/AMS over an IP-based network to a HART pass-through safety instrumented system input/output (I/O) card to serially-connected safety instrument devices. Deployments that use information technology computers and networks with operational technology (OT) inherit all the cyber security risks associated with information technology, enabling attackers to leverage the information technology systems to target operational technology systems.

Methods used by industry to protect safety instruments from unauthorized modifications include hardware write-protect switches or software write-protect passwords on the instruments, passwords on IMS/AMS platforms that remotely manage safety instruments and a variety of unique protections provided by safety instrumented systems.

This research sought to determine if and how an attacker could exploit an IMS/AMS to change safety instrument configurations and states to create potentially unsafe conditions. Attack paths and security controls were evaluated in two common real-world safety system architectures using four product types, safety instrumented systems, multiplexers, IMS/AMS platforms and safety instruments. Several tests were conducted to determine which architecture could provide better protection from attacks using the available security controls. This chapter presents the research methodology, findings, key recommendations and insights into embedding cyber security analyses in industrial control product and system lifecycles.

2. Project Background and Overview

The Linking the Oil and Gas Industry to Improve Cybersecurity (LOGIIC) Consortium studies cyber security issues in industrial control systems that can impact safety. LOGIIC has completed three projects focused on various aspects of safety systems. Two earlier projects investigated safety instrumented system controllers [11, 12]. The latest project focused on safety instruments and their management [16–18], the subjects of this work.

The LOGIIC Consortium was interested in determining the ability of an attacker to compromise an IMS/AMS platform and use it to

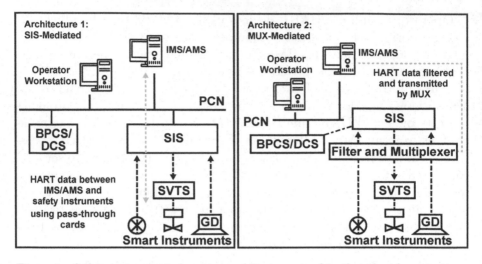

Figure 1. Safety instrumented system architectures used in the oil and gas sector.

alter safety instrument configurations to create unsafe operating conditions, render the safety instruments inoperable and/or seize control from operators. Instead of uncovering specific vulnerabilities in specific vendor products, the objective was to understand if different safety instrumented system architectures and configurations had inherent risks. Another objective was to evaluate the available protections (security controls), identify protection gaps and recommend design alternatives, configuration changes and policies and procedures to reduce the risk of cyber attacks on deployed safety instrumented systems.

The research focused on two safety instrumented system reference architectures typically found in the oil and gas industry. Figure 1 shows the two reference architectures. In Architecture 1, the safety instrumented system and IMS/AMS are in the process control network (PCN). However, safety instruments are not accessible directly on this network. HART data is passed between the IMS/AMS and safety instrument devices through the safety instrumented system using a pass-through I/O card.

In Architecture 2, the safety instrumented system is not accessible via the process control network. Instead, access is via a basic process control system (BPCS) or distributed control system (DCS). As a result, the IMS/AMS cannot communicate with the safety instrumented system or safety instruments over the process control network. The IMS/AMS is connected to a multiplexer using a serial cable and HART data is passed between the IMS/AMS and safety instruments through the multiplexer, bypassing the safety instrumented system entirely.

Analysis of the architectures led to the formulation of the following hypothesis:

> An architecture in which a safety instrumented system mediates communications between an IMS/AMS and the safety instrument devices it manages can better mitigate device vulnerabilities than an architecture in which the IMS/AMS communicates with the devices through a multiplexer.

A series of questions were crafted whose answers could provide evidence to prove or disprove the hypothesis. The questions were examined in the context of the two reference architectures to expose risks associated with the architectures and to determine which architecture posed less risk. Section 4.5 discusses the questions and the findings.

A key goal of the LOGIIC Consortium is to help vendors improve product security, which enhances the security of systems deployed by LOGIIC member companies. Fostering good vendor relationships is essential. Surreptitiously acquiring and evaluating products without vendor consent would damage relationships and hinder product improvements. Therefore, the research was conducted with the full support and cooperation of safety instrumented system product vendors. This impacted the evaluation design because the product sample set could not be random. Instead, the instruments used were representative of the products used by LOGIIC member companies.

LOGIIC member companies identified six safety instrumented system product types for the study and proposed candidates for each type. The product types included safety instrumented systems, IMS/AMS platforms, transmitters, fire detectors, gas detectors and "smart" valve positioners. Vendor decisions to participate or not participate in the research affected the final set of products used in the evaluation.

The assessments were limited in scope and time. Motivated adversaries invest ample resources and time to analyze targeted products, enabling them to discover undocumented commands and software and firmware vulnerabilities to exploit in attacks. In contrast, the assessments performed in this research engaged partial knowledge and conducted hands-on testing over a few weeks.

3.   Assessment Methodology

A subset of vendor products was assigned to each of the four assessments. Each product was used in one or two assessments. Architecture 1 and 2 systems were configured using the same set of products for each assessment. These are referred to as "assessment system pairs."

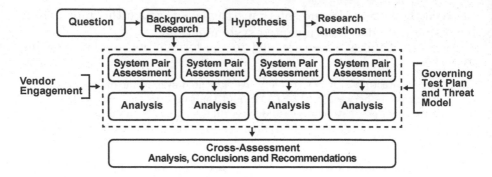

Figure 2.   Overall assessment methodology.

Figure 2 shows the overall methodology that assessed four pairs of instantiated safety instrument systems. The results were cross-analyzed to identify common issues with all assessment system pairs.

Figure 3 shows the system pair assessment methodology. Standard industry assessment methods were employed to flesh out test cases specific to instantiated safety-instrumented-system-mediated and multiplexer-mediated system pairs. The two systems in each pair were evaluated using each test case and the results were collected and analyzed.

All the assessments used the same assessment roles, threat model, rules of engagement and high-level test cases. These were captured in a test plan template that served as the basis of the detailed test plan for each assessment. The use of common templates helped ensure consistency across the assessments.

Test cases were executed at the component and system levels for each assessment system pair using the available security controls. The results of each of the four assessments were analyzed. Finally, the results across the four assessments were analyzed to draw generalized conclusions.

The test case corpus was designed to use the selected products to achieve the effects described in the hypothesis questions. The test cases covered instruments, communications and systems. The instrument and communications tests were used in the system test cases. Instrument test cases focused on command abuse. Each instrument was examined during the discovery phase to identify a sample set of commands in the HART common, universal and device-specific sets that an attacker could use to create one or more of the effects considered in the assessment questions. Table 1 shows examples of command functions that were employed. The same set of device common and universal commands (where possible) were employed to provide more consistency across assessments.

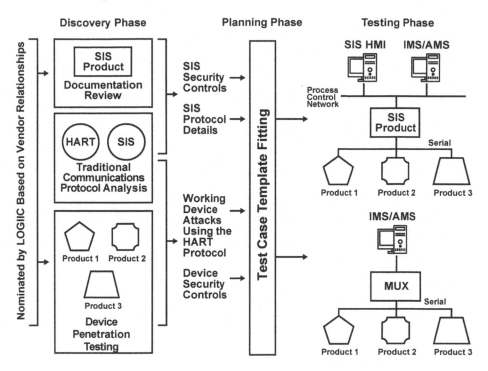

Figure 3. System pair assessment methodology.

The communications test cases examined the use of encrypted and unencrypted network traffic. Tests focused on network attack prevention and bypassing communications encryption. For example, when considering application-layer encryption between the safety instrumented system and IMS/AMS, malware executed as part of the IMS/AMS through a Trojan dynamic-link library (DLL) to send unauthorized commands. Some encryption implementation tests were conducted to assist vendors in securing their products. For example, the tests considered the use of self-signed certificates, unidirectional versus bidirectional authentication, and whether cryptographic components had known vulnerabilities (e.g., older Transport Layer Security (TLS) protocol versions). Specific product implementation issues were not considered in the general architecture measurements.

The system test cases applied each available security control to the instrument test cases to determine the effect of the security control on each attack. Attacks were executed with and without security controls and then serially with each applicable security control. In essence, the security controls were used as "test control knobs" to determine which

Table 1. Test cases abusing device commands to modify configurations and states.

States	Configuration Modifications	Reset/Evasion
Disable write protect	Password and pin code values	Wipe device alert logs
Place in firmware upgrade mode	Valve high-low cut off values	Wipe device history
Place in fixed current mode	Partial stroke values	Reset device change bit
Enable write protect	Alarm settings	
Reset device repetitively	Valve positioner feedback values	
Place in loop current mode	Valve positioner calibration	
Force offline	Valid range limits	
Conduct partial stroke test	Relay latching behavior	
Value position (override)	Polling address	
	Scaling factors	

controls would cause attacks to fail. The security controls included various write protection methods, IMS/AMS authentication, mechanisms disallowing connections from unauthorized hosts and various encryption schemes. Device-native write protection was the only protection common to the system pair. Since multiplexers have no security controls, device-native write protection was the only protection mechanism tested on the Architecture 2 system. Tests were also conducted to determine if attackers could bypass security controls. Interested readers are referred to [16, 17] for more details about the assessment methodology.

4. Research Findings

This section discusses recurring issues found in all or most assessments regardless of the vendor products. Detailed findings are available in the final project report [17]. Nearly all the findings are in the "insecure by design" category. The findings cover four areas, device command processing, IMS/AMS operator workstations, communications and protocols, and security control performance. The findings are discussed as they relate to the assessment questions and the MITRE Common Weakness Enumeration (CWE) database of common-knowledge system design and implementation flaws [13].

4.1 Device Command Processing

The research discovered that device command processing is inherently risky. All nine devices in the sample set processed unchecked commands on the assumption that all the received commands were from legitimate sources. None of the devices implemented authentication or authenticated sessions. In the absence of device write protection and other external protective measures, attackers can execute any device-supported HART command at will from an IMS/AMS host platform. The conclusion is that safety instruments, in general, are subject to configuration integrity attacks.

All the devices implemented a combination of common, universal and device-specific HART commands. Some inconsistencies were observed in device implementations of HART common commands, likely due to the lack of clarity in the HART specification. Many devices implemented undocumented device-specific commands, including some that operated as toggles, which means that an attacker would not have to determine the valid command parameters to execute malicious commands.

Table 1 shows the successful test case attacks using device commands. Individual devices were subjected only to the attacks associated with supported HART commands. Some devices were subjected to additional device-specific command attacks (not discussed here.)

4.2 IMS/AMS Operator Workstations

An IMS/AMS workstation is a trusted platform that can be used to launch practically any attack against a safety instrumented system or other systems connected to a process control network. An IMS/AMS workstation uses device definitions (DDs) and device type managers (DTMs) for device management. Device definitions contain ASCII text files used by an IMS/AMS to perform a limited set of device configurations. Device type managers contain executable dynamic link libraries (DLLs) and text-based configuration files that provide the software needed to configure unique device features. These third-party dynamic link libraries are loaded into IMS/AMS process space so that they run as part of the IMS/AMS.

Attackers can use third-party device definition files and device type manager plugins to attack safety instrumented systems on IMS/AMS platforms as shown in Figure 4. Device type manager plugins are often

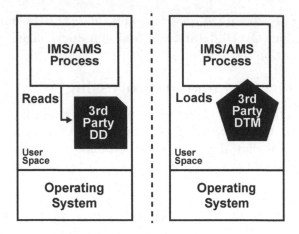

Figure 4. IMS/AMS device management.

distributed publicly on vendor websites. The evaluated systems performed little or no checks before loading the plugins.

Table 2. Summary of security issues related to IMS/AMS platforms.

Security Issue	Enabled Attacker Capability
Malware embedded in and installed alongside device type manager software. Installation requires administrator privileges.	Run co-resident malware with administrator privileges.
No publisher or cryptographic verification of third-party plugins.	Load Trojan dynamic link library and run in IMS/AMS process space.
Lack of digitally-signed IMS/AMS components.	Load and run Trojan IMS/AMS components.
Poor attack visibility – IMS/AMS logging varies from no logging to comprehensive logging.	Attack without leaving much evidence. Possibly evade detection.

Table 2 summarizes the security issues discovered for IMS/AMS platforms. In addition to directly compromising an IMS/AMS platform, an attacker could install co-resident malware along with legitimate device type manager components. When security controls that prevent unauthorized device modifications are not installed, an attack can bypass IMS/AMS authentication mechanisms to impact device functions. Tro-

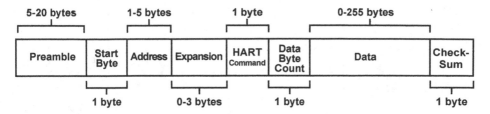

Figure 5. HART protocol packet structure.

jan device definitions and device type managers were introduced that successfully altered the configurations of 78% of the tested devices.

4.3 Safety Instrumented System Communications

An IMS/AMS and safety instrumented system communicate with devices using the HART protocol enveloped in HART-IP or a vendor-proprietary IP-based protocol. The research investigated the HART 5, HART 7 and HART-IP protocols and found security issues in all three protocols.

HART Protocol. The IMS/AMS in Architectures 1 and 2 use the HART protocol to communicate with devices. The HART protocol has no built-in security features such as authentication and encryption.

Figure 5 shows the HART protocol packet structure. It has a preamble field for synchronization and carrier detect, start delimiter that designates the start of the packet, device address, expansion field, number representing a HART command, data size field for the data, data field and a one-byte XOR checksum for packet integrity; the one-byte XOR checksum requires a low level of effort to recompute after packet modification. Cleartext HART packets are enveloped in cleartext HART-IP or other vendor-proprietary protocol packets for transport across IP-based networks.

Security-relevant commands are not standardized. Vendors implement write protection, logging and alerting in non-standard and insecure ways, which complicate monitoring and detection of rogue configuration changes made over a network using the HART-IP protocol.

Standard, open-source penetration testing tools are available, including Wireshark parsers for HART-IP [21] and WirelessHART [20]. Additionally, the HART protocol specification is available online at [5]. Using these resources, an attacker can intercept, craft, modify, inject and replay HART commands into an IP stream at will to alter device configurations when adequate protections are not in use. HART commands can also be injected through a serial connection with a multiplexer.

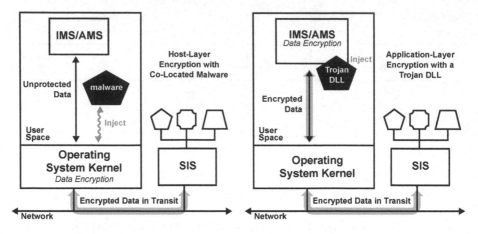

Figure 6. Unauthorized device modification.

HART-IP. HART-IP only applies to Architecture 1. In Architecture 1, the IMS/AMS communicates with devices over an IP-based network using HART-IP or a vendor-proprietary protocol that envelops HART packets. The HART-IP protocol has no security mechanisms and does not encrypt network packets. When coupled with Address Resolution Protocol (ARP) spoofing to intercept network packets, an attacker can create a man-in-the-middle connection to modify commands going to devices and send false information to the IMS/AMS, which is displayed to the operator. A new HART-IP protocol specification that supports encrypted network traffic was released during the research [4], but it was not assessed.

Vendor-Proprietary Secure Communications. Some safety instrumented systems offer a proprietary encrypted communications feature. Network packet encryption significantly improves network security and stops password sniffing, man-in-the-middle, packet replay and other attacks initiated from non-IMS/AMS platforms. However, enabling encrypted communications is not straightforward and blinds common network monitoring solutions. Furthermore, encrypted communications mechanisms can be bypassed using co-located malware or Trojan device type managers as discussed in Section 4.2.

Figure 6 shows the opportunities available to an attacker to make unauthorized device modifications. The opportunities include leveraging the trust relationships between the IMS/AMS and safety instrumented systems and employing co-located malware or Trojan dynamic link libraries to send malicious commands through established encrypted tunnels.

4.4   Security Control Performance

Security controls that prevent unauthorized device changes were available at four locations in the two architectures: devices, IMS/AMS workstations, communications mediator (safety instrumented system only) and network. The protection mechanisms worked best when they were positioned close to the devices. In the sample set, three devices had hardware-only write protection, five had software or hybrid software/hardware write protection, one had independent hardware and software write protection, and one had no native write protection of any kind.

Tables 3 and 4 shows the effectiveness of device security control measures and the residual gaps. No single security measure comprehensively protected the entire safety instrumented systems.

All the safety instrumented systems tested in this research provided mechanisms for blocking HART commands with varying degrees of granularity. Each safety instrumented system tested also offered a unique set of protective features that, if implemented correctly, could help mitigate some the risk related to unauthorized modifications of device configurations. Additional details are not provided to maintain vendor confidentiality.

The most effective combined set of mechanisms for preventing unauthorized device modifications are hardware-based write protection, limiting device configuration commands to authorized applications on authorized hosts, and encrypting communications between the IMS/AMS and safety instrumented system. While none of the three mechanisms on its own provides 100% protection across the system, the three mechanisms together significantly reduce the cyber risk.

4.5   Assessment Questions and Findings

Section 2 discussed the hypothesis that drove the development of the assessment questions. This section lists the assessment questions and the findings for each question.

Q. 1: Can an attacker compromise IMS/AMS platforms? Yes. An attacker can install a Trojan IMS/AMS dynamic link library, device definition or device type manager on all the assessed IMS/AMS platforms if appropriate security procedures are not followed.

Table 3.   Device security control effectiveness and residual gaps.

Hardware-Based Device Write Protection
Applicable Architectures: Architectures 1 and 2
Function: Device will not process device update commands while the switch is in the protect position
Attacks Prevented: Unauthorized updates sent to the target device from anywhere in the PCN, including when attached to the multiplexer
Devices Protected: Single
Residual Gaps: Some maintenance type commands on some devices
Bypassable: No
Collateral Damage: None

Software-Based Device Write Protection
Applicable Architectures: Architectures 1 and 2
Function: Device will not process device update commands until the device is unlocked by entering a passcode
Attacks Prevented: Unauthorized updates sent to the target device from anywhere in the PCN, including when attached to the multiplexer
Devices Protected: Single
Residual Gaps: Some maintenance type commands on some devices
Bypassable: Yes, sniffing or guessing the passcode
Collateral Damage: None

IMS/AMS User Authentication
Applicable Architectures: Architectures 1 and 2
Function: IMS/AMS will not send update commands to devices without authentication
Attacks Prevented: Unauthorized updates through hands-on access to the IMS/AMS
Devices Protected: All
Residual Gaps: Commands sent from locations other than the IMS/AMS
Bypassable: Yes, running co-resident malware on the IMS/AMS host platform
Collateral Damage: None

Device Common and Universal Write Protection: SIS-Enforced Run Mode
Applicable Architectures: Architecture 1
Function: SIS blocks HART common and universal write commands
Attacks Prevented: Unauthorized common and universal command updates sent to any device from anywhere in the PCN
Devices Protected: All
Residual Gaps: Unauthorized updates using HART device-specific commands; some maintenance type common and universal commands on some devices
Bypassable: Generally no, depends on the implementation
Collateral Damage: None

Table 4. Device security control effectiveness and residual gaps (continued).

Device-Specific Write Protection: SIS Enforced
Applicable Architectures: Architecture 1
Function: SIS blocks all HART device-specific commands, including read commands
Attacks Prevented: Unauthorized device-specific command updates sent to any device from anywhere in the PCN
Devices Protected: All
Residual Gaps: Unauthorized updates using HART common and universal commands
Bypassable: Generally no, depends on the implementation
Collateral Damage: Breaks operator user interfaces that display device-specific values due to read blocking

---

Limit Device Connections to Authorized Hosts
Applicable Architectures: Architecture 1
Function: Whitelisting or required authentication mechanism blocks connections from unauthorized hosts
Attacks Prevented: Updates sent to any device from unauthorized hosts in the PCN
Devices Protected: All
Residual Gaps: Some maintenance type commands on some devices; unauthorized updates from authorized hosts (e.g., IMS/AMS)
Bypassable: For whitelisting, via spoofing or using an allowed IP address
Collateral Damage: None

IMS/AMS to SIS Communications Encryption: Host-Level
Applicable Architectures: Architecture 1
Function: Uses public/private key exchange to authenticate senders and receivers; encrypts network-based communications
Attacks Prevented: Unauthorized updates from PCN-attached hosts that cannot establish encrypted sessions with the SIS
Devices Protected: All
Residual Gaps: Co-resident malware can make unauthorized device changes
Bypassable: Yes, using co-resident malware on the IMS/AMS host
Collateral Damage: Blinds network monitoring

IMS/AMS to SIS Communications Encryption: Application-Layer
Applicable Architectures: Architecture 1
Function: Uses public/private key exchange to authenticate senders and receivers; encrypts network-based communications
Attacks Prevented: Unauthorized updates from co-located malware on the IMS/AMS and from PCN-attached hosts that cannot establish encrypted session with the SIS
Devices Protected: All
Residual Gaps: Trojan DLLs and IMS/AMS software components can make unauthorized device changes
Bypassable: Yes, using Trojan trusted components on the IMS/AMS host
Collateral Damage: Blinds network monitoring

Q. 2: Can an attacker gain administrator privileges on IMS/ AMS platforms?   Yes. Administrator privileges are required to install a device type manager in every IMS/AMS platform tested. Installing a Trojan device type manager would give an attacker the ability to run malware with administrator privileges on the host operating system.

Q. 3: Can an attacker gain remote control of an IMS/AMS? Yes. Installation of a malicious Trojan device type manager was demonstrated in all the assessed IMS/AMS platforms. The malware was remotely controlled from another point in the network and was able to modify instrument configurations.

Q. 4: Can an attacker compromise an IMS/AMS software/system from the IMS/AMS host platform or via remote means? Yes. A Trojan device definition or device type manager can be installed from removable media. The ability to install Trojan components in all the assessed IMS/AMS platforms was demonstrated.

Q. 5: Can an attacker affect smart instruments by remotely controlling the IMS/AMS software using stolen or cached credentials with or without IMS/AMS administrator privileges? This is unnecessary. The ability to install remotely-controlled Trojan device type managers in all the assessed IMS/AMS platforms was demonstrated. No stolen or cached credentials were required other than installing the Trojan.

Q. 6: Can an attacker intercept a safety instrument password using keystroke analysis, memory leakage or network sniffing? Yes. Safety instrument passwords were captured by sniffing the network and using a keylogger on some IMS/AMS platforms. Network sniffing is feasible in Architecture 1. The attack was blocked when optional safety instrumented system encrypted communications were employed. Eavesdropping with a serial-connected multiplexer in Architecture 2 requires access to the serial communications and cannot be done directly from the network. Ethernet-connected multiplexers are subject to eavesdropping; however, such multiplexers were not assessed. Serial communications are not encrypted.

Q. 7: Can an attacker bypass the physical lock or password of a safety instrument to make changes to the instrument?   Yes and no. Physical instrument write-protect locks could not be bypassed using network-only access during the allotted time. All the tested software-based write protection mechanisms, including passwords, passcodes and write-protect toggles implemented in software, were bypassed. Devices implemented software write protection using HART device-specific commands. Using hardware-based write protection or Architecture 1 with active security controls blocked this attack.

Q. 8: Can an attacker affect a smart instrument using a vulnerability exploit? Yes. This is due to the lack of authorization checking when executing device commands that affect smart instrument state.

Q. 9: Can an attacker change an instrument parameter to an unsafe setting while evading detection of the parameter change? Yes, in many instances. Device settings were changed and the change bit was immediately reset to acknowledge the change on all the devices that supported the feature. This prevented the IMS/AMS from giving any visual indication of the change. Detection was mainly limited to IMS/AMS logging for *post facto* analysis. The amount of logging varied significantly for each product. In some cases, log entries inappropriately attributed changes to legitimate system components instead of malware. Alarming on changes was less common than logging. Some safety instrumented systems in Architecture 1 provided additional logging capability. The multiplexer in Architecture 2 provided no additional logs or alerts.

Q. 10: Can an attacker cause an instrument to give a false reading (e.g., change the range on the instrument to send the wrong analog signal to the safety instrumented system)? Yes. Devices were placed in the fixed current mode and sent false values to the safety instrumented system. Some attacks leveraged HART common or universal commands and worked across multiple vendor devices. The attack was blocked using hardware-based write protection or Architecture 1 with active safety instrumented system security controls.

Q. 11: Can an attacker force an instrument into the commissioning mode to send the attacker-specified value to the safety instrumented system? Yes. Devices were placed in the fixed current mode and sent designated values to the safety instrumented system. The attack was blocked using hardware-based write protection or Architecture 1 with active safety instrumented system security controls.

Q. 12: Can an attacker cause an instrument to fail to execute authorized parameter and/or state update commands? Yes. Devices were rendered unreachable and, therefore, failed to execute parameter update commands. Some attacks leveraged HART common or universal commands and worked across multiple vendor devices. This attack was blocked using hardware-based write protection or Architecture 1 with active safety instrumented system security controls.

Q. 13: Can an attacker cause an instrument to go offline or otherwise become unresponsive? Yes. Some devices were forced offline, which rendered them unreachable or completely unresponsive. Some attacks leveraged HART common or universal commands and worked across multiple vendor devices. This attack was blocked using hardware-based write protection or Architecture 1 with active safety instrumented system security controls.

Q. 14: Can an attacker change a device password? Yes. Passcodes were changed on all the devices that supported passcodes. If a passcode was already set, it was guessed and then changed. This attack was blocked using Architecture 1 with active safety instrumented system security controls.

Q. 15: Can an attacker lock the administrator out of controlling a safety instrument? Yes. Passcodes on devices were changed without operator knowledge. On some devices, passcodes were changed to strings that could not be typed using a keyboard, making it even more difficult for operators to regain control. This attack was blocked using Architecture 1 with active safety instrumented system security controls.

4.6   Architecture Comparison

The Architecture 1 results varied depending on the use of safety instrumented system protection features. None of the tested safety instrumented systems provide complete protection against the attacks. However, using a safety instrumented system with one or more protection features reduces the risk more than the multiplexer-based Architecture 2. When no safety instrumented system protection measures are employed, the results are equivalent to those for Architecture 2.

The research found little to prevent an attacker from making harmful changes to safety instruments when using Architecture 2. The multiplexer does not protect against rogue device command execution. It partially protects all the tested safety instrumented systems against long command strings crafted to overload device input parsers. The

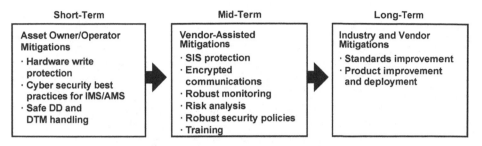

Figure 7. Recommended risk mitigation roadmap.

only completely effective way to prevent unauthorized changes is to use hardware-based device write protection.

4.7 Common Weakness Enumeration Findings

The assessment findings were mapped to the MITRE Common Weakness Enumeration (CWE) [13] to determine the scope of the security issues that were discovered. All the issues mapped to one or more CWEs.

Table 5 shows the CWEs commonly found across most of or all four assessments. Some products have unique security issues covered by other CWEs (not shown).

The MITRE CWEs cover system design and implementation flaws recognized by the cyber security/cyber operations communities. These security issues do not appear to be common knowledge in the safety instrumented system community. At the same time, operational technology environments have unique operational requirements for process efficiency and safety. It is believed that both communities would benefit from a joint discussion to help address the unique security needs of industrial control systems.

5. Recommendations

This section presents detailed actions intended to help safety instrumented system owners and operators to improve the overall security of deployed safety instrumented systems and manage cyber risk [17]. Figure 7 shows the recommended risk mitigation roadmap for safety instrumented systems. The actions are categorized as high-priority short-term, mid-term and long-term actions.

The recommended short-term actions are:

- Follow the International Electrotechnical Commission (IEC) 61511-1 Standard for safety instrumented system functional safety, which

Table 5.   Common Weakness Enumerations (CWEs) found in the assessments.

CWE	Description
15	Improper Verification of Cryptographic Signature
311	Missing Encryption of Sensitive Data
20	Improper Input Validation
319	Cleartext Transmission of Sensitive Information
200	Exposure of Sensitive Information to an Unauthorized Actor
347	Improper Verification of Cryptographic Signature
223	Omission of Security-Relevant Information
419	Unprotected Primary Channel
261	Weak Encoding of Password
474	Use of Function with Inconsistent Implementations
262	Not Using Password Aging
521	Weak Password Requirements
267	Privilege Defined with Unsafe Actions
522	Insufficiently Protected Credentials
268	Privilege Chaining
523	Unprotected Transport of Credentials
269	Improper Privilege Management
602	Client-Side Enforcement of Server-Side Security
284	Improper Access Control
653	Insufficient Compartmentalization
285	Improper Authorization
656	Reliance on Security Through Obscurity
287	Improper Authentication
703	Improper Check or Handling of Exceptional Conditions
288	Authentication Bypass Using an Alternate Path or Channel
707	Improper Neutralization
290	Authentication Bypass by Spoofing
754	Improper Check for Unusual or Exceptional Conditions
294	Authentication Bypass by Capture-Replay
778	Insufficient Logging
295	Improper Certificate Validation
807	Reliance on Untrusted Inputs in a Security Decision
300	Channel Accessible by Non-Endpoint
829	Inclusion of Functionality from Untrusted Control Sphere
302	Authentication Bypass by Assumed-Immutable Data
862	Missing Authorization
305	Authentication Bypass by Primary Weakness
922	Insecure Storage of Sensitive Information
306	Missing Authentication for Critical Function
923	Improper Restriction of Communications Channel to Intended Endpoints
307	Improper Restriction of Excessive Authentication Attempts
924	Improper Enforcement of Message Integrity During Transmission
308	Use of Single-Factor Authentication
940	Improper Verification of Source of a Communications Channel

requires devices to be write-protected unless safety review permits read/write (Section 11.6.4) [9]. Use hardware write-protected switches on all devices where available. Only disable write protection during maintenance and testing.

- Apply cyber security best practices to IMS/AMS platforms to prevent attackers from exploiting their trust relationships with safety instrumented systems to launch attacks. Use network segregation or a host-based firewall to prevent remote access.

- Avoid using vendor device type managers in safety-critical applications where possible, opting instead for device definition files. Where device type managers are currently in use, verify their pedigrees and the integrity of all device type manager files. To avoid compromised device definitions and device type managers that may be placed by attackers on outward-facing vendor websites, request device definitions and device type managers that are provided by vendor representatives from a vendor-internal repository. Request cryptographic hashes to verify the integrity of all device definition and device type manager installers. Request vendors to sign all individual files. Verify the integrity of device type managers and device definitions before installation on IMS/AMS platforms. Download all device definitions and device type managers from the Internet using HTTPS.

The recommended mid-term actions are:

- Use safety instrumented systems to mediate communications between IMS/AMS platforms and safety instruments where possible (Architecture 1). Work with safety instrumented system vendors to identify and implement protection measures that reduce the attack surfaces and risk.

- Implement mechanisms that permit only authorized hosts to connect to safety instruments via safety instrumented systems to prevent unauthorized hosts from making changes.

- Encrypt communications between an IMS/AMS and safety instrumented system where possible to avoid network-based attacks that steal passwords and change device commands in transit.

- Implement a robust monitoring system to detect and raise alerts about safety instrument device changes and unexpected states.

- Conduct a complete consequences-based risk analysis of all operational safety instrumented systems using the research findings of this work to identify residual risks that are not mitigated by deployed security controls. Asset owners and operators should identify and implement additional mitigations based on risk.

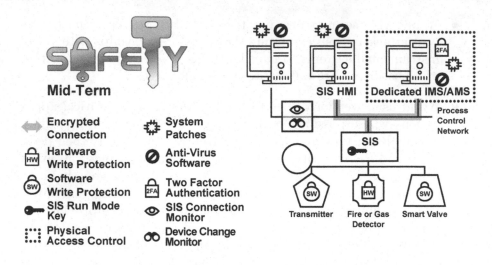

Figure 8. Layered defense-in-depth approach for safety instrumented systems.

- Create a robust security policy for safety instrumented systems. Train operators on the policy to avoid inadvertently introducing malware into safety instrumented system environments.

The recommended long-term actions, which require vendor product and industry-level changes, include:

- Implement the secure HART-IP protocol [4].

- Implement vendor-proprietary encrypted protocols.

The detailed set of recommendations are provided in the final project report [17]. The following are the summary recommendations for the various stakeholders:

- **Asset Owners and Operators:** Asset owners and operators should protect safety instrumented systems from dangerous conditions induced by attacks using a disciplined, holistic approach to security design. While a fully-secure, zero-risk state can never be achieved, risk can be reduced by applying multiple overlapping protections that limit the overall attack surface (based on Architecture 1), by identifying gaps where residual risk exists and by monitoring and alerting for evidence of attacks that are attempting to or have taken advantage of the gaps. Figure 8 shows a layered defense-in-depth approach to security that orchestrates prevention and detection mechanisms to fortify the overall environment against network-based, insider and supply chain attacks.

As demonstrated in Tables 3 and 4, Architecture 2 has fewer options for layering security mechanisms. Its use of a serial-based multiplexer obviates network-based and safety-instrumented-system-based mitigations and a multiplexer provides no security features. The only means to stop unauthorized device modification attacks is to use built-in device protections. These issues render IMS/AMS compromises difficult to stop or detect. Asset owners and operators who must use Architecture 2 should consider disconnecting their IMS/AMS platforms from process control networks to reduce the risk of compromise by network-based attacks. Strict policies and procedures should be used in both architectures to protect against supply chain compromises of the trusted platforms.

- **Safety System Operators:** Humans are often the weakest link in system security. Social engineering is used to deceive operators into accidentally introducing malware into systems. This risk is typically managed by training, limiting access and implementing security controls. Operators should be educated about security-relevant features of safety instrumented systems as well as security policies and procedures.

- **Safety Instrumented System Product Vendors:** Safety instrumented system product vendors should evaluate and refine safety instrumented system standards and designs to address modern realistic attack paths and motivated attackers. Safety instrumented system designs should be assessed for common exploitable weaknesses found in the MITRE CWE. Weaknesses should be addressed to shore up products.

- **IMS/AMS Product Vendors:** IMS/AMS product vendors should improve their IMS/AMS platforms to reduce the risks of compromise and attacks over process control networks. Signed components and safety checking of third-party device type managers should be implemented.

- **Safety Instrument Vendors:** Safety instrument vendors should implement non-bypassable physical write-protected switches on all new products. Individual device type manager files should be cryptographically signed. Provide a cryptographic hash with each device type manager file to IMS/AMS vendors and operators for verification.

- **Safety Instrumented System Vendors:** Safety instrumented system vendors should provide thorough documentation, training

SIL 1: Rated for use to avoid relatively minor incidents.

SIL 2: Rated for use to avoid more serious but limited incidents, some of which may result in severe injury or death to one or more persons.

SIL 3: Rated for use to avoid serious incidents involving multiple fatalities and/or serious injuries.

SIL 4: Rated for use to avoid disastrous accidents (note: not achievable for electronically programmable devices).

Figure 9. IEC 61511-1 safety integrity level ratings for safety instrumented systems.

and hands-on support in securely configuring safety instrumented systems. Additional security controls to address the gaps listed in Tables 3 and 4 should be evaluated and implemented.

- **International Electrotechnical Commission:** The IEC 61508 Standard should be revised to require non-bypassable write protection mechanisms. Also, the IEC 61511 Standard should reinforce the requirement for non-bypassable write protection. The device read/write mode should not be permitted above the Safety Integrity Level 2 (SIL 2). Figure 9 shows the IEC 61511-1 SIL ratings for safety systems; each level represents an order of magnitude reduction in risk [9].

- **Device Type Manager Standards Body:** The device type manager standards body should encourage all vendors to provide asset owners and operators with device definition and device type manager installer cryptographic hashes and a method for verifying the hashes. All device definitions, device type managers and configuration files should be cryptographically signed.

- **HART Standards Body:** The HART standards body should augment the HART protocol command specifications to include a means to differentiate device-specific read and write commands. This is needed to enable external protection mechanisms to block commands that update configurations while not blocking read-only commands. The standards body should work with vendors to develop standard HART commands for configuring security-relevant mechanisms.

6.   Discussion

The industrial control system community has an excellent track record of conducting rigorous safety analyses based on standards. However, safety analyses have not traditionally considered cyber attacks that could impact safety. For example, proof testing is an industry practice used to uncover systematic errors in safety instrumented systems [7]. Vendors specify what should be tested and when, but cyber security concepts are not included.

Attacks against safety instrumented systems can have dire consequences and these systems have already been the subject of such attacks. White hat security analysts have also focused on safety instrumented systems. In 2013, Bolshev and Malinovsky [2] presented their findings on HART, HART-IP, IMSs and device type managers. They concluded that the HART and HART-IP protocols are insecure. As in the case of this research, they found ways to attack IMS platforms through device type managers. In 2014, Bolshev [1] presented his work on HART as an attack vector at DEF CON Russia. Since these works were disseminated nine years ago, the security issues have neither been discussed openly nor addressed. While there are some overlaps with this research related to the findings, this research has focused on information technology interfaces to operational technology systems and has found additional security issues.

U.S. Department of Energy National SCADA Test Bed personnel have examined security defenses for SCADA systems [6]. They found two issues in common with the findings of this research, cleartext communications and weak or no authentication. Had their recommended mitigations been applied to safety instrumented systems, some of the security problems discovered in this research would not have persisted. Such findings need to be shared effectively with the industrial control system community. One approach is the LOGIIC Consortium model, in which industrial control system product vendors participate in assessments and are made aware of the issues that are discovered. The industrial control system community should also consider alternative methods for effective knowledge transfer.

All the phases of the industrial control product and system lifecycles should incorporate cyber security analyses because it is much less costly in terms of lives, dollars and reputation to find and fix problems early in a lifecycle instead of after deployment. Vendors should include adversary-minded cyber security experts in the design process to ensure that designs are free of common-knowledge vulnerabilities [14] and design weaknesses [13] that can be leveraged by attackers. Proof testing and other safety analysis processes should evolve to incorporate cyber security expertise and relevant concepts. Vendors and asset owners should engage penetration testers to periodically assess products and deployed systems to ensure they are not subject to current and future

ICS-CERT advisories [3, 14]. Passing these tests should be required by the IEC 61508 and IEC 61511 Standards to receive and maintain a SIL 2 or higher rating (Figure 9).

7.   Conclusions

This research has evaluated attack paths and security controls in common safety instrumented system architectures. Four instantiated system pairs, each using different products, were tested, following which cross-system analysis was performed to illuminate recurring issues that affect the broader industry. The evaluation was conducted with full cooperation from safety instrumented system and device vendors and security experts. Recurring product-independent vulnerabilities were identified in all the safety instrumented systems tested due to insecure designs of safety instruments, IMS/AMS plugin mechanisms and the HART protocol. The design flaws enable attackers to bypass all software-based device-native write protection mechanisms.

Hardware-based device write protection is the most effective security control, but it was absent in 66% of the sample set. All the assessed safety instrumented systems offer write protection that can be used in safety-instrumented-system-mediated systems. As a result, Architecture 1 can provide better protection for safety instrument devices if security controls are enabled and configured correctly. However, if no safety instrumented system security controls are employed in Architecture 1, the safety instrumented system acts as a pass-through, just like the multiplexer in Architecture 2. In this case, Architecture 1 provides no added security benefits over Architecture 2 aside from the opportunity to perform network-based monitoring. Safety instrumented system security controls are not well known or understood in operational environments. While safety instrumented system security controls are available and can provide protection, they are often not used.

The industrial control system community has the opportunity now to plan for and address cyber threats during all the stages of the safety instrumented system lifecycle. It is time to enhance traditional safety instrumented system standards and processes to include cyber security concepts and analyses that will fortify safety instrumented systems against cyber attacks before they are deployed in operational systems.

The opinions, findings, conclusions and recommendations expressed in this chapter are those of the authors, and should not be interpreted as representing the official policies or endorsements, either expressed or implied, or position of the U.S. Department of Homeland Security, U.S. Government or the participating oil and gas companies.

Acknowledgements

The LOGIIC Consortium is a partnership between the U.S. Department of Homeland Security (DHS) Science and Technology Directorate and member companies in the U.S. oil and gas sector. This project was co-funded by the U.S. Department of Homeland Security under Contract no. HSHQDC-16-C-00034. The authors thank DHS Program Manager Mr. Gregory Wigton for his guidance and support. The authors also thank the LOGIIC Consortium members for providing leadership, domain expertise and funding. Additionally, the authors thank the Project 12 test director and subject matter experts who conducted the hands-on assessment portions of the project.

References

[1] A. Bolshev, HART as an attack vector: From current loop to application layer, presented at *DEF CON Russia* (`www.slideshare. net/dgpeters/17-bolshev-1-13`), 2014.

[2] A. Bolshev and A. Malinovsky, HART (in)security: How one transmitter can compromise a whole plant, presented at the *International Practical Infosecurity Conference* (`www.slideshare.net/ DefconRussia/alexander-bolshev-alexander-malinovsky-har t-insecurity`), 2013.

[3] Cyber Security and Infrastructure Security Agency, ICS-CERT Advisories, Arlington, Virginia (`www.cisa.gov/uscert/ ics/advisories`), 2022.

[4] FieldComm Group, Section 10.2: HART-IP security, in *HART Communication Protocol Network Management Specification*, Austin, Texas, pp. 92–97, 2020.

[5] FieldComm Group, HART Protocol Specifications, Austin, Texas (`www.fieldcommgroup.org/hart-specifications`), 2021.

[6] R. Fink, D. Spencer and R. Wells, Lessons Learned from Cyber Security Assessments of SCADA and Energy Management Systems, Technical Report INL/CON-06-11665, National SCADA Test Bed, Idaho National Laboratory, Idaho Falls, Idaho, 2006.

[7] P. Goteti, Proof testing safety instrumented systems, presented at the *2018 Spring Purdue Process Safety and Assurance Center Conference* (`engineering.purdue.edu/P2SAC/presentations/d ocuments/Proof_Testing_Safety_Instrumented_Systems.pdf`), 2018.

[8] A. Greenberg, Feds uncover a "Swiss Army Knife" for hacking industrial control systems, *Wired*, April 13, 2022.

[9] International Electrotechnical Commission, IEC 61511-1 Ed. 2.1. 2017: Functional Safety – Safety Instrumented Systems for the Process Industry Sector – Part 1: Framework, Definitions, System, Hardware and Application Programming Requirements, Geneva, Switzerland, 2017.

[10] B. Johnson, D. Caban, M. Krotofil, D. Scali, N. Brubaker and C. Glyer, Attackers deploy new ICS attack framework "TRITON" and cause operational disruption to critical infrastructure, Mandiant, Reston, Virginia (`www.mandiant.com/resources/att ackers-deploy-new-ics-attack-framework-triton`), December 14, 2017.

[11] LOGIIC Consortium, Cyber Security Implications of SIS Integration with Control Networks, Technical Report, SRI International, Menlo Park, California, 2011.

[12] A. McIntyre, LOGIIC Safety Instrumented Systems Final Public Report, Technical Report, SRI International, Menlo Park, California, 2018.

[13] MITRE, Common Weakness Enumeration (CWE), Bedford, Massachusetts (`cwe.mitre.org`), 2022.

[14] MITRE, Cybersecurity Vulnerability Enumeration (CVE), Bedford, Massachusetts (`cve.mitre.org`), 2022.

[15] RealPars, What is a safety instrumented system? Rotterdam, The Netherlands (`www.youtube.com/watch?v=W2YUNnfATBY`), 2018.

[16] L. Tinnel and M. Cochrane, Getting to the HART of the matter: An evaluation of real-world safety system OT/IT interfaces, attacks and countermeasures, *Proceedings of the Cyber Security Experimentation and Test Workshop*, pp. 27–35, 2021.

[17] L. Tinnel and U. Lindqvist, LOGIIC Project 12 Safety Instrumentation Final Report, Technical Report, SRI International, Menlo Park, California, 2021.

[18] L. Tinnel and U. Lindqvist, When safety instrument control goes rogue, presented at the *Industrial Control Systems Joint Working Group 2021 Spring Virtual Meeting* (`www.youtube.com/watch?v=PeRvdC07VYw`), 2021.

[19] U.S. Chemical Safety and Hazard Investigation Board, Investigation Report: Refinery Explosion and Fire (15 Killed, 180 Injured), Report no. 2005-04-I-TX, Washington, DC (`www.csb.gov/file.aspx?DocumentId=5596`), 2007.

[20] R. Wightman, WirelessHART-Parser, GitHub (`github.com/reid mefirst/WirelessHART-Parser`), 2017.

[21] Wireshark Foundation, Highway Addressable Remote Transducer over IP (HART-IP), Davis, California (`wiki.wireshark.org/HART-IP`), 2020.

Chapter 4

TRUSTED VIRTUALIZATION-BASED PROGRAMMABLE LOGIC CONTROLLER RESILIENCE USING A BACKFIT APPROACH

James Cervini, Daniel Muller, Alexander Beall, Joseph Maurio, Aviel Rubin and Lanier Watkins

Abstract   Industrial control systems perform vital cyber-physical functions in critical infrastructure assets. Programmable logic controllers, which are prominently found in industrial control environments, execute the operational control logic of cyber-physical systems. Due to the continued escalation of cyber attacks targeting industrial control systems and programmable logic controllers, strengthening the trust and resilience of these systems is paramount.

This chapter proposes an approach that leverages virtualization, cryptographic attestation, software-defined networking, security orchestration and a proprietary programmable logic controller runtime application to advance programmable logic controller trust and resilience while facilitating integration in deployed systems. A proof-of-concept capability demonstrated on a physical industrial control system testbed validates the approach. The experimental results confirm that the approach is viable for industrial control applications.

Keywords: Industrial control systems, virtualization, security

1.   Introduction

Programmable logic controllers (PLCs) are real-time systems that receive inputs from sensors, execute pre-programmed logical routines and produce outputs that ultimately drive physical actuators. These devices and their control loops operate diverse physical processes, supporting industrial control systems in critical infrastructure assets in the energy, chemicals, manufacturing, water and wastewater sectors. Given the con-

© IFIP International Federation for Information Processing 2022
Published by Springer Nature Switzerland AG 2022
J. Staggs and S. Shenoi (Eds.): Critical Infrastructure Protection XVI, IFIP AICT 666, pp. 103–117, 2022.
https://doi.org/10.1007/978-3-031-20137-0_4

stant targeting of these vital systems and processes, there is a compelling need to research methods that increase their resilience against cyber attacks. Additionally, cost and uptime requirements often result in sparse upgrade cycles of programmable logic controllers in the operational technology domain. Therefore, research must investigate the applicability of security approaches for deployed proprietary systems. This chapter proposes an approach that leverages virtualization and trusted computing to enhance operational technology systems. The enhancements enable these systems and the processes they control to be more resilient, flexible, secure and cost-effective.

Virtualization provides a guest environment segmented from host machine hardware by using a hypervisor to interpret and allocate the available computing resources. The segmentation provides several benefits. The lack of reliance on a specific host contributes to a dynamic virtual environment that can rapidly change hosts as needed to ensure maximum uptime. Also, the isolation between guest and host can mitigate malicious processes from spreading to host hardware. Additionally, the hardware abstraction provided by virtualization is cost effective compared with installing and maintaining dedicated hardware for each process that could be virtualized. Indeed, the ability to virtually test and seamlessly merge software updates and configuration changes with little or no downtime is highly desirable for operational technology systems.

This research has three principal contributions. It is first to cryptographically attest a virtualized programmable logic controller using a trusted platform module (TPM). Additionally, it proposes a virtualized programmable logic controller environment generation approach that leverages existing system hardware and software artifacts to streamline backfit deployments. Also, it is the first to engage automated security orchestration to respond to failures of programmable logic controllers in performing cryptographic attestation.

2.   Related Work

The hard and soft real-time performance requirements imposed in operational technology environments clash with added layers of software complexity introduced by virtualization. As additional software processes are introduced to support programmable logic controller virtualization, the ability to guarantee real-time control loop performance is reduced. Previous research has attempted to address this problem by utilizing a real-time optimized environment and highlighting virtual programmable logic controller feasibility [3]. In contrast, this work explores the trust and resilience functionality enabled by the proven virtual programmable logic controller feasibility using an approach that is readily implemented in deployed systems.

Other research has conducted experiments with cloud-based virtual programmable logic controllers that demonstrate their feasibility for soft real-time systems [8]. However, the previous research only demonstrated performance feasibility whereas the cryptographic attestation proposed in this work can be applied to address trust concerns associated with cloud utilization.

Previous research efforts have proven the feasibility of attestation using the physics of control processes [7, 9]. In contrast, the programmable logic controller attestation approach developed in this research does not observe the physical system state and could be implemented in combination with other attestation methods. Additionally, this research utilizes security orchestration and software-defined networking (SDN) in combination with the attestation outcome for virtualized programmable logic controllers.

In an earlier paper, Cervini et al. [2] described an automated resilience approach that employs containerized programmable logic controllers. In contrast, the approach described in this chapter uses virtualization to achieve additional security isolation. A shortcoming of the earlier work is the manual generation of containerized programmable logic controller logic [2]. This shortcoming is addressed in the proposed approach by leveraging existing software artifacts for automated virtual programmable logic controller generation. Finally, Cervini et al. [2] state that cryptographic attestation and subsequent response actions should be researched to guarantee system integrity. This avenue is pursued in this research via the cryptographic attestation of virtual programmable logic controller configurations.

3. Virtualization for Trust and Resilience

This section describes the programmable logic controller virtualization and remote programmable logic controller attestation using a trusted platform module.

3.1 PLC Virtualization

Three criteria must be satisfied to virtualize a programmable logic controller. The primary criterion is that the virtual programmable logic controller should mirror the control behavior of the physical programmable logic controller with high fidelity. Additionally, the virtual programmable logic controller should employ existing hardware and installed wiring to achieve system control. Also, the process for virtualizing the physical programmable logic controller should be automatable and support the ingestion of system software artifacts. These criteria assure that a virtual programmable logic controller will function properly and minimize the cost and effort associated with its deployment.

In order to virtualize a programmable logic controller while conforming to the three criteria, an architecture was designed that leverages a software variant of the programmable logic controller. Specifically, the Allen Bradley SoftLogix programmable logic controller runtime application is employed. Virtualizing the programmable logic controller in software enables it to inherit the ability to seamlessly interface with the existing programmable logic controller ecosystem, including its software and hardware. As a result, the virtualized software programmable logic controller runtime application requires minimal effort to ingest and execute logical artifacts of the deployed programmable logic controller and the virtualized programmable logic controller can interface with its installed hardware endpoints to meet the second and third criteria. Moreover, due to the ease of preexisting logic utilization, no logic reprogramming has to be performed. The execution of identical logic ensures that the control loop of the virtual programmable logic controller results in identical process execution and conforms to the first criterion.

Ultimately, the outcome is the implementation of a logically-equivalent virtualized software programmable logic controller. The virtualized programmable logic controller utilizes existing input and output hardware and wiring to drive the control system, all the while being enhanced with the adaptability of virtualization to threats, isolation protection and reduced costs.

3.2   Remote TPM-Based Attestation

An additional benefit of virtualization is the ability to implement diverse security and trust mechanisms on a host and runtime application that would be unavailable to a proprietary physical programmable logic controller. Due to the potentially-critical processes operated by programmable logic controllers, trusting the devices is paramount to having confidence in process continuity and outcomes.

However, the reliance on virtualization for enhanced resilience potentially introduces new vulnerabilities unique to the information technology domain. Therefore, a method for affirming the trust of virtual programmable logic controllers is imperative. This can be accomplished by executing a virtual programmable logic controller on a host with Trusted Platform Module (TPM) version 2.0. A trusted platform module leverages cryptographic keys generated during the manufacturing process to perform remote attestation, a technique that ensures the legitimacy of a networked device and its software. This research employs a hardware-based trusted platform module instead of software solutions used in previous research [1, 10].

Remote attestation engages a challenger host system that attempts to verify the internal state of another attester system. The end goal of attestation is to enable the attester to generate a signed trusted platform module quote that proves to the challenger that the internal state of the system matches the expected state [5]. The virtual programmable logic controller testbed used in this research implements remote attestation where a Linux orchestration server functions as the challenger and an Intel Next Unit of Computing (NUC) hosting the virtual programmable logic controller functioned as the attester.

Figure 1 shows the attestation process. The first step in the attestation process is a one-time device registration. In this step, the challenger sends a request to register with the attester and the attester generates an endorsement key (EK) along with an attestation identity key (AIK) pair. The asymmetric endorsement key is unique to the trusted platform module on the device. The attestation identity key is generated by the trusted platform module and signed by the endorsement key. To ensure that the challenger does not register with an imposter, a trusted third-party can perform certificate validation of the attester.

The next step in the registration is to compute the reference hash for the challenger. The reference hash is computed using the platform configuration registers (PCRs) in the trusted platform module. These registers can only be modified using a hash extension, which overwrites previous values. Since extension is the only path to overwrite values, the platform configuration register hash values reflect the entire history of the hash extensions [11]. The attester is sent the specific platform configuration registers to use in its hash computation. One set of the registers is left untouched and is used to identify the trusted platform module hardware; the other set of registers is extended with the hash of a file that reflects the logic used by the virtual programmable logic controller. The file reflecting the logic is a proprietary Allen Bradley project file with the ACD extension. The ACD file, which is contained in the SoftLogix program, is named `slot02.acd`. Slot 02 in the SoftLogix program corresponds to the central processing unit (CPU) of the virtual programmable logic controller and the ACD file in the file path location corresponds to the logic programmed on the CPU. After the hash is computed, the public attestation identity key and hash are sent to the challenger, completing the registration process.

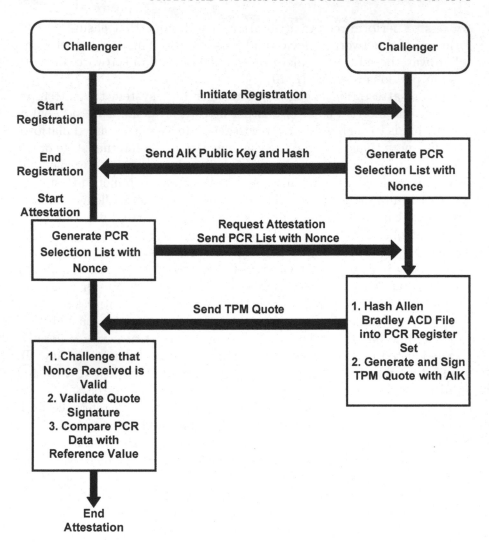

Figure 1. Attestation process.

After the registration is complete, the challenger can verify the internal state of the attester at any time. This is accomplished by the challenger sending a request to the attester to read the platform configuration registers from which the computed hash was derived along with a generated random nonce. The attester computes the hash of the current ACD file for Slot 02 and overwrites the hash in the platform configuration registers corresponding to the device software. With the platform configuration registers updated, the attester generates a trusted platform monitor quote for the challenger using the platform configuration register values and signs it with the private attestation identity key.

Upon receiving the trusted platform module quote, the challenger checks that the nonce and quote signature are valid. Next, it verifies that the platform configuration register values it received match the hash computed during the registration process. If any of the checks fail, the internal state of the system has been modified. If all the checks pass, then the internal state reflects what is expected and the attestation is successful.

The result of the virtual programmable logic controller attestation check is passed to a security information and event management (SIEM) system that aggregates various system indicators and facilitates mitigation responses. If the SIEM reports that the virtual programmable logic controller failed to cryptographically attest its trustworthiness, it is not given control of the physical system and response actions could be taken to mitigate the situation.

4.   Experiments and Results

This section describes the experimental environment and the virtual programmable logic controller resilience experiments and results.

4.1   Experimental Environment

Figure 2 shows the experimental environment. The environment includes a power distribution testbed that accepts user inputs over a human-machine interface (HMI) to open and close contactors and manipulate power flow to a target load. An Allen Bradley 1756 ControlLogix programmable logic controller chassis is employed. The Allen Bradley programmable logic controller was selected because it has a large market share, rendering the experimental results immediately applicable to thousands of deployed systems due to backfit considerations [4].

Virtual programmable logic controller creation was initiated by launching the SoftLogix 5800 programmable logic controller runtime application on a Windows 10 virtual machine. Windows was utilized to satisfy the SoftLogix operating system requirements. SoftLogix processes were set up in Windows with real-time process priority, mitigating interruptions caused by other operating system processes. The virtual programmable logic controller was hosted on an Intel NUC running the Ubuntu 20.04 operating system. The Allen Bradley proprietary software Studio 5000 retrieved the logic and configuration from the physical programmable logic controller. All the hardware references in the original logic and configuration were changed to the virtual programmable

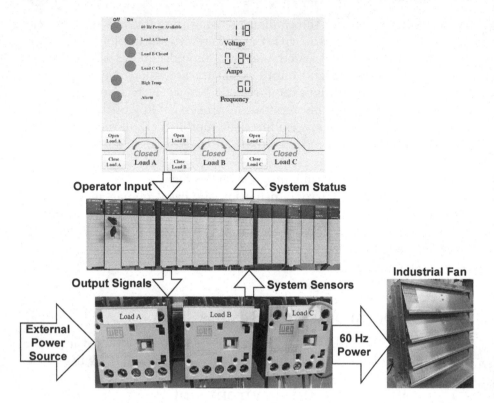

Figure 2. Experimental environment.

logic controller instance and remote input/output (I/O). Nothing precludes the reconfiguration process from being completely automated. Note that, despite the reliance on a proprietary programmable logic controller, several vendors offer comparable runtime products, and the proposed approach could support a runtime substitution to a preferred vendor or open-source runtime solution [6]. The programmable logic controller runtime application was virtualized using VMware ESXi and executed as a high-priority, real-time operating system process. Figure 3 shows the virtual programmable logic controller host architecture.

The Intel NUC hosting the virtual programmable logic controller has TPM 2.0 hardware, which was used to validate the Ubuntu 20.04 host operating system as well as the logic file of the virtual programmable logic controller. Snapshots of the configured and attested virtual programmable logic controller states were taken for use in the experiments.

Supplemental to the trusted virtualized programmable logic controller was a security environment that enabled automated alerting, analysis

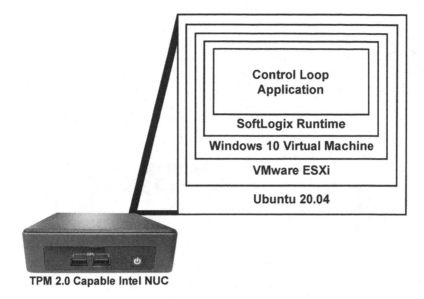

Figure 3. Virtual programmable logic controller host architecture.

and response actions. The environment comprised a rule-based intrusion detection system, software-defined network controller and switch, and a security orchestration, automation and response (SOAR) tool. The intrusion detection system was configured with a ruleset that detected programmable logic controller modifications and transmitted alerts. The software-designed network controller was programmed to redirect network traffic from the physical programmable logic controller to the virtual programmable logic controller via commands sent to the software-defined network switch. The SOAR tool was configured with automated actions to ingest intrusion detection alerts, request the status of the virtual programmable logic controller attestation, interface with the software-defined network controller to enact network modifications and prompt operators to perform manual actions. Figure 4 shows the automated security implementation of the control system network.

4.2 Resilience Experiments and Results

The experiments began by confirming system functionality while under the control of the virtual programmable logic controller. Initially, the virtual programmable logic controller failed to control the system. However, it was quickly discovered that the logical variables of the virtual programmable logic controller were initialized to zero because the default variable values of the physical programmable logic controller were not

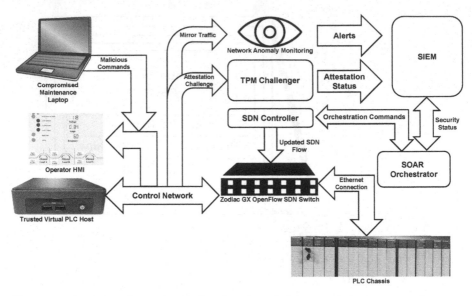

Figure 4. Automated security implementation of the control system network.

inherited properly. The problem was corrected and the expected system functionality was achieved under virtual programmable logic controller control.

Next, an attack model was applied. The attack leveraged trusted access to reprogram the programmable logic controller, resulting in reduced system functionality. Specifically, any loads that were powered on would lose power after 10 seconds. Additionally, without proper cyber situational awareness, such an incident might be investigated as a hardware failure, resulting in system assets remaining unpowered for extended periods of time. This trusted, but malicious, configuration represented a witting or unwitting insider threat, trusted device compromise or supply chain compromise.

The attack model was exercised in three scenarios. The first scenario executed the attack against the physical programmable logic controller with no resilience enhancements. The attack modified the programmable logic controller programming, which resulted in the expected degradation of system behavior. Utilization of network situational awareness tools enabled the timely identification of the rogue machine and the diagnosis of anomalous system behavior. Even so, the configuration change due to the attack persisted until manual reconfiguration was performed. In a real-world environment, manual reconfiguration can take hours to weeks to perform depending on the system complexity and scale, damage caused and process sensitivity. Live duplicate systems are a common redundancy method, but they are susceptible to the same attack because they use identical hardware and software.

In the second scenario, the physical programmable logic controller was compromised again; however, the network situational awareness tools enabled automated system recovery by leveraging the trusted virtual programmable logic controller approach. This contrasts with the first scenario, where utilizing the same network data only resulted in threat identification and system behavior diagnosis. The attack triggered a SOAR workflow, which requested the attestation status of the virtual programmable logic controller. Given that the virtual programmable logic controller configuration was untouched, it passed the attestation check and was given responsibility for the system control loop via the software-defined network orchestration by SOAR. The software-defined network reconfiguration took place after the operator was prompted to remove the infected programmable logic controller CPU. The CPU removal further purged the system of malicious artifacts and ensured no input/output conflicts with the remaining programmable logic controller chassis. These corrective actions took mere seconds to perform and resulted in the expected control system behavior.

In the third scenario, the attack was executed against the physical and trusted virtual programmable logic controllers. Due to the trusted status of the compromised maintenance laptop, the malicious configuration was accepted by both devices. However, when SOAR executed its workflow for transitioning system control from the physical programmable logic controller to the virtual programmable logic controller, the workflow commanded an attestation check of the virtual programmable logic controller. The virtual programmable logic controller failed to attest due to the discrepancy between the expected configuration and loaded malicious configuration.

The failure to attest resulted in the complete loss of trust in the virtual programmable logic controller configuration and the SOAR workflow diverged to compensate. Specifically, SOAR made an operator recommendation to revert to the snapshot of the virtual programmable logic controller in a known good configuration. While this action was passed to an operator, it could easily be automated by scripting or invoking an application programming interface. After reverting to the snapshot state, the device passed the attestation check and was given physical system control via software-defined network orchestration by SOAR after the programmable logic controller chassis CPU was removed. This corrective action took one minute to complete, resulting in the semi-automated transition to a trusted system. The system performed as expected and all the operator inputs produced the appropriate outputs.

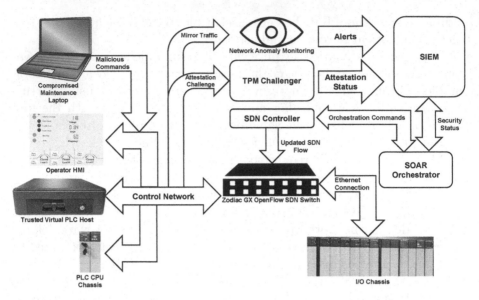

Figure 5.   Automated security architecture with virtual PLC failover support.

In scenarios two and three, the speed of the automated process was limited by the removal of the infected CPU by the operator. This was easily remedied by moving the physical CPU to a separate programmable logic controller chassis and using the remote input/output protocol to control the inputs and outputs. The process could have been automated fully by having the virtual and physical programmable logic controller CPUs use remote input/output through the software-defined switch. However, this would have required reconfiguration of the deployed programmable logic controller, unlike the tested method that is immediately applicable to deployed systems. Figure 5 shows the automated security architecture with seamless virtual programmable logic controller failover support.

5.   Conclusions

The initial misconfiguration of the virtual programmable logic controller due to the lack of variable initialization values highlights the need for automated validation of virtual programmable logic controller generation. The validation can be performed using a simulation environment for virtual programmable logic controller execution or an automated comparison of the cryptographic hashes between the physical and virtual programmable logic controller logic programs. Additionally, because the runtime application of a proprietary programmable logic controller was never meant to be virtualized, its licensing model would be more cost-effective at scale. This is because a physical machine would be dedicated to a single software instance instead of a single physical machine potentially running multiple virtual instances. This is a shortcoming that is subject to change with market demands as the feasibility of the proposed approach continues to be proven and successful technology pilots occur, potentially leading to a site-wide licensing model.

Comparing the outcomes in scenarios one and two showcases the automated resilience benefits provided by the virtual programmable logic controller approach. This is evidenced by the control process continuity and execution speed advantages associated with automated recovery over manual recovery. Furthermore, comparing the outcomes between scenarios two and three accentuates the need for system trust. This also demonstrates the flexibility of a virtual programmable logic controller in terms of control process continuity despite the initial virtual programmable logic controller compromise by a trusted host. It is worth noting that the added flexibility of a virtual programmable logic controller facilitates the implementation of additional security mechanisms that a proprietary programmable logic controller would not support, reducing the likelihood of compromise and introducing new host-based data sources. The trusted flexibility of the proposed approach coupled with the ability to augment deployed proprietary environments would enable programmable logic controllers to take dynamic actions to manage their critical processes. This could play a pivotal role in securing deployed and future systems while providing the cost-savings and high-availability benefits of virtualization.

Future research will investigate the automated validation of virtual programmable logic controllers to ensure that attested configurations conform to the demands of physical processes. Data fusion, which can help correlate virtual programmable logic controller attestation with additional data sources, should be investigated to define a holistic solution that provides trust indicators for system processes. For example, associating physical sensor data with an attestation failure could quantify the impact of an unauthorized change to a physical process. Data fusion could also contribute to effective automated recovery methods due to the understanding of physical system state. Moreover, as additional data sources and indicators are ingested, an autonomic decision engine could orchestrate process continuity actions cooperatively with the manually-developed rulesets deployed in this research. This would enable the mitigation of anomalous events that fall outside the parameters of the defined ruleset.

This research has sought to validate the computational speed of the virtualization approach in the context of soft real-time applications. Additional testing and tuning will be performed to maximize performance. Due to the diversity of operational technology systems, experiments and pilots involving environments of various scales and operational requirements should be performed to explore the breadth of applicability of the proposed programmable logic controller virtualization approach.

References

[1] F. Armknecht, A. Sadeghi, S. Schulz and C. Wachsmann, A security framework for the analysis and design of software attestation, *Proceedings of the ACM SIGSAC Conference on Computer and Communications Security*, 2013.

[2] J. Cervini, A. Rubin and L. Watkins, A containerization-based backfit approach for industrial control system resiliency, *Proceedings of the IEEE Symposium on Security and Privacy Workshops*, pp. 246–252, 2021.

[3] T. Cruz, P. Simoes and E. Monteiro, Virtualizing programmable logic controllers: Toward a convergent approach, *IEEE Embedded Systems Letters*, vol. 8(4), pp. 69–72, 2016.

[4] T. Dawson, Who were the leading vendors of industrial controls in 2017? Interact Analysis, Raunds, United Kingdom (`int eractanalysis.com/who-were-the-leading-vendors-of-indus trial-controls-in-2017`), November 2018.

[5] A. Francillon, Q. Nguyen, K. Rasmussen and G. Tsudik, A minimalist approach to remote attestation, *Proceedings of the Design, Automation and Test in Europe Conference and Exhibition*, 2014.

[6] S. Fujita, K. Hata, A. Mochizuki, K. Sawada, S. Shin and S. Hosokawa, OpenPLC-based control system testbed for PLC whitelisting, *Artificial Life and Robotics*, vol. 26(1), pp. 149–154, 2021.

[7] H. Ghaeini, M. Chan, R. Bahmani, F. Brasser, L. Garcia, J. Zhou, A. Sadeghi, N. Tippenhauer and S. Zonouz, PAtt: Physics-based attestation of control systems, *Proceedings of the Twenty-Second International Symposium on Research in Attacks, Intrusions and Defenses*, pp. 165–180, 2019.

[8] O. Givehchi, J. Imtiaz, H. Trsek and J. Jasperneite, Control-as-a-service from the cloud: A case study for using virtualized PLCs, *Proceedings of the Tenth IEEE Workshop on Factory Communication Systems*, 2014.

[9] M. Salehi and S. Bayat-Sarmadi, PLCDefender: Improving remote attestation techniques for PLCs using a physical model, *IEEE Internet of Things Journal*, vol. 8(9), pp. 7372–7379, 2021.

[10] A. Seshadri, A. Perrig, L. van Doorn and P. Khosla, SWATT: Software-based attestation for embedded devices, *Proceedings of the IEEE Symposium on Security and Privacy*, pp. 272–282, 2004.

[11] tpm2-software community, Remote attestation (`tpm2-software.github.io/tpm2-tss/getting-started/2019/12/18/Remote-Attestation.html`), December 18, 2019.

III

ADDITIVE MANUFACTURING SYSTEMS

Chapter 5

ATTACK-DEFENSE MODELING OF MATERIAL EXTRUSION ADDITIVE MANUFACTURING SYSTEMS

Alyxandra Van Stockum, Elizabeth Kurkowski, Tiffany Potok, Curtis Taylor, Joel Dawson, Mason Rice and Sujeet Shenoi

Abstract   The use of additive manufacturing in the critical infrastructure makes it an attractive target for cyber attacks. However, research on additive manufacturing threats has tended to focus on specific vulnerabilities and specific attacks against specific systems. The narrow scope hinders the understanding of the attack vectors that constitute the attack surfaces as well as the various targets and impacts of attacks. This results in vulnerabilities, potential attacks and countermeasures being overlooked during security analyses.

This research addresses the limitations by focusing on material extrusion, the most common additive manufacturing process. A material extrusion workflow (process chain) that comprehensively covers the design, slicing and printing phases is specified. Analysis of the workflow in conjunction with attack and defense frameworks yields attack-defense models for the three material extrusion phases. The attack-defense models, which specify the attack vectors, attack vector vulnerabilities and countermeasures, attack surfaces, system targets, target vulnerabilities and vulnerability countermeasures, and attacks and attack impacts, directly support risk identification, risk assessment and analysis, and risk mitigation and planning.

Three material extrusion printers ranging from hobbyist to industrial systems are used as case studies. Four attacks on the printers during the design, slicing and printing phases are described, including vulnerability identification, exploit development and countermeasures. The case studies demonstrate the effectiveness of attack-defense modeling and its ability to clarify and bolster the cyber security and risk management postures of material extrusion additive manufacturing environments.

Keywords: Additive manufacturing, material extrusion, attack-defense modeling

© IFIP International Federation for Information Processing 2022
Published by Springer Nature Switzerland AG 2022
J. Staggs and S. Shenoi (Eds.): Critical Infrastructure Protection XVI, IFIP AICT 666, pp. 121–153, 2022.
https://doi.org/10.1007/978-3-031-20137-0_5

1.   Introduction

Additive manufacturing is a multi-step process for building physical objects (parts) from computer-aided designs [24]. Unlike traditional subtractive manufacturing that removes material to create parts, additive manufacturing applies material layer by layer to build parts. Additive manufacturing combines manufacturing automation and custom part creation in ways that subtractive manufacturing cannot accomplish [10].

Additive manufacturing is a key component of Industry 4.0 – the fourth industrial revolution [6]. Industry 4.0 is the digital transformation of manufacturing and production industries characterized by the intelligent networking of machines that bridges the physical and digital worlds via cyber-physical systems that define and implement the manufacturing steps for flexible and customizable part production. The digital transformation supports autonomous decision-making and real-time monitoring of assets and processes. Additive manufacturing enables new capabilities in product design, prototyping, remote control, predictive maintenance, system monitoring and more.

Additive manufacturing is a multibillion-dollar industry [13]. Many critical infrastructure sector industries rely on additive manufacturing for mission-critical parts. The incorporation of additive manufacturing systems and their products in the critical infrastructure makes them attractive targets for hackers, criminal entities and nation-state actors.

In general, there are two types of additive manufacturing threats. The first are threats that use additive manufacturing for malicious purposes – concealing illicit objects such as drugs or explosives in printed parts, and creating objects such as untraceable "ghost guns" and spoofed biometrics of fingerprints and facial features [9]. The second are threats against additive manufacturing – intellectual property theft, part sabotage and additive manufacturing environment sabotage [24]. This research focuses on the threats against additive manufacturing, which are more serious in the context of the critical infrastructure.

Several researchers have investigated threats against additive manufacturing. However, the research efforts have primarily examined specific vulnerabilities and specific attacks against specific additive manufacturing systems [3, 7, 25]. Also, the research primarily focuses on firmware and stereolithography (STL) design file manipulations [5]. The research is interesting and important – it provides valuable insights into threats and their mitigation, and stimulates efforts at securing additive manufacturing systems. However, the deficiency is that the research efforts do not adopt holistic perspectives of additive manufacturing systems, let alone families of additive manufacturing systems corresponding to the seven standard additive manufacturing processes [10].

The narrow focus is problematic. The consideration of a specific additive manufacturing system instead of an additive manufacturing process hinders the overall understanding of the attack vectors that constitute the attack surface as well as the various targets and impacts of attacks. The lack of comprehension and comprehensiveness can result in vulnerabilities, potential attacks and countermeasures being overlooked during security analyses, negatively impacting risk management efforts.

This research attempts to address the limitations by focusing on the most common additive manufacturing process – material extrusion, also called fused deposition modeling or fused filament fabrication [12]. The material extrusion process involves heating material and depositing it on a print bed via an extruder layer by layer according to G-code toolpath instructions. The research comprehensively models the material extrusion workflow (process chain) over three additive manufacturing phases: (i) design, (ii) slicing and (iii) printing. The fourth phase, postprocessing, is not considered because an analysis of the material extrusion process reveals that the overwhelming majority of cyber threats target the earlier design, slicing and printing phases.

The material extrusion workflow facilitates the specification of attack-defense models for complex material extrusion additive manufacturing systems. An attack-defense model is created for each phase by specifying the original attack surface and implemented attack vector countermeasures to establish the current attack surface. Next, the system targets that can be accessed using the current attack surface are identified. Following this, the material extrusion workflow and the MITRE ATT&CK Knowledge Base [14] are employed to identify vulnerabilities in the targets and potential attacks that exploit the vulnerabilities. Next, countermeasures based on the MITRE D3FEND Knowledge Graph [15] are identified to combat the attacks. Attacks without adequate countermeasures would be successful and their potential negative impacts are specified. The attack-defense model directly supports three key risk management steps, risk identification, risk assessment and analysis, and risk mitigation and planning [16].

Three material extrusion printers are used as case studies in this research. The first is a material extrusion printer with a price point of $25,000 that is used in industry. The second is a fused filament fabrication printer priced at $4,000 that is commonly used in laboratory environments. The third is a $300 fused filament fabrication printer primarily used by educators and hobbyists.

Four real attacks on the material extrusion printers are described in detail. The first is a printer-independent, design phase attack that causes part sabotage. The second is a man-in-the-middle attack that targets the first printer during the slicing phase. The third is a G-code toolpath file modification attack that targets the second printer during the slicing phase. The fourth is a malware implant attack that targets the third printer during the printing phase. The case studies demonstrate the effectiveness of attack-defense modeling and its ability to help understand and bolster the cyber security postures and risk management of material extrusion additive manufacturing environments.

2.   Additive Manufacturing Workflow

The ability to rapidly design and create complex parts with intricate internal structures have led to dramatic increases in the use of additive manufacturing by industries across the critical infrastructure sectors. Additive manufacturing offers environmental, socioeconomic and technical advantages compared with traditional manufacturing [24]. The advantages include speed, accuracy, efficiency and cost savings. Additive manufacturing also results in less wasted material compared with traditional manufacturing. Parts can be printed on-site and on-demand without the added financial and temporal costs of off-site production.

Design files used for additive manufacturing can be shared to allow for reliable repeatability, enabling the printing of precisely the same parts by any capable printer. A design file can be used to print a part with identical properties (shape, size, weight and internal structures) anywhere in the world. Large warehouses of additive manufacturing printers, known as "print farms," are used to increase the number of print jobs completed simultaneously to further improve efficiency [24].

Figure 1 presents a generic additive manufacturing workflow (process chain). The workflow comprises four phases: (i) design, (ii) slicing, (iii) printing and (iv) post-processing:

- During the design phase, a 3D design of the desired part, including its shape, size, weight and other intricate details, is created using computer-aided design (CAD) software. Parts are designed for a range of uses from hobbyist toys and medical prosthetics to mission-critical components and weapons. The design details of the parts are saved in stereolithography (STL) design files. Part design files are often archived in online databases, enabling users to upload and download designs for dissemination and printing by compatible printers, respectively.

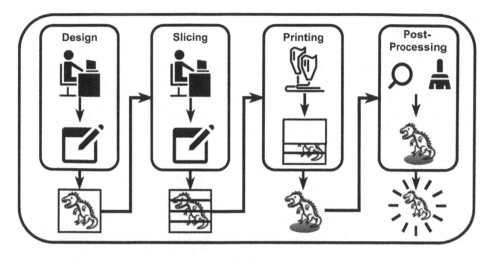

Figure 1. Additive manufacturing workflow.

- During the slicing phase, an STL design file is processed by a slicer, a type of computer-aided manufacturing (CAM) software. The slicing software divides the STL design file into segments of geometric code (G-code). Each G-code segment conveys the toolpath instructions for printing a slice of the part. Segments of the G-code file are sent directly to a printer or the entire file may be stored on removable storage media for subsequent input to a printer.

- During the printing phase, the printer firmware executes the G-code toolpath instructions to control actuator movements. The printer builds the part by depositing printing material (filaments) layer by layer according to the instructions that determine characteristics such as extruder motion, material temperature, thickness and distribution speed.

- During the post-processing phase, quality control and part finalization steps are performed, for example, to improve part strength and obtain the desired part finish. These steps are heavily dependent on the printer technology, material types and printed parts.

3. Additive Manufacturing Threats

This section discusses the two principal types of threats involving additive manufacturing systems: (i) threats that leverage additive manufacturing for malicious purposes and (ii) threats that target additive manufacturing environments.

3.1   Threats Leveraging Additive Manufacturing

Additive manufacturing can be used for nefarious purposes such as concealing illicit objects [9]. This is accomplished by pausing the printing process, inserting an illicit object inside the unfinished part and continuing the print job to hide the illicit object. Example illicit objects include explosives, illegal drugs and espionage devices.

Untraceable weapons such as "ghost guns" can be printed without serial numbers and other identifying information [9]. Digital part files for handguns and assault rifles have been available on the Internet for almost a decade. Accessories can be printed for illegal modifications to weapons. The perpetrator of the October 2019 synagogue shooting in Halle, Germany used improvised guns that incorporated 3D-printed components [4].

A novel feature of additive manufacturing is the ease with which parts can be reverse engineered to create digital part files for producing counterfeit parts. Additionally, modifications can be introduced in the reverse-engineered part files to produce hazardous items.

Biometric authentication devices scan human features such as fingerprints, handprints, retinas and faces. Additive manufacturing can be used to print high-quality spoofed fingerprints, handprints and facial features that defeat biometric authentication [9].

3.2   Threats Against Additive Manufacturing

The primary threats against additive manufacturing are intellectual property theft, part sabotage and additive manufacturing environment sabotage [24].

Researchers have theorized attacks that compromise the intellectual property of 3D-printed parts [1, 2, 8, 21]. One approach is to steal a digital part file from a control device that interfaces with a 3D printer. Another is to steal a part file directly from a printer. Yet another approach is to use a man-in-the-middle attack to steal a part file during its transfer from a control device to a printer over a network. Additionally, it is possible to scan a part and create a part file to replicate the part at will.

Sabotage attacks may target printed objects as well as print environments. Zeltmann et al. [25] discuss the potential risks and impacts of embedded defects and orientation changes on part strength. Moore et al. [17] analyzed a variety of open-source 3D printer software products.

They employed static and dynamic code analyses to reveal vulnerabilities such as buffer overflows and unencrypted communications that could be used to compromise printed parts. Additionally, they discovered weaknesses that could be exploited to manipulate G-code in toolpath files to sabotage parts.

Belikovetsky et al. [3] leveraged a phishing attack to install a backdoor on a control device. The backdoor enabled compromises of STL design files that resulted in weakened objects being printed. This attack was subsequently confirmed by Sturm et al. [22] who used malware to modify STL design files, leading to the premature failure of printed objects.

Moore et al. [18] implanted malicious code in 3D printer firmware. The modified firmware ignored incoming print commands, substituted malicious print commands and manipulated printer feed rates. The research amply demonstrated the negative impacts that malicious firmware can have on printed parts as well as on print environments.

As early as 2013, Xiao [23] demonstrated the malicious modification of a print environment. The firmware in a RepRap Prusa desktop 3D printer was changed to make the printer believe that the extruder temperature was twice as high as the actual temperature.

Pearce et al. [19] installed Trojan bootloaders in more than 100 Marlin-compatible commercial 3D printers to modify their print environments and compromise printed part integrity. The bootloaders scanned the firmware for certain byte patterns in the G-code and triggered manipulations that reduced printer extrusion rates and reordered G-code commands.

Most research in additive manufacturing has investigated weaknesses and avenues for attacks against design files and firmware. The narrow body of research involving real attacks focuses on STL design file manipulations and firmware modifications. In contrast, this research, in addition to demonstrating working attacks, presents an additive manufacturing attack-defense model that supports the discovery and exploitation of vulnerabilities in diverse material extrusion printers as well as the articulation of appropriate countermeasures.

4. Material Extrusion Additive Manufacturing

The additive manufacturing workflow differs based on printing technology, print material and other characteristics. Several types of additive manufacturing technologies have been developed, each with specific use cases, benefits and challenges. This research focuses on material extrusion additive manufacturing.

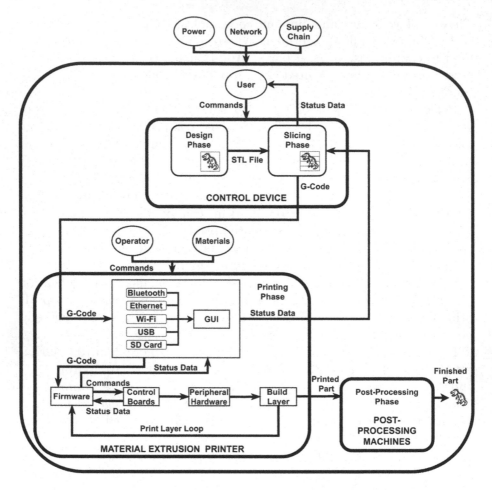

Figure 2. Material extrusion additive manufacturing workflow.

Material extrusion, also called fused deposition modeling or fused filament fabrication, is the most common additive manufacturing process [12]. The process involves heating print material and using an extruder to deposit it on a print bed layer by layer. Material is deposited along three dimensions according to the G-code instructions. Material extrusion is primarily used for printing prototypes, household items, toys, games and products with rough surface finishes.

Figure 2 shows the material extrusion additive manufacturing workflow. It comprises the four additive manufacturing phases: design, slicing, printing and post-processing. However, to provide background information and support the creation of the attack-defense model specified later, details about the four phases are only provided for material extrusion additive manufacturing.

The control device in Figure 2 is responsible for the design and slicing phases of material extrusion. The design phase inputs include electric power, network communications, supply chain components and user commands to the control device. The principal design phase output is the STL design file, which is transmitted to the slicing phase for processing by the slicer.

The slicing phase inputs include electric power, network communications, supply chain components and control device user commands, as well as the STL design file input from the design phase. Since the slicing software acts as an interface between the control device and printer, it receives print status data inputs from the printer during the printing phase. The slicing phase also outputs status data to the control device user who interacts with the slicing software.

The material extrusion printer is responsible for the printing phase. The printing phase inputs include electric power, network communications, supply chain components, printer operator commands and extruder materials. The G-code file, a key printer input, is transmitted by the slicing software remotely via Bluetooth, Ethernet or Wi-Fi, or manually by a printer operator via a USB device or SD card. The printer also receives status data from the firmware as the part is printed.

During the printing phase, the printer firmware processes the G-code file. The firmware communicates G-code toolpath instructions to the control boards, which control the peripheral hardware that prints the part layer by layer (in a loop) until all the G-code instructions are executed. The firmware sends status data as necessary to the printer.

The printing phase outputs the printed part to the post-processing phase, which may have multiple automated/manual sub-phases depending on the part and its desired properties. The post-processing phase receives inputs such as electric power, network communications, supply chain components, materials and technician/operator commands. The output of the post-processing phase, indeed the ultimate product of the material extrusion additive manufacturing workflow, is the finished part.

Post-processing operations are highly specific to the print materials and parts. Additionally, an analysis of the material extrusion process conducted in this research revealed that the overwhelming majority of cyber threats target the earlier design, slicing and printing phases. Therefore, the post-processing phase is considered to be out of scope in this research and is not described in detail in the material extrusion workflow in Figure 2.

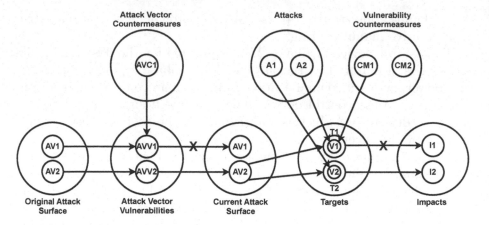

Figure 3.   Attack-defense model components.

5.   Attack-Defense Modeling

This section describes an attack-defense model of the security environment of a complex cyber-physical system. The model specifies key components such as attack vectors, attack vector vulnerabilities and countermeasures, attack surfaces, system targets, target vulnerabilities and vulnerability countermeasures, and attacks and attack impacts. The model directly supports three key risk management steps, risk identification, risk assessment and analysis, and risk mitigation and planning (the remaining two steps are risk allocation and risk monitoring and control) [16].

Figure 3 shows the components of an attack-defense model. An attack vector gives an adversary cyber or physical access to one or more targets in the system of interest. The collection of possible attack vectors comprises the original attack surface of the system ([AV1, AV2]).

An attack vector (AV2) is effective when it exploits an attack vector vulnerability (AVV2) to achieve the desired access. However, if an attack vector countermeasure (AVC1) is implemented to combat an attack vector vulnerability (AVV1), the associated attack vector (AV1) is ineffective. The collection of effective attack vectors comprises the current attack surface of the system ([AV2]).

An attacker can leverage effective attack vectors in the current attack surface to access targets in the system ([T1, T2]). Having gained access to a target, the attacker proceeds to launch an attack that exploits a vulnerability in the target. If appropriate countermeasures that address the target vulnerability are implemented, the attack is unsuccessful; otherwise, the attack is successful and causes negative impacts.

In Figure 3, attack A2 that exploits vulnerability V1 in target T1 is unsuccessful because vulnerability countermeasure CM1 is implemented for vulnerability V1. However, attack A1 that exploits vulnerability V2 in target T2 is successful because no countermeasures are implemented for vulnerability V2, resulting in impact I2.

The attack-defense model of a cyber-physical system is created by specifying the original attack surface and implemented attack vector countermeasures to obtain the current attack surface. Next, the system targets that can be accessed using the current attack surface are identified. Following this, a cyber-physical system workflow as in Figure 2 and the MITRE ATT&CK Knowledge Base [14] are employed to identify vulnerabilities in the targets and possible attacks. Countermeasures based on the MITRE D3FEND Knowledge Graph [15] are then identified to combat the attacks. Attacks without adequate countermeasures would be successful and their potential negative impacts on the system are specified.

Attack-defense modeling effectively conveys the security environment of a complex cyber-physical process such as material extrusion manufacturing. It clearly specifies the attack vectors that provide access to targets and the attack vector countermeasures that combat the vulnerabilities exploited by attack vectors to reduce the overall attack surface. Having identified the targets reachable by attacks, it clarifies the target vulnerabilities that could be exploited and demands that countermeasures be considered to address the vulnerabilities, defeating the attacks and reducing or eliminating the negative impacts.

6. Material Extrusion Attack-Defense Model

This section specifies a general attack-defense model for material extrusion additive manufacturing systems. The overall model includes separate models for the design, slicing and printing phases. Each model comprises the current attack surface (set of attack vectors), targets, target vulnerabilities, attacks, vulnerability countermeasures and attack impacts. Note that the current attack surface includes all the attack vectors because it is assumed that no attack vector countermeasures are implemented.

A graphical representation of an attack-defense model with circles and arrows as shown in Figure 3 offers clarity. However, in the case of the attack-defense models for the design, slicing and printing phases, the graphical representations are cumbersome because there are large numbers of vulnerabilities, attacks and vulnerability countermeasures.

Alternatively, attack-defense models may be presented as tables with columns: attack vectors, targets, target vulnerabilities, attacks, vulnerability countermeasures and impacts. The tables simplify the presentation while providing details of individual vulnerabilities, attacks and vulnerability countermeasures. A table may not provide a comprehensive description of all the vulnerabilities, attacks and vulnerability countermeasures, but it does provide significant examples to understand the security environment, including the gaps that must be filled by adding new rows to the table. Additionally, the tables are readily implemented in an automated system for presenting the security environment of an material extrusion additive manufacturing system and evaluating vulnerability countermeasures and attack impacts for various targets.

Another significant advantage of the tabular representation compared with its graphical counterpart is its ability to express one-to-many, many-to-one and many-to-many relationships involving target vulnerabilities, attacks and vulnerability countermeasures. One example is a single attack that can exploit multiple vulnerabilities on multiple targets. Another is a single target vulnerability that can be exploited by multiple attacks. Yet another example is a single vulnerability countermeasure that can be applied to address multiple target vulnerabilities.

6.1   Design Phase Attack-Defense Model

Table 1 shows an attack-defense model table created for the design phase of the material extrusion workflow. The attack vectors in the attack-defense table correspond to the four design phase inputs in the workflow, power supply, network, supply chain and user. The targets, control device, design software and STL design file, correspond to the three design phase components whose compromise can impact an STL design file, which is the output of the design phase.

A target reachable by an attack vector may have vulnerabilities. An attack exploits one or more vulnerabilities. A vulnerability countermeasure addresses one or more vulnerabilities and combats the associated attacks.

As seen in Table 1, the three principal impacts of attacks on the design phase are intellectual property theft, part sabotage and print environment sabotage. Note that power supply attacks only result in part sabotage because they prevent the STL design file from being created. In contrast, the network, supply chain and user attack vectors may ultimately result in intellectual property theft, part sabotage and print environment sabotage. Intellectual property theft occurs when an STL design file is exfiltrated. Part sabotage occurs when the 3D surface geo-

Table 1. Design phase attack-defense table.

Attack Vectors	Targets	Vulnerabilities	Attacks	Vulnerability Countermeasures	Impacts
Power supply	Control device	Unprotected power supply	Power shut off	Backup power supply	PS
			Power surge	Power surge protection	PS
Network	Control device	Memory access	File modification	Access control	IPT, PS, PES
		Root access	File theft	Access control	IPT
		Open ports	File theft	Port security	IPT
	Design software	Software access	Malware implant	Integrity checking	IPT, PS, PES
	STL design file	No STL file integrity checking	STL file modification	Integrity checking	IPT, PS, PES
			STL file replacement	File hashing	IPT, PS, PES
		Memory access	STL file modification	Access control	IPT, PS, PES
Supply chain	Control device	Operating system access	Malware implant	Integrity checking	IPT, PS, PES
		Firmware access	Malware implant	Integrity checking	IPT, PS, PES
		Network access	Malware implant	Integrity checking	IPT, PS, PES
		Physical access	Malware implant	Integrity checking	IPT, PS, PES
			Parasitic device implant	Physical inspection	IPT, PS, PES
	Design software	Software access	Malware implant	Integrity checking	IPT, PS, PES
	STL design file	Vendor USB drive	Malware implant	USB port security	IPT, PS, PES
			Malicious STL file	USB port security	IPT, PS, PES
User	Control device	Physical access	Malware implant	Integrity checking	IPT, PS, PES
			Parasitic device implant	Physical inspection	IPT, PS, PES
			Erroneous use	User training	IPT, PS, PES
			Memory modification	Quality control	IPT, PS, PES
			File theft	Access control	IPT
	Design software	Physical access	Malware implant	Integrity checking	IPT, PS, PES
			Erroneous STL file	User training	IPT, PS, PES
			Malicious STL file	Access control	IPT, PS, PES
				Quality control	IPT, PS, PES
	STL design file	Physical access	Erroneous STL file	User training	IPT, PS, PES
			Malicious STL file	Access control	IPT, PS, PES
				Quality control	IPT, PS, PES

IPT: Intellectual property theft, PS: Part sabotage, PES: Print environment sabotage

metry encoded in an STL design file is manipulated. Print environment sabotage occurs (for example) when malware is incorporated in an STL design file to target slicing software, causing it to incorporate malicious G-code instructions that impact the print environment.

6.2   Slicing Phase Attack-Defense Model

Table 2 shows an attack-defense model table created for the slicing phase of the material extrusion workflow. The attack vectors in the attack-defense table correspond to the four slicing phase inputs in the material extrusion workflow, power supply, network, supply chain and user. The targets, control device, slicing software and G-code file, cor-

Table 2.   Slicing phase attack-defense table.

Attack Vectors	Targets	Vulnerabilities	Attacks	Vulnerability Countermeasures	Impacts
Power supply	Control device	Unprotected power supply	Power shut off	Backup power supply	PS, PES
			Power surge	Power surge protection	PS, PES
Network	Control device	Memory access	File modification	Access control	IPT, PS, PES
		Root access	File theft	Access control	IPT
		Open ports	File theft	Port security	IPT
	Slicing software	Software access	Malware implant	Integrity checking	IPT, PS, PES
		No printer authentication	Man-in-the-middle	Printer authentication	IPT, PS, PES
			ARP spoofing	Network authentication	IPT, PS, PES
		Print queue access	Print queue modification	Print queue access control	IPT, PS, PES
	G-code file	No G-code file integrity checking	G-code file modification	Integrity checking	IPT, PS, PES
			G-code file replacement	File hashing	IPT, PS, PES
		Memory access	G-code file modification	Access control	IPT, PS, PES
Supply chain	Control device	Operating system access	Malware implant	Integrity checking	IPT, PS, PES
		Firmware access	Malware implant	Integrity checking	IPT, PS, PES
		Network access	Malware implant	Integrity checking	IPT, PS, PES
		Physical access	Malware implant	Integrity checking	IPT, PS, PES
			Parasitic device implant	Physical inspection	IPT, PS, PES
	Slicing software	Software access	Malware implant	Integrity checking	IPT, PS, PES
	G-code file	Vendor USB drive	Malware implant	USB port security	IPT, PS, PES
			Malicious G-code file	USB port security	IPT, PS, PES
User	Control device	Physical access	Malware implant	Integrity checking	IPT, PS, PES
			Parasitic device implant	Physical inspection	IPT, PS, PES
			Erroneous use	User training	IPT, PS, PES
			Memory modification	Quality control	IPT, PS, PES
			File theft	Access control	IPT
	Slicing software	Physical access	Malware implant	Integrity checking	IPT, PS, PES
			Erroneous G-code file	User training	IPT, PS, PES
			Malicious G-code file	Access control	IPT, PS, PES
				Quality control	IPT, PS, PES
	G-code file	Physical access	Erroneous G-code file	User training	IPT, PS, PES
			Malicious G-code file	Access control	IPT, PS, PES
				Quality control	IPT, PS, PES

IPT: Intellectual property theft, PS: Part sabotage, PES: Print environment sabotage

respond to the three slicing phase components whose compromise can impact the G-code file, which is the output of the slicing phase.

As shown in Table 2, the three principal impacts of attacks on the slicing phase are intellectual property theft, part sabotage and print environment sabotage. Power supply attacks result in part sabotage and print environment sabotage due to the dependence of the slicing software on the control device. Attacks leveraging the access provided by the network, supply chain and user attack vectors result in intellectual property theft, part sabotage and print environment sabotage. Intellectual property theft occurs when a G-code or control device file is exfiltrated. Part sabotage occurs when a G-code file is modified to alter the toolpath, which modifies the printed part. Print environment sabotage occurs when the environment is disturbed by modifying a G-code file or by directly interacting with the printer.

Attacks during the slicing phase that modify a G-code toolpath file are a concern because G-code determines the toolpath and print environment variables such as temperature and fan speed. Alterations to a G-code file can result in part sabotage and print environment sabotage regardless of the intent of the alteration. The direct connection between the slicing software and a printer provides an avenue for accessing the print environment. Attacks against the direct connection between the slicing software and a printer can result in the exploitation of several vulnerabilities.

6.3   Printing Phase Attack-Defense Model

Table 3 shows the attack-defense model table for the printing phase of the material extrusion workflow. The attack vectors in the attack-defense table correspond to the four design phase inputs in the material extrusion workflow, power supply, network, supply chain and operator. As seen in the table, the targets vary based on the attack vector. The potential targets include the control device, printer, printer firmware, peripheral hardware, print layer, control boards and printer material. Each target represents a printing phase component whose compromise can impact the printing process and print environment, which collectively produce the final printed part.

Table 3 shows the three principal impacts of attacks on the printing phase, intellectual property theft, part sabotage and print environment sabotage. The most concerning impacts of successful attacks against the printing phase are part sabotage and print environment sabotage. Attacks against the power supply can be used to target vulnerabilities in the control device and printer. The impacts of successful attacks against the power supply are part sabotage and print environment sabotage.

The network attack vector may provide an attacker with access to targets such as a printer, printer firmware, peripheral hardware and print layer. Communications between slicing software and a printer are commonly unencrypted, and therefore, subject to eavesdropping, interference and malicious modification of G-code and status data in transit unless strong access controls are implemented.

The supply chain attack vector may enable an attacker to access a printer, printer firmware, control boards, peripheral hardware, print layer and printer material. Physical access to a printer via the supply chain provides opportunities to implant malware and parasitic devices. A malware implant may involve malicious modifications to printer

Table 3. Printing phase attack-defense table.

Attack Vectors	Targets	Vulnerabilities	Attacks	Vulnerability Countermeasures	Impacts
Power supply	Control device	Unprotected power supply	Power shut off	Backup power supply	PS, PES
			Power surge	Power surge protection	PS, PES
	Printer	Unprotected power supply	Power shut off	Backup power supply	PS, PES
			Power surge	Power surge protection	PS, PES
Network	Printer	No control device authentication	HTTP packet spoofing	Control device authentication	IPT, PS, PES
	Printer firmware	No integrity checking	Firmware implant	Integrity checking	IPT, PS, PES
		Remote update access	Firmware implant	Integrity checking	IPT, PS, PES
		Firmware access	Firmware implant	Integrity checking	IPT, PS, PES
	Peripheral hardware	No access control	Data modification	Access control	IPT, PS, PES
	Print layer	No access control	G-code layer theft	Access control	IPT
			G-code modification	Access control	IPT, PS, PES
Supply chain	Printer	Physical access	Malware implant	Integrity checking	IPT, PS, PES
			Parasitic device implant	Physical inspection	IPT, PS, PES
	Printer firmware	No integrity checking	Firmware implant	Integrity checking	IPT, PS, PES
		Firmware access	Firmware implant	Integrity checking	IPT, PS, PES
	Control boards	Physical access	Malware implant	Integrity checking	IPT, PS, PES
			Parasitic device implant	Physical inspection	IPT, PS, PES
	Peripheral hardware	Physical access	Faulty hardware implant	Physical inspection	IPT, PS, PES
	Printer material	Physical access	Faulty material	Quality control	IPT, PS, PES
Operator	Printer	Physical access	Malware implant	Integrity checking	IPT, PS, PES
			Parasitic device implant	Physical inspection	IPT, PS, PES
	Printer firmware	Firmware access	Firmware implant	Integrity checking	IPT, PS, PES
		Physical access	Erroneous use	Operator training	IPT, PS, PES
			Malicious use	Access control	IPT, PS, PES
	Control boards	Physical access	Erroneous use	Operator training	IPT, PS, PES
			Malicious use	Access control	IPT, PS, PES
	Peripheral hardware	Physical access	Erroneous use	Operator training	IPT, PS, PES
			Malicious use	Access control	IPT, PS, PES
	Print layer	Physical access	Erroneous use	Operator training	IPT, PS, PES
			Malicious use	Access control	IPT, PS, PES
	Printer material	Physical access	Erroneous use	Operator training	IPT, PS, PES
			Malicious use	Access control	IPT, PS, PES

IPT: Intellectual property theft, PS: Part sabotage, PES: Print environment sabotage

firmware that could alter printer functionality, thereby sabotaging print jobs and the print environment.

The operator attack vector enables an attacker to access a printer, printer firmware, control boards, peripheral hardware, print layer and printer material. Operators often have unfettered access to the targets, providing opportunities to erroneously or maliciously interfere with printed parts and the print environment.

7. Material Extrusion Case Studies

This section describes the three material extrusion printers used as case studies to demonstrate the effectiveness of the attack-defense model and help understand the cyber security and risk management postures of material extrusion additive manufacturing environments. For security reasons, certain details about the printers and their environments are obfuscated.

7.1 Printer Annamieke

Printer Annamieke is a proprietary material extrusion printer. The printer facilitates efficient and durable printing with plastic and metallicized-plastic materials. An Annamieke printer has a unique device name and serial number, neither of which can be changed.

Printer Annamieke is typically used in industry because of its size and $25,000 price. The printer comes equipped with proprietary software for slicing STL design files to produce G-code toolpath files, and for interfacing between the control device and printer.

A vulnerability in the network discovery process utilized by the proprietary interface software and printer was exploited to obtain a man-in-the-middle position. Attacks that exploit the vulnerability result in intellectual property theft, part sabotage and print environment sabotage.

7.2 Printer Beatrijs

Printer Beatrijs is an industrial fused filament fabrication printer. It uses a dual extruder and a partially-enclosed environment to print parts using a variety of materials, including plastics, wood and stainless steel. The printer costs approximately $4,000 and is commonly used in laboratory environments.

Printer Beatrijs is equipped with open-source slicing and printer interface software that allows for reliable and persistent access. A vulnerability discovered in the open-source slicing and interface software enables the unauthorized modification of G-code toolpath files in control device memory [11]. Modifications to the G-code toolpath file during the slicing phase, before it is sent to the printer, can result in part sabotage and print environment sabotage.

7.3 Printer Cathelijne

Printer Cathelijne is a fused filament fabrication printer with a single extruder capable of printing with plastic or wood filament. The printer

has an open design and comes with a removable print bed, built-in filament tray, patent extruder, touch screen and multiple communications
modes, including USB cable, USB drive, Ethernet and Wi-Fi.

Printer Cathelijne is primarily used by educators and hobbyists due
to its low $300 price and ease of use. It has proprietary slicing and
interface software and printer firmware.

Printer Cathelijne is vulnerable to several attacks, including firmware
modification, remote code execution and malware implants.

8.   Material Extrusion Attacks

Attack-defense models for the design, slicing and printing phases were
created for the three printers in the case study. The attack-defense models comprise the attack vectors, targets, target vulnerabilities, attacks,
vulnerability countermeasures and attack impacts. Since the models
were developed from a common process workflow, the attack vectors,
targets and attack impacts are common to all three printers. However,
differences exist in the target vulnerabilities between printers due to differences in printer designs, features and implementations. As a result,
the target vulnerabilities, attacks and vulnerability countermeasures in
the attack-defense models vary from printer to printer.

This section describes four exemplar attacks in the printer attack-
defense models. The first exemplar attack is a design phase attack on
a control device that is printer-independent. The second and third exemplar attacks, which focus on the slicing phase, are unique to printers
Annamieke and Beatrijs, respectively. The fourth exemplar attack targets the printing phase of printer Cathelijne.

8.1   Design Phase Attack

During the design phase, a 3D rendering of a part is created using
computer-aided design software running on a control device that is independent of the eventual printer. The 3D rendering of the part is saved
on the control device as an STL design file. Vulnerabilities in the control
device that creates and/or stores the STL design file can enable attacks
on the STL design file, which is the output of the design phase.

A classic attack is to modify an STL design file to sabotage the resulting printed parts. The attack, first demonstrated by Belikovetsky et
al. [3], leveraged general infiltration methods to target a control device
hosting an STL design file. Access to the control device (target) was
gained using a phishing attack (network attack vector) and the data
alteration attack exploited a ZIP file vulnerability (target vulnerability). Specifically, the STL design file was modified to introduce a void in

Table 4. STL design file attack.

Attack Vectors	Targets	Vulnerabilities	Attacks	Vulnerability Countermeasures	Impacts
· · ·	· · ·	· · ·	· · ·	· · ·	· · ·
Network	· · ·	· · ·	· · ·	· · ·	· · ·
	STL design	· · ·	· · ·	· · ·	· · ·
	file	Memory access	STL file modification	Access control	IPT, PS, PES
		· · ·	· · ·	· · ·	· · ·
	· · ·	· · ·	· · ·	· · ·	· · ·
· · ·	· · ·	· · ·	· · ·	· · ·	· · ·

IPT: Intellectual property theft, PS: Part sabotage, PES: Print environment sabotage

the part as it was printed (attack), causing a time-delayed part failure (attack impact).

Attacks on an STL design file during the design phase can be executed independently of a printer. Table 4 shows a portion of the design phase attack-defense model corresponding to the STL design file attack. The impacts of the STL design file attack include part sabotage as well as intellectual property theft (theft of the STL design file) and print environment sabotage (malware implant in the STL design file). Table 4 also shows that an access control countermeasure can address the vulnerability and counter the STL design file attack, eliminating the negative impacts.

8.2 Slicing Phase Attacks

The slicing software hosted on a control device transforms an STL design file to a G-code toolpath file for eventual printing. The slicing software may also act as an interface between the control device and a compatible printer. Penetration tests revealed that the slicing software systems designed for the Annamieke and Beatrijs printers had vulnerabilities that could be exploited during the slicing phase to cause intellectual property theft, part sabotage and print environment sabotage.

Printer Annamieke Man-in-the-Middle Attack. A control device may connect to an Annamieke material extrusion printer via a Wi-Fi or Ethernet link, or directly via a cable. However, dynamic or static connections via a Wi-Fi network are most common. If the network is configured for the Dynamic Host Configuration Protocol (DHCP), an IP address is automatically assigned to the printer. Otherwise, a user

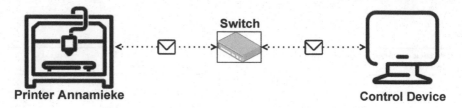

Figure 4.   Legitimate connection between the slicing software and printer Annamieke.

may manually enter a static IP address in the printer user interface and enter the same IP address in the proprietary printer interface software.

The control device executes slicing/interface software developed for an Annamieke printer. The software searches the network for a compatible printer and establishes a connection if one is discovered. The software then slices the STL design file to create a printer-compatible G-code toolpath file. The software may be used to view, resize or place a 3D rendering on the print bed. Additionally, the software provides data about the connected printer, including its name, material status, print status, print history and current print job data.

The exemplar attack developed for the Annamieke printer slicing phase leverages local network connectivity as the attack vector to target the slicing software. Analysis of the material extrusion workflow using the MITRE ATT&CK Knowledge Base led to the discovery of a vulnerability in how the slicing software establishes a connection with the Annamieke printer. Specifically, the software and printer Annamieke use plaintext HTTP communications without authentication to establish their connection. This vulnerability is exploited to obtain a man-in-the-middle position before or after the connection between the slicing software and printer Annamieke is established.

During its execution, the slicing software spawns a network process that sends Simple Service Discovery Protocol (SSDP) multicast messages in the local network looking for compatible printers. Upon receiving the message, printer Annamieke sends a plaintext HTTP response containing its printer name, serial number and IP address. The software stores the data received from printer Annamieke and proceeds to establish a connection as shown in Figure 4. After the connection is established, printer Annamieke sends the slicing software status reports about the printer material status and extruder location and temperature. Additionally, the slicing software sends user commands to and requests status data from printer Annamieke.

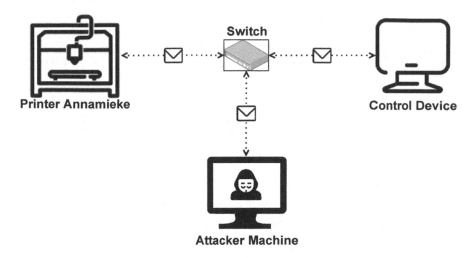

Figure 5. Printer Annamieke man-in-the-middle attack position.

An attacker can leverage the lack of encryption and authentication to assume a man-in-the-middle position between the slicing software and printer Annamieke. This is accomplished by actively monitoring the local network traffic from an attacker-controlled machine for SSDP multicast messages sent by the slicing software to find a compatible printer. Upon detecting an SSDP message and the response from printer Annamieke, a spoofed response is created by the attacker claiming to be printer Annamieke (using the unique identifiers in the Annamieke response packet), but replacing the legitimate IP address with the IP address of the attacker-controlled machine. Figure 5 shows the attacker-controlled machine after it has assumed a man-in-the-middle position during initial session establishment.

Note that the attacker can also assume a man-in-the-middle position after a legitimate connection is established between the slicing software and printer Annamieke. This is because the slicing software allows dynamic updates to IP addresses and only requires the printer name, unique identification number and IP address to update the connection, all of which can be captured from network traffic. The attacker then hijacks the legitimate connection between the slicing software and printer Annamieke by sending a packet to replicate an Annamieke IP address update. Finally, the attacker maintains persistence by establishing network traffic forwarding rules on the attacker-controlled machine to ensure that all communications are forwarded through the attacker-controlled machine.

Table 5.   Printer Annamieke man-in-the-middle network attack.

Attack Vectors	Targets	Vulnerabilities	Attacks	Vulnerability Countermeasures	Impacts
...	...	...	...	...	...
Network	...	...	...	...	...
	Slicing	...	...	...	...
	software	No printer authentication	Man-in-the-middle	Printer authentication	IPT, PS, PES
		...	...	...	...
	...	...	...	...	...
...	...	...	...	...	...

IPT: Intellectual property theft, PS: Part sabotage, PES: Print environment sabotage

Table 5 shows a portion of the slicing phase attack-defense model corresponding to the printer Annamieke man-in-the-middle network attack. Intellectual property theft is perpetrated by copying the G-code toolpath file from the man-in-the-middle position. Part sabotage and print environment sabotage are accomplished by modifying the G-code file during its transmission. Table 5 also shows that a device authentication countermeasure can counter the printer Annamieke man-in-the-middle network attack, eliminating the negative impacts.

Printer Beatrijs G-Code File Modification Attack.   Printer Beatrijs uses open-source slicing/interface software that is employed by many other additive manufacturing printers. Analysis of the material extrusion workflow using the MITRE ATT&CK Knowledge Base led to the discovery of a vulnerability in the open-source slicing software [11].

Specifically, after the G-code is generated by the slicing software, but before it is saved on the control device hosting the slicing software, the entire G-code toolpath file is stored unencrypted as ASCII characters in the heap memory of the control device. Root access to the control device enables the ASCII representation of the G-code in heap memory to be modified while the user views the 3D rendering of the G-code using the slicing software.

A tool was created to locate and extract the ASCII G-code in heap memory, and reconstruct the G-code toolpath layers in ascending order by layer number [11]. The tool also facilitates surreptitious alterations of the G-code such as excluding infill from certain layers and reducing the extruder temperature when certain layers are printed. When the user saves the G-code toolpath file to the control device, the modified

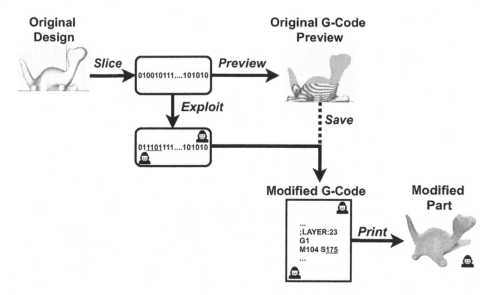

Figure 6. Printer Beatrijs G-code file modification attack workflow.

G-code in heap memory is saved instead of the original version. Figure 6 shows the printer Beatrijs G-code file modification attack workflow.

Table 6. Printer Beatrijs G-code file modification attack.

Attack Vectors	Targets	Vulnerabilities	Attacks	Vulnerability Countermeasures	Impacts
· · ·	· · ·	· · ·	· · ·	· · ·	· · ·
Network	· · ·	· · ·	· · ·	· · ·	· · ·
	G-code file	· · ·	· · ·	· · ·	· · ·
		Memory access	G-code file modification	Access control	IPT, PS, PES
		· · ·	· · ·	· · ·	· · ·
	· · ·	· · ·	· · ·	· · ·	· · ·
· · ·	· · ·	· · ·	· · ·	· · ·	· · ·

IPT: Intellectual property theft, PS: Part sabotage, PES: Print environment sabotage

Table 6 shows a portion of the slicing phase attack-defense model corresponding to the G-code file modification attack against the Beatrijs printer. Intellectual property theft is perpetrated by copying the ASCII version of the G-code toolpath file from heap memory. Part sabotage and print environment sabotage are accomplished by modifying the G-code file in heap memory.

Experiments revealed that G-code modifications that cause infill to be excluded from certain layers and the extruder temperature to be reduced while printing certain layers have significant ramifications [11].

In the infill exclusion experiments, excluding infill from just five of the 127 total layers in printed plastic cylinders yielded a 10.6% reduction in the average failure force under compression. Excluding infill from 25 of the 127 layers yielded a 19.9% reduction in the average failure force under compression. In both instances, the mass reductions were negligible (within standard error) and no perceptible differences were visible between the original and modified cylinders.

In the temperature reduction experiments, G-code was modified to reduce the extruder temperature slightly (from the normal 198°C to the new 190°C) when just seven centrally-located layers of the 530 total layers of plastic parts were printed. No perceptible differences were visible between the original and modified parts. However, the average breaking force under tensile testing dropped by 14% for the modified parts.

Table 6 shows that a G-code file hashing vulnerability countermeasure can counter the printer Beatrijs G-code file modification attack, eliminating the negative impacts.

8.3   Printing Phase Attack

The control board of a Cathelijne printer has a debug port for analyzing printer activity and errors. The supply chain attack vector enables physical access to a Cathelijne printer control board (target). Physical access to the control board is a critical vulnerability that enables malware to be implanted using the debug port. Note that physical access could also be leveraged to attack the printer after it is operational at the print facility. Table 7 shows a portion of the printing phase attack-defense model corresponding to the printer Cathelijne malware implant attack.

The printer Cathelijne malware implant attack requires a debug port connection. Jumper cable connections are made between the RX, TX and ground pins of the debug port and an FTDI Basic chip connected to a laptop running a Windows operating system. The FTDI Basic chip converts the serial communications from the debug port to the USB protocol, enabling them to be monitored via a PuTTY application that offers a terminal emulator, serial connection and network file transfers to the Windows laptop.

Table 7. Printer Cathelijne malware implant attack.

Attack Vectors	Targets	Vulnerabilities	Attacks	Vulnerability Countermeasures	Impacts
. . .	. . .	. . .	. . .	. . .	. . .
Supply chain	. . .	. . .	. . .	. . .	. . .
	Printer	. . .	. . .	. . .	. . .
		Physical access	Malware implant	Integrity checking	IPT, PS, PES
		. . .	. . .	. . .	. . .
	. . .	. . .	. . .	. . .	. . .
. . .	. . .	. . .	. . .	. . .	. . .

IPT: Intellectual property theft, PS: Part sabotage, PES: Print environment sabotage

The next steps in the attack are to interrupt the boot process and modify the boot settings to execute a shell instead of the Linux operating system. After the `PuTTY` terminal displays the communications from the debug port, the printer boot process is interrupted by depressing the escape key repeatedly. Following this, the new boot environment variables are set by issuing the following two commands in sequence:

- `setenv bootargs 'noinitrd root=/dev/mmcblk0p2 rootfstype=ext4 init=/bin/sh/ rootwait console=ttyS0, 115200n8'`

- `saveenv`

The `printenv` command is executed to confirm that the environment variables have been set.

Printer Cathelijne is restarted after confirming that the environment variable has been changed to execute a shell at bootup. When the terminal prompts for a username and password, the default credentials provided in the Cathelijne printer manual are entered, enabling access to the printer filesystem. The filesystem access enables any file to be moved to a USB drive plugged into the printer. In this case, the `/etc/shadow` file is moved to the USB drive and a forensic tool is used to decrypt the file to obtain root credentials.

Next, a USB drive is used to implant malware in printer Cathelijne. This is accomplished by navigating to the `/media` directory and copying the malware file to the `/bin/obfuscated` directory. Leveraging root access via the operating system shell, a startup script is modified to connect the printer to the Wi-Fi network and execute the malware as

```
Options

        find       -->  "find"      [start directory] [filename/dirname]
        download   -->  "download"  [filename]
        upload     -->  "upload"    [filename]
        die        -->  "die"

Received data.
```

Figure 7.   Malware command terminal options.

a persistent background process. Printer Cathelijne is then rebooted to launch the malware. The malware executes whenever printer Cathelijne boots up.

The executing malware establishes a client-server connection between the printer and a remote attacker-controlled device. When the attacker device executes the client code, a user interface with malware command options is presented. Figure 7 shows the four malware command options, find, download, upload and die.

```
Options

        find       -->  "find"      [start directory] [filename/dirname]
        download   -->  "download"  [filename]
        upload     -->  "upload"    [filename]
        die        -->  "die"

--> find / corporate_secrets

The server sent the following data:

/data/corporate_secrets
/opt/corporate_secrets
/media/corporate_secrets
/etc/corporate_secrets
/root/corporate_secrets
/media/thelogic/corporate_secrets
/etc/ssh/corporate_secrets
/etc/wpa_supplicant/corporate_secrets
```

Figure 8.   Malware find command execution results.

The find command searches through directories for filenames. Figure 8 shows the execution results of a find command that searches the Cathelijne printer filesystem for directory names and/or filenames con-

```
Options

        find       -->  "find"      [start directory] [filename/dirname]
        download   -->  "download"  [filename]
        upload     -->  "upload"    [filename]
        die        -->  "die"

--> download /data/corporate_secrets as stolen_data

Received data.
```

Figure 9. Malware **download** command execution results.

taining **corporate_secrets**. Options are provided to prune directory paths in the file-search tree to shorten the search time.

Intellectual property theft is perpetrated using the **download** command to transfer files from the printer to the remote attacker-controlled device. Figure 9 shows the downloading of the **corporate_secrets** file discovered using the **find** command. The downloaded file is given the name **stolen_data**.

The **upload** command enables files to be moved to the printer filesystem. The files may include G-code files to print sabotaged parts, firmware files to sabotage the print environment and malware files with sophisticated functionality.

```
Options

        find       -->  "find"      [start directory] [filename/dirname]
        download   -->  "download"  [filename]
        upload     -->  "upload"    [filename]
        die        -->  "die"

--> upload /etc/altered_firmware_file

File written to path on server.
```

Figure 10. Malware **upload** command execution results.

Figure 10 shows **/etc/altered_firmware_file** being uploaded from the attacker-controlled device to the working directory of the printer. It was observed that an uploaded file overwrites an existing file with the same name in the printer directory. This feature can be exploited to overwrite the Wi-Fi configuration files in the **/etc/wpa_suplicant**

```
Options

        find       --> "find"      [start directory] [filename/dirname]
        download   --> "download"  [filename]
        upload     --> "upload"    [filename]
        die        --> "die"

--> die

Server exiting.
```

Figure 11. Malware **die** command execution results.

directory or any other system configuration files. As a result, any number of file manipulations and malware updates could be performed to alter the physical, storage and network behavior of the printer.

The **die** command halts malware execution until the printer is re-booted. Figure 11 shows the **die** command execution results. The command to halt execution enables the malware to remain dormant for an extended period of time to prevent the discovery of an open network port on the Cathelijne printer. The malware is reactivated automatically when the printer is rebooted.

The malware can be deployed on any Linux kernel running on an ARM or x86 architecture, which enables it to target a variety of printers. The case study demonstrates how a supply chain attack vector and physical access vulnerability can enable malware that causes intellectual property theft, part sabotage and print environment sabotage to be implanted.

Table 7 shows that integrity checking can address the physical access vulnerability and counter the printer Cathelijne malware implant attack, eliminating the negative impacts.

9.   Discussion

Material extrusion additive manufacturing is a complex cyber-physical process system. Attempting to secure the process system in a robust and (ideally) comprehensive manner requires a holistic perspective provided by a workflow that describes the operational phases, their systems and subsystems, and inputs and outputs. In the case of material extrusion additive manufacturing, separate workflows were created for its three principal phases, design, slicing and printing. Based on their workflows, separate attack-defense models were constructed for the three material extrusion phases.

Each attack-defense model comprises a set of attack vectors, targets, target vulnerabilities, attacks, vulnerability countermeasures and attack impacts. The specification of the attack surface is the first step in developing an attack-defense model. The attack surface is the collection of attack vectors that provide cyber or physical access to targets. The attack vectors and targets are clearly discernible in the process workflow. At this juncture, the vulnerabilities exploited by the attack vectors must be identified and the countermeasures that would address the vulnerabilities and combat the associated attack vectors must be specified. Attack vectors for which no countermeasures are implemented constitute the current attack surface, which provides insights into the accessible targets and types of access.

An attack framework is employed to identify target vulnerabilities and devise potential attacks that exploit the vulnerabilities. Simultaneously, a defense framework is used to identify countermeasures that combat the attacks by addressing the vulnerabilities they exploit. Attacks without adequate countermeasures would be successful and their potential negative impacts on the system are specified.

Attack-defense models are often represented graphically, but the graphical models developed for the design, slicing and printing phases were cumbersome. Alternative representations of the attack-defense models as tables with attack vectors, targets, target vulnerabilities, attacks, vulnerability countermeasures and impacts columns proved to be superior. The tables simplify the presentation while providing details about vulnerabilities, attacks and vulnerability countermeasures.

Considerable effort was invested in creating the attack-defense model tables for the design, slicing and printing phases of material extrusion additive manufacturing. The tables are large and detailed, but they are certainly not comprehensive specifications of the vulnerabilities, attacks and vulnerability countermeasures. What is important is that they provide adequate examples to understand the security environments and the gaps in the security analysis that must be filled by adding new rows to the tables.

Finally, the three attack-defense model tables provided deep insights that contributed immensely to the vulnerability discovery, exploit development and countermeasure identification efforts in this research on material extrusion additive manufacturing. Vulnerability discovery, exploit development and countermeasure identification are essential to security analyses of cyber-physical systems. In this light, a construct, such as the attack-defense model, that advances vulnerability discovery, exploit development and countermeasure identification, has considerable value.

10.   Conclusions

Additive manufacturing systems, which produce mission-critical parts used in the critical infrastructure, are exposed to cyber threats that perpetrate intellectual property theft, part sabotage and print environment sabotage. Research on additive manufacturing threats has tended to focus on specific vulnerabilities and specific attacks against specific systems. The narrow scope hinders the overall understanding of the attack surfaces and targets, causing vulnerabilities, potential attacks and countermeasures being overlooked during security analyses.

This research addresses the limitations in the context of material extrusion additive manufacturing, the most common additive manufacturing process. A material extrusion workflow that comprehensively covers the design, slicing and printing phases is specified. Analysis of the workflow in conjunction with attack and defense frameworks (MITRE ATT&CK Knowledge Base and MITRE D3FEND Knowledge Graph) yield detailed attack-defense models for the design, slicing and printing phases of material extrusion systems. The attack-defense models, which specify the attack vectors, attack vector vulnerabilities and countermeasures, attack surfaces, system targets, target vulnerabilities and vulnerability countermeasures, and attacks and attack impacts, directly support risk identification, risk assessment and analysis, and risk mitigation and planning. Although the attack-defense models are very detailed, they do not specify all the target vulnerabilities, attacks and vulnerability countermeasures. However, they provide adequate examples to understand the threat environment and security posture, and the gaps that must be filled to make the models more comprehensive.

The case studies involving three material extrusion printers ranging from a $300 hobbyist device to a $25,000 industrial system demonstrate the effectiveness of attack-defense modeling at advancing vulnerability discovery, exploit development and countermeasure identification as well as its ability to clarify and bolster the cyber security and risk management postures of material extrusion additive manufacturing environments.

Future research will focus on vulnerability discovery, exploit development and countermeasure identification for a larger subset of additive manufacturing systems. It will also develop workflows and attack-defense models for the remaining six standard additive manufacturing processes.

Acknowledgement

This research was supported by the National Science Foundation under Grant no. DGE 1501177 and by UT-Battelle under Contract no. DE-AC05-00OR22725 with the U.S. Department of Energy.

References

[1] M. Al Faruque, S. Chhetri, A. Canedo and J. Wan, Acoustic side-channel attacks on additive manufacturing systems, *Proceedings of the Seventh ACM/IEEE International Conference on Cyber-Physical Systems*, 2016.

[2] M. Al Faruque, S. Chhetri, S. Faezi and A. Canedo, Forensics of Thermal Side Channels in Additive Manufacturing Systems, CECS Technical Report #16-01, Center for Embedded and Cyber-Physical Systems, University of California, Irvine, Irvine, California, 2016.

[3] S. Belikovetsky, M. Yampolskiy, J. Toh, J. Gatlin and Y. Elovici, dr0wned – Cyber-physical attack with additive manufacturing, presented at the *Eleventh USENIX Workshop on Offensive Technologies*, 2017.

[4] M. Berger, The attack on a German synagogue highlights the threat posed by do-it-yourself guns, *The Washington Post*, October 11, 2019.

[5] S. Bridges, K. Keiser, N. Sissom and S. Graves, Cyber security for additive manufacturing, *Proceedings of the Tenth Annual Cyber and Information Security Research Conference*, article no. 14, 2015.

[6] A. Damani, The fundamentals and impact of Industry 4.0, *Forbes*, June 24, 2020.

[7] Q. Do, B. Martini and K. Choo, A data exfiltration and remote exploitation attack on consumer 3D printers, *IEEE Transactions on Information Forensics and Security*, vol. 11(10), pp. 2174–2186, 2016.

[8] A. Hojjati, A. Adhikari, K. Struckmann, E. Chou, T. Nguyen, K. Madan, M. Winslett, C. Gunter and W. King, Leave your phone at the door: Side channels that reveal factory floor secrets, *Proceedings of the ACM SIGSAC Conference on Computer and Communications Security*, pp. 883–894, 2016.

[9] Homeland Security Advisory Council, Final Report of the Emerging Technologies Subcommittee 3D-Printing, U.S. Department of Homeland Security, Washington, DC, 2020.

[10] Hybrid Manufacturing Technologies, Seven Families of Additive Manufacturing (According to ASTM F2792 Standards), McKinney, Texas (`www.additivemanufacturing.media/cdn/cms/7_families_print_version.pdf`), 2021.

[11] E. Kurkowski, A. Van Stockum, J. Dawson, C. Taylor, T. Schulz and S. Shenoi, Manipulation of G-code toolpath files in 3D printers: Attacks and mitigations, in *Critical Infrastructure Protection XVI*, J. Staggs and S. Shenoi (Eds.), Springer, Cham, Switzerland, pp. 155–174, 2022.

[12] Manufactur3D Magazine, The seven types of additive manufacturing technologies, Thane, India (`manufactur3dmag.com/7-types-additive-manufacturing-technologies`), April 6, 2018.

[13] T. McCue, Additive manufacturing industry grows to almost $12 billion in 2019, *Forbes*, May 8, 2020.

[14] MITRE Corporation, ATT&CK for Industrial Control Systems, Bedford, Massachusetts (`collaborate.mitre.org/attackics/index.php/Main_Page`), 2021.

[15] MITRE Corporation, D3FEND: A Knowledge Graph of Cybersecurity Countermeasures, Bedford, Massachusetts (`d3fend.mitre.org`), 2021.

[16] K. Molenaar, S. Anderson and C. Schexnayder, Guidebook on Risk Analysis Tools and Management Practices to Control Transportation Project Costs, NCHRP Report 658, The National Academies Press, Washington, DC, 2010.

[17] S. Moore, P. Armstrong, T. McDonald and M. Yampolskiy, Vulnerability analysis of desktop 3D printer software, *Proceedings of the 2016 Resilience Week*, pp. 46–51, 2016.

[18] S. Moore, W. Glisson and M. Yampolskiy, Implications of malicious 3D printer firmware, *Proceedings of the Fiftieth Hawaii International Conference on System Sciences*, 2017.

[19] H. Pearce, K. Yanamandra, N. Gupta and R. Karri, FLAW3D: A Trojan-Based Cyber Attack on the Physical Outcomes of Additive Manufacturing, arXiv: 2104.09562 (`arxiv.org/abs/2104.09562`), 2021.

[20] N. Shevchenko, B. Frye and C. Woody, Threat Modeling for Cyber-Physical System-of-Systems: Methods Evaluation, Software Engineering Institute, Carnegie Mellon University, Pittsburgh, Pennsylvania (`resources.sei.cmu.edu/library/asset-view.cfm?assetid=526365`), 2018.

[21] C. Song, F. Ling, Z. Ba, K. Ren, C. Zhou and W. Xu, My smartphone knows what you print: Exploring smartphone-based side-channel attacks against 3D printers, *Proceedings of the ACM SIGSAC Conference on Computer and Communications Security,* pp. 895–907, 2016.

[22] L. Sturm, C. Williams, J. Camelio, J. White and R. Parker, Cyber-physical vulnerabilities in additive manufacturing systems: A case study attack on the .STL file with human subjects, *Journal of Manufacturing Systems,* vol. 44(1), pp. 154–164, 2017.

[23] C. Xiao, Security attack on 3D printing, presented at the *xFocus Security Conference* (`www.claudxiao.net/Attack3DPrinting-Claud-en.pdf`), 2013.

[24] M. Yampolskiy, W. King, J. Gatlin, S. Belikovetsky, A. Brown, A. Skejellum and Y. Elovici, Security of additive manufacturing: Attack taxonomy and survey, *Additive Manufacturing,* vol. 21, pp. 431–457, 2018.

[25] S. Zeltmann, N. Gupta, N. Tsoutsos, M. Maniatakos, J. Rajendran and R. Karri, Manufacturing and security challenges in 3D printing, *Journal of the Minerals, Metals and Materials Society,* vol. 68(7), pp. 1872–1881, 2016.

Chapter 6

MANIPULATION OF G-CODE TOOLPATH FILES IN 3D PRINTERS: ATTACKS AND MITIGATIONS

Elizabeth Kurkowski, Alyxandra Van Stockum, Joel Dawson, Curtis Taylor, Tricia Schulz and Sujeet Shenoi

Abstract   Additive manufacturing or 3D printing is commonly used to create mission-critical parts in the critical infrastructure. This research focuses on threats that target the key slicing step of additive manufacturing, when design files that model part geometry are converted to G-code toolpath files that convey instructions for printing parts layer by layer. The research leverages a hitherto unknown slicing software vulnerability where G-code corresponding to part slices is stored as plaintext ASCII characters in heap memory during execution. The vulnerability was discovered in two open-source, full-featured slicing software suites that support many 3D printers.

Experiments with a toolkit developed to target slicing software in real time demonstrate that the attacks are surreptitious and fine-grained. Two attacks, temperature modification and infill exclusion, performed against G-code generated for fused filament fabrication printers demonstrate the ability to sabotage printed parts as well as print environments. Although the vulnerability can be mitigated using strong authentication and access controls along with G-code obfuscation, the ability to automate surreptitious, fine-grained attacks that degrade printed parts in ways that are imperceptible to the human eye and undetectible by non-destructive testing methods is a serious concern.

Keywords: Additive manufacturing, fused filament fabrication, G-code attacks

1. Introduction

Additive manufacturing (AM) or 3D printing is the process of depositing layers of material to create 3D objects. Additive manufacturing is a

© IFIP International Federation for Information Processing 2022
Published by Springer Nature Switzerland AG 2022
J. Staggs and S. Shenoi (Eds.): Critical Infrastructure Protection XVI, IFIP AICT 666, pp. 155–174, 2022.
https://doi.org/10.1007/978-3-031-20137-0_6

rapidly-growing segment of the manufacturing sector; its market value increased by 21.2% to $11.867 billion in 2019 alone [11].

Additive manufacturing is a competitive alternative to traditional subtractive manufacturing with many economic and environmental advantages. It enables complex internal structures to be created during a single print run due to the layer-by-layer part printing process. To obtain similar results, traditional manufacturing often requires the creation and assembly of multiple individual parts. Additively-manufactured parts often have improved mechanical properties due to high resolution control over internal structures [6]. Additive manufacturing enables rapid prototyping due to quick design-to-product times as well as on-demand low volume or high-volume production. Also, additive manufacturing has less material wastage than subtractive manufacturing.

Additive manufacturing is heavily utilized in many critical infrastructure sectors, including energy, healthcare, transportation and defense [3–5, 8, 16]. However, a 2021 cyber security audit of defense additive manufacturing systems by the Inspector General of the U.S. Department of Defense [7] determined that all the reviewed sites did not consistently manage or secure their systems to prevent unauthorized changes and ensure the integrity of design data.

This research focuses on threats targeting the key slicing step of additive manufacturing. During this step, part design files that model part geometry are converted to G-code toolpath files that cover printer actions and parameters such as extruder movements in each print layer, print speed, melt block temperature, material extrusion amount and fan speed. G-code toolpath files may be targeted by deleting sections of code (data destruction attacks) or by modifying the code (data integrity attacks), potentially sabotaging printed parts and print environments.

This research leverages a hitherto unknown vulnerability that G-code corresponding to part slices is stored as plaintext ASCII characters in heap memory during execution. The vulnerability was discovered in two open-source, full-featured slicing software suites that support many 3D printers. Exploiting the vulnerability requires root access (full code execution privileges) to the controller machine that executes the slicing software. The attacks access the runtime process image, scan the image memory, extract the plaintext G-code, perform various modifications to the G-code and write the code back to image memory.

Experiments using a toolkit developed to target slicing software in real time demonstrate that the attacks are surreptitious (difficult to detect) and fine-grained (able to target specific layers of printed parts). The two experimental attacks, temperature modification and infill exclusion, performed against G-code generated for fused filament fabrication

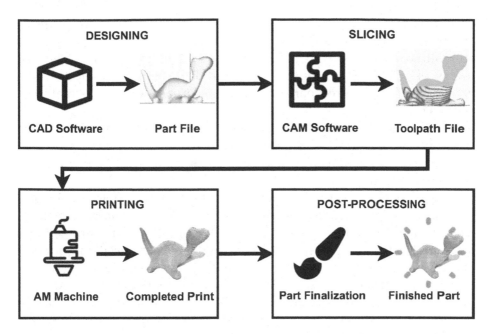

Figure 1. Additive manufacturing process chain.

printers demonstrate the ability to sabotage printed parts and print environments. The temperature modification attacks, which reduced the extruder head temperature from 198°C to 190°C while printing just seven of the 530 total layers, resulted in a 14% drop in the average tensile strength. The infill exclusion attacks, which excluded infill from five and 25 layers of the 127 total layers of printed parts, reduced the average compressive strengths by 10.6% and 19.9%, respectively. The ability to automate surreptitious, fine-grained attacks that significantly degrade printed parts in ways that are imperceptible to the human eye and undetectible by nondestructive testing methods demands systematic efforts at securing additive manufacturing systems from cyber threats.

2. Background and Related Work

This section describes the additive manufacturing process chain and research focused on attacking the process chain.

2.1 Additive Manufacturing Process Chain

The additive manufacturing process chain has four steps: designing, slicing, printing and post-processing. Figure 1 shows the steps in the process chain.

The designing step uses computer-aided design (CAD) software to create a part design model that is specified as a part file. The popular stereolithography (STL) part file format uses triangles to model the geometry of a part [10]. The more advanced 3MF file format captures the geometry of the desired part as well as its properties such as materials and colors [1].

During the slicing step, a part file is imported by computer-aided manufacturing (CAM) software. In additive manufacturing, this software is referred to as a slicer because it cuts the 3D-part model into 2D layers for printing.

The slicer enables a user to specify various print options before generating a toolpath file for a printer. Print options of interest include adding support material, specifying infill properties and characteristics such as density and pattern, and selecting the print speed and orientation. Support material is necessary when a print orientation causes part overhangs. Other print settings such as infill characteristics and print speed can affect the strength and other mechanical properties of the printed parts. All these features are eventually encoded in a toolpath file for printing. The toolpath commands, commonly called G-code, cover printer actions and parameters such as extruder movements, print speed, melt block temperature, material extrusion amount and fan speed.

During the printing step, a printer follows the instructions in a toolpath file to print a part. The printing time varies based on part size, geometry and material.

After a part is printed, one or more post-processing steps may be performed. In some cases, post-processing simply involves removing the support material and sanding rough edges. In other cases, especially for metal parts, annealing is performed to obtain the desired mechanical properties. The final post-processing step is quality control, which ensures that a printed part meets the design specifications.

2.2   Process Chain Attacks

Due to the relative youth of the field, security research on additive manufacturing systems is limited. Attacks on additive manufacturing fall into two main categories, theft of technical data and sabotage of parts or print environments [20]. While malicious attacks against 3D printers are rare, several potential attacks during the first three steps of the process chain have been theorized. Attacks during the last (fourth) post-processing step are possible. However, they are highly specific to the printing materials and parts. Therefore, they are rarely discussed in the literature. In any case, they are outside the scope of this research.

During the designing step, attacks typically target part design files. For example, Belikovetsky et al. [2] proposed a phishing attack to install a backdoor on the computer hosting the design software; the backdoor is leveraged to compromise the STL part design file and weaken the printed parts. Sturm et al. [18] demonstrated that malicious STL file modifications can cause printed parts to fail prematurely.

Zeltmann et al. [21] theorized several attacks during the slicing step. These include embedding defects and changing part orientations when the printing slices are created, sabotaging the parts created during the printing step.

Attacks targeting the printing step focus heavily on modifying 3D-printer firmware. Xiao [19] modified the firmware of a desktop RepRap Prusa printer to alter the temperature feedback loop, leading the printer to believe that the extruder temperature was double the real temperature.

Moore et al. [13] performed static and dynamic code analyses of Cura 3D, ReplicatorG, Repetier-Host and Marlin 3D-printer firmware that revealed several vulnerabilities in their code bases. These included buffer overflows and unencrypted host-printer communications. The security implications of these vulnerabilities include theft of technical data and part sabotage. Moore and colleagues also noted that weaknesses in the G-code structure provide opportunities for printed part manipulation. In subsequent work, Moore et al. [14] introduced malicious modifications to Marlin 3D-printer firmware. The modified firmware ignored incoming print commands, substituted malicious print commands in place of legitimate commands and manipulated extruder feed rates.

Pearce et al. [15] used a Trojan bootloader to infiltrate Marlin-compatible 3D printers and compromise the integrity of printed parts. The attack leveraged bootloader control over the initial printer firmware installation. The bootloader was able to scan for and modify byte patterns in the firmware, triggering G-code manipulations that reduced the extrusion rate and reordered print commands.

Rais et al. [17] developed novel attacks on fused filament fabrication printers. Their dynamic thermal and localized filament kinetic attacks were executed by a printer firmware rootkit that modified G-code toolpath instructions. The attacks had minimal footprints, but the damage to the printed parts was significant.

The research efforts described above and other research in additive manufacturing theorize potential attacks against design files and printer firmware, but few actually implement proof-of-concept attacks. In contrast, this research, which focuses on toolpath files created during the slicing step, allows for generalizable, surreptitious attacks that leverage weaknesses in slicing software. The research has also developed a tool for deploying the attacks on real 3D-printer process chains.

3.   G-Code Toolpath File Attack Surface

This research targets G-code toolpath files by deleting sections of the G-code (data destruction attacks) or modifying the G-code (data integrity attacks). Both types of attacks change print layer information, sabotaging the printed parts.

An attack vector is a means for gaining access to a target, in this case, an entire G-code toolpath file or portions of its code. The attack surface of a G-code toolpath file is the collection of attack vectors that target the designing, slicing and printing steps of the process chain. Since the three steps are chained, an attack vector that provides access to a component or service during a preceding step provides indirect access to a G-code toolpath file in a later step. For example, gaining access to CAD software in the designing step enables malicious modifications to the part design file, which are encoded in the G-code toolpath file used during the slicing step.

The following attack vectors provide (direct or indirect) access to the G-code toolpath file/code during the designing, slicing and printing steps:

Designing Step Attack Vectors.

- **Access to CAD Software from Controller Computer:** An attacker can introduce malicious modifications to CAD software and/or its runtime process image that change part files unbeknownst to a user.

- **Access to CAD Software via Network:** An attacker can introduce malicious modifications to CAD software and/or its runtime process image that change part files unbeknownst to a user.

- **Access to CAD Software via Remote Software Update:** An attacker can introduce malicious modifications to a CAD software update that change part files unbeknownst to a user.

- **Access to Part Files from Controller Computer:** An attacker can introduce malicious modifications by manually editing part files unbeknownst to a user.

- **Access to Part Files via Network:** An attacker with remote access to a controller computer can introduce malicious modifications by manually editing part files unbeknownst to a user. If the part files are transferred to another controller computer for slicing, an attacker can assume a man-in-the-middle position to introduce malicious modifications to part files during transfer.

Slicing Step Attack Vectors.

- **Access to Slicing (CAM) Software from Controller Computer:** An attacker can introduce malicious modifications to slicing software and/or its runtime process image that change G-code toolpath files unbeknownst to a user. The attacks developed in this research can leverage this attack vector to target the runtime process image of slicing software.

- **Access to Slicing (CAM) Software via Network:** An attacker can introduce malicious modifications to slicing software and/or its runtime process image that change G-code toolpath files unbeknownst to a user. The attacks developed in this research can leverage this attack vector to target the runtime process image of slicing software.

- **Access to Slicing (CAM) Software via Remote Software Update:** An attacker can introduce malicious modifications to a CAM software update that change G-code toolpath files unbeknownst to a user. The attacks developed in this research can leverage this attack vector to target the runtime process image of slicing software.

- **Access to Toolpath Files from Controller Computer:** An attacker can introduce malicious modifications by manually editing G-code toolpath files unbeknownst to a user.

- **Access to Toolpath Files via Network:** An attacker with remote access to a controller computer can introduce malicious modifications by manually editing G-code toolpath files unbeknownst to a user. An attacker can also assume a man-in-the-middle position to introduce malicious modifications to G-code toolpath files during transfer to a printer.

Printing Step Attack Vectors.

- **Access to Toolpath Files via Network:** Networked printers enable users to remotely issue print commands and monitor the print status. An attacker with remote access can maliciously modify G-code toolpath commands unbeknownst to a user.

- **Access to Toolpath Files from Printer:** An attacker can introduce malicious modifications by manually editing G-code toolpath files unbeknownst to a user.

- **Access to Toolpath Files via Printer Firmware:** An attacker can introduce malicious modifications to printer firmware that change G-code toolpath files unbeknownst to a user.

4.   G-Code Toolpath File Exploitation

This section describes a vulnerability discovered in slicer software from multiple vendors that can be exploited to attack G-code toolpath files during the slicing step. Exploiting the vulnerability requires access to the runtime process image of the slicing software from the controller computer or network.

4.1   Software Execution Vulnerability

The slicing software vulnerability is that G-code corresponding to part slices is stored in an unprotected manner as plaintext ASCII characters in heap memory during execution. The vulnerability was discovered in slicing software suites from two vendors. The software suites were selected because they are open-source, full-featured and support many 3D printers. For security reasons, details about the slicing software suites are obfuscated. The two slicing software suites are referred to as Alpha and Beta.

4.2   Software Execution Attack

The attacker requires root access (full code execution privileges) to the controller machine that executes the slicing software. The attack accesses the runtime process image, scans the image memory, extracts the plaintext G-code, modifies the G-code and writes it back to image memory.

Figure 2 shows the details of the slicing software execution attack. An unsuspecting user loads a part file, slices the part and previews the G-code toolpath data using the slicer graphical user interface. While the user is previewing the slice layers, the attack modifies the G-code in runtime process image memory. Since the memory modifications occur in the background, the graphical user interface continues to present the original unmodified slices.

After previewing the G-code, the unsuspecting user proceeds to save the G-code to a file. However, the modified G-code in heap memory is saved to the toolpath file instead of the original G-code.

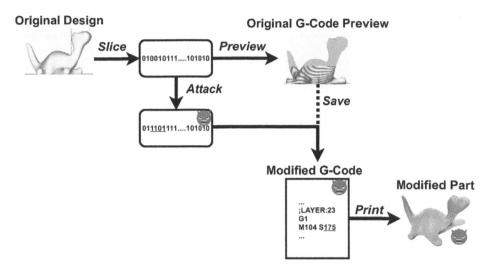

Figure 2. Slicing software execution attack.

A toolkit was created to launch slicing software execution attacks. The toolkit conducts the attack in two phases, layer identification and layer modification:

- **Layer Identification:** The first attack phase involves scanning the slicer process heap memory address range for plaintext G-code layers. The goal is to reconstruct the original G-code toolpath file to the extent possible.

  Each slicer has a slightly different format for header data that can be used to extract summary data about a print. Each slicer also has specific start and end delimiters for a toolpath layer that can be used to track G-code in heap memory. When a G-code layer is being processed, all the data associated with the layer is stored in consecutive pages in memory. However, successive layers are not necessarily stored contiguously. Therefore, the individual layers of G-code in memory have to be identified. Algorithm 1 specifies the layer identification procedure.

- **Layer Modification:** After the G-code is reconstructed from memory, modifications are made to the code. Since G-code has a standard format [9], it is straightforward to implement attacks given a complete G-code reconstruction. Layer modification involves parsing the reconstructed G-code, making the malicious G-code modifications and writing the modified G-code back to the same locations in memory.

Algorithm 1: Identify G-code layers in process heap memory.

Input: startAddress: Start address of slicer process heap memory
Output: layerTable: Hash table containing layer information
layerTable ← LayerStruct[]
page ←initialPage(startAddress)
while *page ≠ End of Memory* **do**
    page ← getNextPage()
    if *startConditionExists* **then**
        layer ← **new** LayerStruct
        layer.id ←parseID()
        layer.start ← getStartLocation()
        while *!endConditionExists* **do**
            layer.contents ← layer.contents + page
            page ← getNextPage()
        end
        layer.contents ← layer.contents + page
        layerTable[layer.id] ← layer
    end
end

Since this methodology can modify G-code at the instruction level, it is possible to execute fine-grained attacks that significantly degrade printed parts in a manner that is undetectible by visual inspection and other nondestructive testing methods.

5.   G-Code Toolpath File Attacks

This section discusses the temperature modification and infill exclusion attacks that were performed against G-code generated for fused filament fabrication printers. The attacks were chosen for their ability to sabotage printed parts as well as print environments [17], demonstrating the serious impacts of G-code manipulation.

5.1   Temperature Modification Attacks

A temperature modification attack modifies the extrusion head temperature during printing. The temperature at which a part is printed determines its physical properties such as layer adhesion and material phase transformation. An extreme temperature modification from the baseline temperature for a given material can cause air gaps to form between printed layers that are visible to the naked eye.

A temperature modification attack also impacts the print environment. Altering the extruder head temperature affects the printer itself.

Prolonged printer operation outside its normal parameters can induce printer component wear, material blockage and premature breakage.

5.2   Infill Exclusion Attacks

An infill exclusion attack alters a printed part by selectively removing material from specified layers. Printed parts may not be completely solid; often they are printed as shells to conserve printing material (filament). In such cases, infill with a pattern such as stars or squares fills the 3D-printed shell. The infill pattern and density affect part strength and durability, so modifying the infill via G-code manipulation impacts the mechanical properties of the part.

It can be difficult to detect infill changes by visually inspecting a completed part. Additionally, removing small percentages of infill from part layers can reduce part strength without a significant reduction in weight, making the modification difficult to detect via nondestructive testing. Indeed, by targeting specific layers of a part during printing, critical areas of the final part can be compromised.

6.   Attack Results and Mitigations

This section describes the results of experiments that used the toolkit to launch slicing software execution attacks on two software suites that create G-code toolpath files for a variety of fused filament fabrication printers. The toolkit, written in C, runs on the same Ubuntu 20.04 virtual machine as the slicing software suites. Since the software execution attack has root access, the toolkit code is able to search for the slicer process ID and attach to the runtime process image in order to scan and modify the memory.

For each slicing software suite, an attack was executed against the first slice on a clean boot of the virtual machine. After the execution, the modified G-code toolpath file was saved for transfer to a printer using an SD card. Modified G-code toolpath files in the temperature modification experiments were submitted to an Ender 3 fused filament fabrication printer. Modified G-code toolpath files in the infill exclusion experiments were submitted to a Prusa i3 Mk3S fused filament fabrication printer. Both the printers employed polylactic acid (PLA) filament as the printing material.

6.1   Attack Effectiveness Experiments

The first set of experiments evaluated toolkit performance. The execution time metric, corresponding to the duration of a successful attack, was used to evaluate attack detectibility based on its impact on user

Table 1. Average attack execution times over ten runs.

Attack	Software	Execution Time
Temperature Modification	Slicer Alpha	22 ms
Temperature Modification	Slicer Beta	32 ms
Infill Exclusion	Slicer Beta	184 ms

experience. An attack attaches to the runtime process image, which freezes slicer software execution, impacting user experience and potentially raising an alarm. In the experiments, temperature modification attacks were executed on G-code generated by slicers Alpha and Beta whereas infill exclusion attacks were only executed on G-code generated by slicer Alpha. The reason for not executing infill exclusion attacks on slicer Alpha is explained below.

Table 1 shows the average durations of the two attacks. The average attack execution times obtained for the temperature modification attacks on Alpha and Beta G-code were 22 ms and 32 ms, respectively. The average attack execution time obtained for the infill exclusion attack on slicer Beta G-code was 184 ms. The low execution times are expected for the temperature modification attacks because only two lines of G-code in two different layers need to be modified to successfully implement the attacks. In contrast, the infill exclusion attacks require considerable time because every line of G-code in multiple layers is modified. Nevertheless, the 22 ms to 184 ms attack execution window is well within the acceptable response time [12], so attack execution would not change the normal user experience. The attacks were also surreptitious because the firmware in the two printers did not raise any exceptions or warnings about malformed G-code produced by the two slicing software suites.

The second set of toolkit performance experiments evaluated the ability of the toolkit to identify G-code in memory corresponding to individual print layers. This is important because the greater the percentage of individual layers detected at runtime, the finer the granularity and more insidious the attacks.

Table 2 shows the average percentages of G-code layers identified for the two slicing software suites. Exceptional G-code layer identification of 99.73% was obtained for slicer Beta. The G-code layer identification of 41.29% for slicer Alpha is modest, but the temperature attacks were, nevertheless, successful. Note that the low layer identification percentage obtained for the G-code generated by slicer Alpha renders infill exclusion

Table 2. Average G-code layers identified over ten runs.

Software	G-Code Layers
Slicer Alpha	41.29%
Slicer Beta	99.73%

attacks infeasible. This is because the attacks require every line of G-code in multiple layers to be modified.

6.2 Temperature Modification Experiments

Temperature modification attacks were launched against G-code tool-path files generated by slicer Alpha. In the attacks, the extruder head temperature was reduced by $8°C$ from the normal operating temperature of $198°C$ while printing just seven centrally-located layers of the 530 total layers of the parts before being returned to the original temperature.

The printer did not indicate any issues with the lower temperature during printing. No discernible pauses in printing occurred while the temperature was decreased and increased. The temperature modifications did not result in any observable differences in the printed parts.

Tensile tests were performed on parts that were printed in the standard ASTM dogbone shape. However, the test samples were modified slightly by printing two holes near the two ends to mount them on a servohydraulic tensile testing system. Ten control samples were printed at the temperature of $198°C$ and ten attack samples were printed with the $8°C$ drop in temperature for seven centrally-located layers.

Table 3. Tensile test results for the temperature modification attacks.

Sample (Temperature)	Average Breaking Force	Standard Deviation	Strength Reduction	$P(T \leq t)$ Two-Tailed Test
Control (198°C)	964.9 N	72.1 N	–	–
Attack (190°C)	829.7 N	29.2 N	14.0%	0.00019

Table 3 shows the results of the tensile tests on the printed samples. The average breaking forces for the control and attack samples were 964.9 N and 829.7 N, respectively. This corresponds to a 14% reduction in the average tensile strength of parts due to the temperature modification attacks. A two-tailed t-test indicated a statistically-significant

Figure 3.   Control and attack samples in the infill exclusion experiments.

difference between the attack and control sample populations. Examination of the attack samples revealed that all the samples failed at the seven layers that were printed when the temperature was reduced.

6.3   Infill Exclusion Experiments

The infill exclusion experiments employed solid ASTM cylinders with 6.35 mm radius and 25.4 mm height printed using G-code toolpath files generated by slicer Beta. Figure 3 shows three sample prints. The cylinder on the left is a control sample. The attack sample in the center had infill excluded from five centrally-located layers of the 127 total layers. The attack sample on the right had infill excluded from 25 centrally-located layers of the 127 total layers.

Printing the control and attack samples took the same amount of time because the extruder head went through the same motions for all the samples, except that no infill was printed in some layers of the attack samples. The reduction in mass due to infill exclusion was negligible. As seen in Figure 3, the only discernible differences are small blobs of extra filament at the attacked layers. However, it is common for parts printed

Table 4. Compresssion test results for the infill exclusion attacks.

Sample (Layers Removed)	Average Failure Force	Standard Deviation	Strength Reduction	P(T≤t) Two-Tailed Test	Average Mass
Control (0)	2,446.7 N	130.9 N	–	–	2 g
Attack (5)	2,187.2 N	53.8 N	10.6%	0.0082	2 g
Attack (25)	1,959.5 N	233.9 N	19.9%	0.00018	1.9 g

via fused filament fabrication to have small masses of extra filament that are broken off or sanded down during the post-processing step.

The attacked cylinders were evaluated by performing compression tests using a universal testing machine. In the experiments, five control samples and 20 attack samples (ten for each of the two attacks) were compressed with increasing force until failure.

Table 4 shows the compression test results. Excluding infill from five of the 127 layers resulted in a 10.6% decrease in the average compressive strength of the printed parts. As expected, excluding infill from 25 of the 127 layers resulted in a significant decrease of 19.9% in the average compressive strength. Two-tailed t-tests indicated statistically-significant differences between each attack sample population and the control sample population.

Figure 4 shows the average compression failure curves for the control and attack samples. Note that the peaks in the curves correspond to the points of part failure. As expected, the average failure force for the control samples is higher than the average failure force for the attack samples. Moreover, the greater the number of layers with excluded infill, the lower the average failure force.

6.4 Discussion

The experimental results demonstrate that slicing software attacks weaken printed parts with little or no discernible differences. Furthermore, temperature modification and infill exclusion are just two of many attacks on G-code in toolpath files. G-code specifies print speed, fan speed and other printer parameters, all of which affect the properties of printed parts. Manipulating printer parameters by modifying G-code could also damage the printer itself.

Executing the slicing software attacks developed in this research requires root access, but it is an attractive attack option despite the many opportunities offered by arbitrary code execution. This is because the

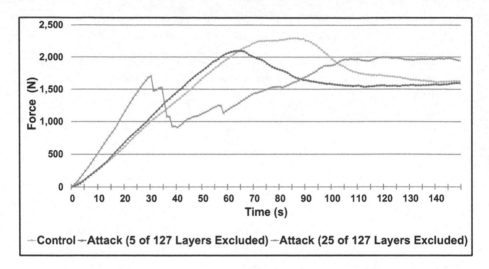

Figure 4. Average failure curves for the infill exclusion attacks.

software execution exploit can be executed and operated autonomously, without the need for Internet access. Also, the current toolkit could be reconfigured as malware that runs in the background and constantly scans runtime process images and manipulates G-code. Although targeted attacks on parts would produce more extreme effects on printed products, the malware would not need to know the precise parts being printed in order to launch attacks such as temperature modification and infill exclusion. Indeed, the malware could run independently and attack parts and print environments with little or no human intervention. Thus, slicing software exploitation can result in surreptitious attacks that are difficult to detect and mitigate.

The main limitations of the slicing software execution attacks are that they apply to ASCII-encoded G-code and require G-code to be extracted from heap memory. As a result, the attacks only target slicers that store dynamic copies of toolpath files. However, this characteristic is common in slicers that permit users to send G-code toolpath files directly to printers and to dynamically manipulate G-code toolpath settings.

Another limitation is that certain layers of G-code were not recoverable in the case of slicer Alpha. Future research will employ reverse engineering to investigate this anomaly and create fine-grained attacks.

Finally, a limitation with direct memory modification is one-to-one byte replacement. This increases the creativity needed to craft attacks. Of course, attacks against G-code could be performed with more freedom using other attack vectors such as direct access to a G-code toolpath file via the network or controller computer. These opportunities eliminate the need to exploit a memory vulnerability, rendering G-code attacks widely applicable and a major concern.

7.   Mitigations

In the experiments, the attacks that modified ASCII-encoded G-code in heap memory leveraged access to slicing software from a controller computer. However, the same exploits could be applied by leveraging access to slicing software from a network or access to a slicing software update. The attack impacts include intellectual property theft as well as part and print environment sabotage.

The first set of mitigations should combat the attack vectors that provide access to a controller computer, network and slicing software update. These are accomplished by instituting strong user authentication and access controls on the controller computer and network, and requiring signed and encrypted slicing software updates. If an attacker breaches these defenses, the next set of defenses should protect ASCII-encoded G-code in heap memory. This is accomplished by obfuscating the G-code in heap memory, which would make it difficult to identify the toolpath layers. Another mitigation technique is to detect and block common behavior sequences (such as scanning runtime process image memory) that occur when attempts are made to identify, extract and modify G-code.

However, G-code attacks beyond modifying code images in heap memory could be launched by leveraging other attack vectors and other vulnerabilities. This emphasizes the need to conduct a comprehensive analysis of the attack vectors, targets, target vulnerabilities and attacks that enable G-code manipulation, along with countermeasures for combating the attack vectors that provide access to targets and attacks that exploit the identified vulnerabilities.

8.   Conclusions

3D printing is commonly used to create mission-critical parts in the energy, healthcare, transportation and defense sectors. A 2021 cyber security audit of U.S. Department of Defense additive manufacturing sites determined that all the reviewed sites did not consistently manage or secure their systems to prevent unauthorized changes and ensure design data integrity. Since additive manufacturing is constantly exposed to cyber threats, it is imperative to continually analyze the attack surface, identify vulnerabilities, devise exploits and institute countermeasures.

This research has identified a novel slicing software vulnerability where G-code corresponding to part slices is stored as plaintext ASCII characters in heap memory during execution. The vulnerability was discovered in two open-source, full-featured slicing software suites that support many 3D printers. Exploiting the slicing software vulnerability requires full code execution privileges (root access) to the controller machine that executes the slicing software. The attacks access the runtime process image, scan the image memory, extract the plaintext G-code, perform various modifications to the G-code and write the code back to image memory.

The temperature modification and infill exclusion attacks demonstrate the ability to sabotage printed parts and print environments. The temperature modification attacks, which reduced the extruder head temperature by just 8°C while printing less than 1.5% of the part layers, resulted in a 14% drop in the average tensile strength. The infill exclusion attacks, which omitted infill from less than 4% of the part layers, reduced the average compressive strength by 10.6%.

Although the discovered vulnerability can be mitigated using strong authentication and access controls along with G-code obfuscation, the ability to automate surreptitious, fine-grained attacks that significantly degrade printed parts in ways that are imperceptible to the human eye and undetectible by nondestructive testing methods is a serious concern. Clearly, strong, systematic efforts must be directed at securing additive manufacturing systems from cyber threats.

Acknowledgement

This research was supported by the National Science Foundation under Grant no. DGE 1501177 and by UT-Battelle under Contract no. DE-AC05-00OR22725 with the U.S. Department of Energy.

References

[1] 3MF Consortium, 3MF Specification, San Francisco, California (3mf.io/specification), 2020.

[2] S. Belikovetsky, M. Yampolskiy, J. Toh, J. Gatlin and Y. Elovici, dr0wned – Cyber-physical attack with additive manufacturing, presented at the *Eleventh USENIX Workshop on Offensive Technologies*, 2017.

[3] I. Birrell, 3D-printed prosthetic limbs: The next revolution in medicine, *The Guardian*, February 19, 2017.

[4] J. Burke, 3D printing off to the races, *Oak Ridge National Laboratory Blog*, Oak Ridge National Laboratory, Oak Ridge, Tennessee (`www.ornl.gov/blog/3d-printing-races`), April 26, 2019.

[5] J. Ellis, 3D-printed nuclear reactor promises faster, more economical path to nuclear energy, *Oak Ridge National Laboratory News*, Oak Ridge National Laboratory, Oak Ridge, Tennessee (`www.ornl.gov/news/3d-printed-nuclear-reactor-promises-faster-more-economical-path-nuclear-energy`), May 11, 2020.

[6] S. Ford, Additive manufacturing technology: Potential implications for U.S. manufacturing competitiveness, *Journal of International Commerce and Economics*, vol. 6(1), pp. 40–74, 2014.

[7] Inspector General, U.S. Department of Defense, Audit of the Cybersecurity of Department of Defense Additive Manufacturing Systems, Washington, DC (`media.defense.gov/2021/Jul/07/2002757308/-1/-1/1/DODIG-2021-098.PDF`), 2021.

[8] J. Keller, The navy can now 3D-print submarines on the fly for SEALs, *Task and Purpose* (`taskandpurpose.com/gear-tech/navy-3d-printing-submarines`), July 31, 2017.

[9] T. Kramer, F. Proctor and E. Messina, The NIST RS274NGC Interpreter – Version 3, NIST Interagency/Internal Report 6556, National Institute of Standards and Technology, Gaithersburg, Maryland, 2000.

[10] Library of Congress, STL (Stereolithography) File Format Family, Washington, DC (`www.loc.gov/preservation/digital/formats/fdd/fdd000504.shtml`), September 9, 2019.

[11] T. McCue, Additive manufacturing industry grows to almost $12 billion in 2019, *Forbes*, May 8, 2020.

[12] R. Miller, Response time in man-computer conversational transactions, *Proceedings of the AFIPS Fall Joint Computer Conference, Part I*, pp. 267–277, 1968.

[13] S. Moore, P. Armstrong, T. McDonald and M. Yampolskiy, Vulnerability analysis of desktop 3D printer software, *Proceedings of the 2016 Resilience Week*, pp. 46–51, 2016.

[14] S. Moore, W. Glisson and M. Yampolskiy, Implications of malicious 3D printer firmware, *Proceedings of the Fiftieth Hawaii International Conference on System Sciences*, 2017.

[15] H. Pearce, K. Yanamandra, N. Gupta and R. Karri, FLAW3D: A Trojan-Based Cyber Attack on the Physical Outcomes of Additive Manufacturing, arXiv: 2104.09562 (`arxiv.org/abs/2104.09562`), 2021.

[16] B. Post, B. Richardson, P. Lloyd, L. Love, S. Nolet and J. Hannan, Additive Manufacturing of Wind Turbine Molds, Document ORNL/TM-2017/290, Oak Ridge National Laboratory, Oak Ridge, Tennessee, 2017.

[17] M. Rais, Y. Li and I. Ahmed, Dynamic thermal and localized filament kinetic attacks on a fused-filament-fabrication-based 3D printing process, *Additive Manufacturing*, vol. 46, article no. 102200, 2021.

[18] L. Sturm, C. Williams, J. Camelio, J. White and R. Parker, Cyberphysical vulnerabilities in additive manufacturing systems: A case study attack on the .STL file with human subjects, *Journal of Manufacturing Systems*, vol. 44(1), pp. 154–164, 2017.

[19] C. Xiao, Security attack on 3D printing, presented at the *xFocus Security Conference* (`www.claudxiao.net/Attack3DPrinting-Claud-en.pdf`), 2013.

[20] M. Yampolskiy, W. King, J. Gatlin, S. Belikovetsky, A. Brown, A. Skejellum and Y. Elovici, Security of additive manufacturing: Attack taxonomy and survey, *Additive Manufacturing*, vol. 21, pp. 431–457, 2018.

[21] S. Zeltmann, N. Gupta, N. Tsoutsos, M. Maniatakos, J. Rajendran and R. Karri, Manufacturing and security challenges in 3D printing, *Journal of the Minerals, Metals and Materials Society*, vol. 68(7), pp. 1872–1881, 2016.

Chapter 7

DETECTING PART ANOMALIES INDUCED BY CYBER ATTACKS ON A POWDER BED FUSION ADDITIVE MANUFACTURING SYSTEM

Elizabeth Kurkowski, Mason Rice and Sujeet Shenoi

Abstract   Additive manufacturing systems are highly vulnerable to cyber attacks that sabotage parts and print environments during the designing, slicing and printing steps of the process chains. Due to the complex cyber-physical nature of additive manufacturing systems, cyber attacks are difficult to detect and mitigate, and impossible to eliminate entirely. Therefore, it is imperative to develop rapid and reliable non-destructive testing methods for detecting anomalies in printed parts.

This chapter describes a novel anomaly detection method developed for a selective laser sintering type of powder bed fusion system. The method does not engage computing-intensive machine learning to detect anomalies, relying instead on three side channels, print bed movement, laser firing time and print chamber temperature, that underlie the physics of selective laser sintering. The side channels provide adequate detection coverage while reducing the sensor requirements; they are also robust to noise, which enhances the detection of printed part anomalies. Experimental results demonstrate the efficacy of the anomaly detection method under attacks that target the mechanical properties of printed parts. The cost of the sensors and peripheral devices is minimal and anomaly detection for each test part requires less than three seconds.

Keywords: Additive manufacturing, powder bed fusion, anomaly detection

1.   Introduction

Additive manufacturing (AM), also referred to as 3D printing, builds parts layer by layer by depositing materials ranging from plastics to met-

© IFIP International Federation for Information Processing 2022
Published by Springer Nature Switzerland AG 2022
J. Staggs and S. Shenoi (Eds.): Critical Infrastructure Protection XVI, IFIP AICT 666, pp. 175–203, 2022.
https://doi.org/10.1007/978-3-031-20137-0_7

als. It offers several advantages over conventional subtractive manufacturing, including intricate customized parts with improved mechanical properties, and rapid prototyping and flexible on-demand manufacturing options, all with reduced material wastage. As a result, additive manufacturing is used to create parts for critical infrastructure assets such as wind turbines [19], jet engines [13] and nuclear reactors [7].

Although few, if any, real-world cyber attacks have been reported against additive manufacturing systems, it is a matter of time before these systems will be targeted by hackers, criminals and nation-state actors to sabotage printed parts and print environments. Indeed, the research literature in additive manufacturing abounds with viable attacks focused on part sabotage and/or print environment sabotage. These attacks focus on the three principal steps in the additive manufacturing process chain, for example, stereolithographic (STL) files in the designing step [4, 25], slicing software and toolpath (G-code) files in the slicing step [14], and printer firmware in the printing step [17, 18, 28].

Due to the complex cyber-physical nature of additive manufacturing systems, cyber attacks are difficult to detect and mitigate, and impossible to eliminate entirely. Therefore, it is imperative to focus on methods that can verify the integrity of printed parts. While quality control using destructive testing is always an option, to reduce the costs related to resources and time, rapid and reliable non-destructive testing methods are needed to detect anomalies in printed parts induced by cyber attacks during the designing, slicing and/or printing steps.

This chapter describes a novel anomaly detection method developed for powder bed fusion, one of the most popular additive manufacturing processes after material extrusion [15]. Unlike material extrusion, which typically extrudes plastic materials, powder bed fusion uses powdered plastic or metallic materials to create parts. Powder bed fusion is generally more expensive than material extrusion, but it is increasingly used to print mission-critical parts for critical infrastructure assets [12].

The anomaly detection method, which is developed for a selective laser sintering type of powder bed fusion system, leverages data from three side channels, print bed movement, laser firing time and print chamber temperature. The three side channels are robust to noise, which increases the probability of detecting printed part anomalies while reducing the number of sensors required to obtain feature data.

The anomaly detection method has two phases, baseline creation and anomaly detection. The baseline creation phase, which involves limited destructive testing of parts, constructs the ground truth for anomaly detection. The non-destructive anomaly detection phase compares side-channel data from test parts against the baseline to identify anomalies. The proposed method does not engage computing-intensive machine learning, relying instead on the three side channels that underlie the physics of selective laser sintering, enhancing anomaly detection coverage as well as detectibility. Additionally, since the detection method does not require access to toolpath control code, it is readily applied to proprietary additive manufacturing systems.

Experimental results using a Sintratec Kit selective laser sintering printer demonstrate the efficacy of the proposed anomaly detection method. Four anomaly creation attacks – void insertion, layer thickness alteration, temperature modification and scanning speed variation – were executed to evaluate the anomaly detection method. The attacks, which were selected based on their effects on the mechanical properties of printed parts, were launched with varying degrees of severity to assess the finest anomaly detection granularities. The proposed method yielded 96.9% accuracy in anomaly detection. The smallest discernible changes were 1.29% for void insertion attacks, 5% for layer thickness alteration attacks, 3.57% for temperature modification attacks and 4.55% for scanning speed variation attacks. Just as significant, the total cost of the sensors and peripheral devices is under $120 and anomaly detection for each test part requires less than three seconds.

2.   Related Work

Side-channel analysis is a well-known methodology that has been leveraged to attack additive manufacturing and related systems [8, 11, 23]. However, it can also be applied to verify the integrity of additively-manufactured parts with limited destructive testing. Vincent et al. [26] proposed a side-channel scheme for detecting Trojans implanted in integrated circuits used in cyber-physical systems. They suggested using structural health monitoring techniques, but did not conduct experiments to demonstrate the effectiveness of the integrity detection scheme.

Wu et al. [27] investigated printed part defects that could be introduced maliciously during the additive manufacturing process chain. They proposed a method that uses machine learning and image classification of software simulation screenshots to examine printed parts layer by layer and detect anomalies.

Al Faruque et al. [1] employed image processing and machine learning on thermal camera images to detect intellectual property theft and sabotage in additive manufacturing systems. The images, which tracked nozzle motion in a fused filament fabrication printer, were essentially used as a side channel to detect potential printed part anomalies. Chhetri et al. [6] used statistical modeling to map toolpath (G-code) instructions to analog (side-channel) emissions in order to detect anomalous operations of a fused filament fabrication printer.

Bayens et al. [2] developed a scheme for detecting malicious infill patterns in a fused filament fabrication printer. The scheme explicitly excluded the analysis of STL and G-code files, focusing instead on side-channel acoustic, magnetic and motion data to train a machine learning model that classified printed part layers as valid or anomalous.

Belikovetsky et al. [3] applied signal processing and machine learning to acoustic side-channel emanations from a fused filament fabrication printer to create a master audio signature for verifying printed part integrity. Gatlin et al. [9] presented a similar side-channel method but, instead of acoustic emanations, monitored the electric current delivered to the motors of a fused filament fabrication printer to detect sabotage attacks. Master power signatures for different types of printed parts were employed as baselines for anomaly detection.

Sturm et al. [24] explored the use of impedance-based monitoring to detect part defects during material jetting additive manufacturing. Sensors were attached directly to the print bed or permanently to parts as they were being printed. The method was able to detect void defects down to 2.28% of printed part volume.

Yu et al. [29] leveraged a multi-modal approach for detecting sabotage attacks on a fused filament fabrication printer. Side-channel data associated with vibrations, acoustics, magnetic fields and electric current were analyzed to obtain correlations between toolpath commands and physical parameters in order to identify anomalous parts.

Brandman et al. [5] generated physical hash values (QR codes) of process parameters and toolpath code for detecting attacks on additive manufacturing systems. Their approach secures proprietary process parameters and printing instructions while performing quality control of printed parts.

Rais et al. [20] developed a framework for detecting low-profile sabotage attacks on fused filament fabrication printers. They analyzed G-code and created a model of expected printer behavior based on nozzle temperature, extruder head position and extruded filament quantity, which is used as a baseline to detect sabotage.

The review of the literature reveals that side-channel data captured during additive manufacturing can be leveraged to detect potential sabotage attacks on printed parts and print environments. The method described in this chapter leverages side-channel print bed movement, laser firing time and print chamber temperature data collected from a selective laser sintering printer to detect printed part anomalies introduced by part and print environment sabotage attacks during the designing, slicing and printing steps.

Much of the previous research relies on side-channel data (e.g., acoustics and magnetic fields) with high levels of noise that negatively impact machine-learning-based anomaly detection. In contrast, the proposed side-channel method does not engage computationally-intensive signal processing and machine learning, and can be applied to proprietary additive manufacturing systems without accessing part designs or toolpath code.

Additionally, practically all the research efforts have focused on fused filament fabrication belonging to the material extrusion class of additive manufacturing processes [16] whereas this work focuses on selective laser sintering, a powder bed fusion process. Finally, the proposed method for detecting the sabotage of selective laser sintering printed parts and environments is applicable to metal powder bed fusion processes such as selective laser melting and direct metal laser sintering used to create mission-critical metal parts for critical infrastructure assets.

3. Powder Bed Fusion

This section describes the powder bed fusion additive manufacturing process and the selective laser sintering printer employed in this research.

3.1 Powder Bed Fusion Process

Powder bed fusion is one of the most popular types of additive manufacturing processes after material extrusion [15]. It is generally more expensive than material extrusion, but is increasingly used to print mission-critical parts for critical infrastructure assets [12].

Powder bed fusion conforms to the same additive manufacturing process chain as material extrusion, which includes the designing, slicing, printing and post-processing steps (Figure 1). However, each step in powder bed fusion may include additional considerations depending on the printing technology and print materials. For example, the designing step in powder bed fusion is distinctive because the printing process allows for more durable parts due to the properties of the print materials employed and increased control over part resolution. Therefore, parts can be designed with finer details for diverse applications.

As in material extrusion, the slicing step in powder bed fusion yields toolpath code that conveys detailed printing information. However, the toolpath commands differ because a laser is used instead of an extruder in the case of material extrusion.

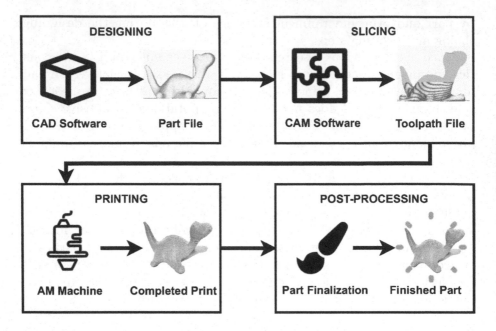

Figure 1. Additive manufacturing process chain.

The printing step in powder bed fusion differs considerably from material extrusion. Figure 2 presents a generic powder bed fusion process. During the printing step, powder particles are fused on a print bed using a laser. The powder delivery system raises fresh powder in the powder bed, following which a rake or roller deposits the powder on top of the fused material in the print bed, creating the base for the next layer of the printed part.

The principal variations in powder bed fusion processes, such as selective laser sintering and selective laser melting, arise from the print material properties and laser power. Selective laser sintering uses a low power laser to sinter layers of plastic particles whereas selective laser melting uses a high power laser to melt metal particles to create parts with smooth surfaces.

The post-processing step in powder bed fusion depends on the print materials. For example, printed parts are annealed in the print bed to obtain the desired mechanical properties. Following annealing, the printed parts are removed and cleaned of excess powder.

3.2   Selective Laser Sintering Printer

This research employed a Sintratec Kit selective laser sintering printer [22] that uses (PA 12) polyamide material to print parts. The powder

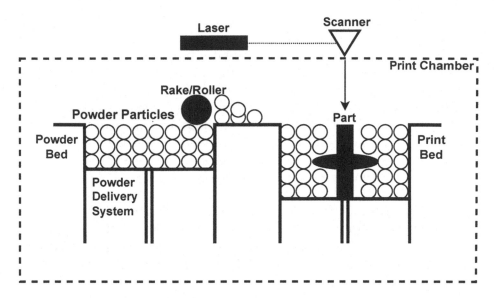

Figure 2. Powder bed fusion process.

delivery system engages a rake to move particles from the powder bed to the print bed, following which galvanometer mirrors deflect beams from a proprietary laser to sinter layers of powder to create a printed part.

A Sintratec Kit has a list price of $6,000, making it the first relatively-affordable selective laser sintering system in the market [21]. However, more important is the fact that the Sintratec Kit research can be leveraged to develop reliable anomaly detection methods for more expensive metal-based selective laser melting systems. Additionally, the Sintratec Kit requires an assembly process, which provides valuable insights into its internal mechanisms that advance side-channel anomaly detection research.

A Sintratec Kit printer comes with the Sintratec Central slicing software, which runs on a Windows machine that communicates with the printer via a USB cable. The software slices a typical part design file (e.g., STL file) to create a toolpath file for printing parts layer by layer. Sintratec Central enables a user to specify the layer height, number of perimeters, perimeter offset, hatching offset and hatching spacing. For live print settings, Sintratec Central allows a user to specify the print chamber temperature, surface temperature and laser scanning speed.

4. Powder Bed Fusion Printer Anomalies

This section discusses the common anomalies seen in parts printed by powder bed fusion printers and the steps in the additive manufacturing process chain where the anomalies may be introduced to sabotage printed parts. Since the additive manufacturing steps are chained, a flaw in the early part design file propagates to and manifests itself as an anomaly in subsequent steps. Understanding where and how anomalies may be induced assists anomaly detection efforts.

This research focuses on detecting anomalies induced by cyber attacks during the designing, slicing and printing steps, and are detectible during or after the printing process. Anomalies introduced during the final post-processing step are outside the scope of this work because they are highly specific to the printing materials and desired parts.

Designing Step Anomalies. Designing step anomalies are introduced by accidental or intentional changes to part design files. The changes require access to the part design computer, part design software and/or saved part design. The principal designing step anomalies are:

- **Part Scaling:** Modification of part dimensions.

- **Voids:** Insertion of open spaces inside a part.

Slicing Step Anomalies. Slicing step anomalies are introduced by accidental or intentional changes to toolpath files. The changes require access to the slicing computer, slicing software and/or toolpath file. The principal slicing step anomalies are:

- **Part Scaling:** Modification of part dimensions.

- **Voids:** Insertion of open spaces inside a part.

- **Part Orientation:** Modification of part orientation on the build platform.

- **Layer Thickness:** Modification of print material quantity deposited in part layers.

Printing Step Anomalies. Printing step anomalies are introduced by printer or material degradation or intentional changes to the printing process. The changes require access to the printer, print materials and/or printing software. The principal printing step anomalies are:

- **Print Material Properties:** Modification of print material quality due to improper storage, inadequate quality control during procurement or poor powder recovery practices.

- **Print Bed Temperature:** Modification of print chamber temperature.

- **Material Surface Temperature:** Modification of powder surface temperature immediately before sintering.

- **Powder Spreading:** Modification of powder distribution in a part layer.

- **Laser Scanning Speed:** Modification of laser sintering speed.

- **Heating/Sintering Times:** Modification of powder heating and/ or sintering times.

5. Anomaly Detection Method

The proposed anomaly detection method leverages three side channels, print bed movement, laser firing time and print chamber temperature, to detect print anomalies. The three side channels are robust to noise, which increases the probability of detecting printed part anomalies while reducing the number of sensors required to obtain feature data.

The anomaly detection method has two phases, baseline creation and anomaly detection. Unlike other additive manufacturing anomaly detection approaches that engage machine learning, the proposed method relies on three important print environment features that underlie the physics of selective laser sintering; this enhances anomaly detection coverage as well as detectibility. Additionally, the detection method does not require access to toolpath control code. As a result, the anomaly detection method is applicable to proprietary additive manufacturing systems.

Figure 3 shows the anomaly detection workflow. The baseline creation phase creates the ground truth based on control part readings and a configuration file containing threshold values for anomaly detection. This is followed by the anomaly detection phase that compares test part readings against the control readings using the threshold values in the configuration file.

The first step in the baseline creation phase is data collection, which gathers raw control data associated with the three features of interest while the control parts are being printed. Meanwhile, a configuration file containing initial detection thresholds is created to customize anomaly detection to print environments and user requirements. For example, some configuration file options enable users to specify the allowable fluctuations in laser firing time and print chamber temperature.

The second step is to conduct destructive testing of each control part to determine whether or not it meets the physical (e.g., size) and mechanical (e.g., tensile strength) specifications. Depending on the statistical requirements, the anomaly detection control data is created by

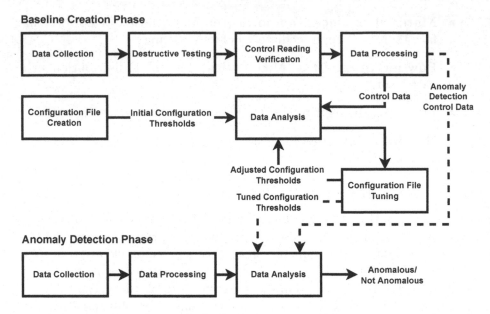

Figure 3. Anomaly detection workflow.

destructively testing control parts from multiple print jobs. The third step in baseline creation is control reading verification during which the readings of control parts that satisfy the specifications upon destructive testing are averaged to create the baseline for anomaly detection. The fourth data processing step transforms the raw part data to a format suitable for data analysis.

The final data analysis and configuration file tuning steps use verified baseline control data in an iterative manner to adjust the configuration thresholds. Verified control data from multiple print jobs are compared against each other in order to adjust the initial configuration thresholds based on applicable constraints. The final tuned configuration thresholds are input to the data analysis step in the anomaly detection phase.

During the anomaly detection phase shown in Figure 3, each subsequent printed (test) part is non-destructively processed by comparing its readings against the baseline readings. The same data collection and data processing steps performed in the baseline creation phase are employed to collect the raw test part data and convert it to a format suitable for anomaly detection. The data analysis step uses the tuned configuration thresholds, test data and anomaly detection control data for every test part layer to determine anomalies. A test part that passes the data analysis step is deemed to be free from anomalies with respect to the measured side-channel data.

Figure 4. Magnet and rotary sensor placement.

Note that the anomaly detection workflow involves destructive testing to create the baseline. Therefore, it is designed to be used in industrial environments that manufacture multiple copies of parts as opposed to hobbyist environments that print single parts.

5.1 Data Collection

Three sensors are employed to obtain side-channel data related to the control and test parts. The first sensor is a magnetic rotary board that works in concert with a small round (diametrically-magnetized) magnet to collect data pertaining to print bed movements. As shown in Figure 4, the magnet sits on the stepper motor that controls the print bed and the sensor board is positioned on top of the magnet. The sensor board communicates with an Arduino Uno device using the I2C protocol. The magnet is rotated and the magnet angle changes whenever the print bed moves. The Arduino Uno device records the magnet angle every 50 ms.

The Sintratec Kit printer used in this research has a proprietary laser that operates in the blue light range. Therefore, an ultraviolet light sensor is employed to determine when the laser is fired. The sensor has a relatively high sampling rate and accurately detects light in the ultraviolet wavelengths. As shown in Figure 5, the ultraviolet light sensor is placed inside the casing where the laser originates. The sensor is connected to a Raspberry Pi 3 computer, which uses the I2C protocol to passively collect ultraviolet index (intensity) measurements every 3 ms.

The third sensor, a thermistor, that can withstand high printing temperatures over extended periods of time, collects print chamber tem-

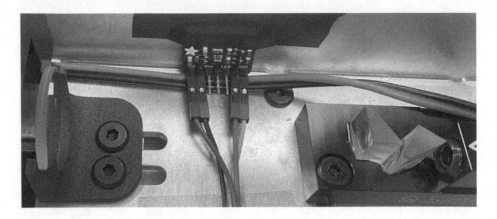

Figure 5.   Light sensor placement.

Figure 6.   Thermistor placement.

perature data. The thermistor shown in the oval region in Figure 6 is positioned to the left of the Sintratec Kit integrated thermistors at the back of the core. The thermistor is connected to the Arduino Uno device that collects five temperature samples every 10 ms and records the average value.

Table 1. Side-channel sensors and data collection devices.

Device	Purpose	Resolution	Sampling Rate
Seeed Studio AS5600 Rotary Sensor	Print bed movement	0.09 °	50 ms
Adafruit SI1145 Light Sensor	Laser firing detection	100 mlx	3 ms
EPCOS/TDK NTC thermistor	Print chamber temperature	0.1 °C	50 ms
Miuzei Arduino Uno	Data collection	–	–
Raspberry Pi 3	Drive data collection	–	–

The Arduino Uno communicates with the Raspberry Pi over a serial connection using a USB cable. The Raspberry Pi runs driver code that initiates scripts that continuously collect raw data provided by the three sensors during the printing process. Data values from the sensors are timestamped and stored in CSV files on a USB storage drive connected to the Raspberry Pi.

Table 1 provides information about the side-channel sensors and data collection devices. Note that emphasis is on employing multiple side channels to enhance anomaly detection coverage. While a single sensor is capable of detecting certain anomalies, using three sensors enables the majority of anomalies to be detected. The combination of sensors enhances detectibility while reducing the hardware requirements.

5.2   Data Processing

The data processing step invokes three main functions to convert the raw side-channel data to a format that supports data analysis:

- **Layer Detection Function:** The layer detection function examines consecutive rotary magnet sensor readings to determine when a new layer of powder is set. A Sintratec Kit printer performs four print bed movements in order to deposit a new layer. Consistent fluctuations in the rotary sensor readings indicate print bed movements. The layer detection function records the timestamped readings associated with powder deposition.

- **Laser-Layer Correlation Function:** The laser-layer correlation function uses the timestamped print layer readings to split the ultraviolet light sensor readings into layers. Since the intent is to detect attacks during sintering, the function records the timestamps of the first and last sintered layers. The timestamps of the first and last sintered layers are correlated with the timestamps of the first and last laser firings, respectively. Laser and layer data collected before and after these two times are discarded.

The laser data values are drawn from a continuous scale based on the ultraviolet index (intensity). Since the focus is only on laser firing, the laser firing data for each layer is simplified by converting it to a string of binary values corresponding to whether (1) or not (0) the laser was fired.

- **Layer-Temperature Correlation Function:** The layer-temperature correlation function analyzes the laser-layer correlated data to split the temperature readings by layer. Since the temperature values do not fluctuate as rapidly as print bed movements and laser firings, the temperature readings are downsampled to about two readings per second.

The time required for data processing depends on the printed part. In the experiments, print jobs required around two hours and processing the data for a job took about ten minutes; this is not an issue because data processing only occurs once per print job. The files containing the processed data from the three sensors are input to the data analysis step to detect anomalies.

5.3   Data Analysis

The data analysis step compares the processed sensor data against the verified control data to determine the existence of anomalies in the printed parts. The thresholds stored in the configuration file are used for the comparisons.

Several variables should be considered when tuning the threshold values used for anomaly detection. The thresholds should be adjusted based on the printer tolerances and desired precision. Sensor sampling rates and error rates impose limits on detection capabilities and the appropriate threshold values. Additionally, allowable tolerances on the final printed parts provide guidance on the flexibility and variance in the part printing process. Ideally, thresholds should be customized to the parts as well as the printer.

Algorithm 1 specifies the anomaly detection procedure using the side-channel data. Most anomalies are detected via straightforward comparisons of layer counts, sintering times and print chamber temperatures. Analyzing the layer counts potentially reveals changes in the layer thick-

---

Algorithm 1: Identify anomalies using side-channel data.

Input: control: Processed control data
Input: test: Processed test data
Input: thresholds: Threshold settings from configuration file
Output: report: Summary of anomalies
anomalies ← []
if *len(control) – len(test)* ≠ *0* then
    anomalies ← (layerCount, 0)
end
for *cLayer, tLayer* **in** *control, test* do
    if *|cLayer.time – tLayer.time|* ≥ *threshold.time* then
        anomalies ← (timing, tLayer.ID)
    end
    if *levenshtein(cLayer.pattern, tLayer.pattern)* ≥ *threshold.firing* then
        anomalies ← (firing, tLayer.ID)
    end
    for *controlTemp, testTemp* **in** *cLayer.temperatures, tLayer.temperatures* do
        if *|controlTemp – testTemp|* ≥ *threshold.temperature* then
            anomalies ← (temperature, tLayer.ID)
        end
    end
end
report ← generateReport(anomalies)
return report

---

ness due to attacks. Variations in the sintering times may point to the existence of voids in printed parts and changes in the laser scanning speed. Temperature deviations greater than the threshold indicate heating-related anomalies in the print chamber.

Voids and other changes to the internal structures of printed parts may be detected by analyzing the laser firing data. The laser firing data for each layer is expressed as a binary string. Levenshtein distances are computed between the test and control binary strings for the corresponding part layers. Distances exceeding a threshold are deemed to be anomalous. Since additive manufacturing is a timing-based process, the Levenshtein distance is a better metric than direct binary string comparison because slight differences in laser firing times can occur due to the heating process or because the ultraviolet light sensor sampling data may not align in exactly the same way for every print.

The data analysis step performs anomaly detection on a per-layer basis. Deviations beyond the set thresholds are flagged as anomalies in a summary file. The summary file lists the anomalies and their types, along with the anomalous part layers. The final report incorporates visualizations that can assist operators in determining if anomalies should be investigated further or if they are likely false positives.

The proposed anomaly detection method does not engage computing-intensive machine learning to detect anomalies. Additionally, it does not require access to toolpath control code, rendering it attractive for proprietary systems such as Sintratec Kit printers for which human-readable control code is not available. Just as significant, the total cost of the sensors and peripheral devices is under $120 and anomaly detection for each test part requires less than three seconds.

6.   Anomaly Creation Attacks

Anomaly creation attacks were executed to evaluate the effectiveness of the proposed anomaly detection method. The attacks were selected based on their effects on the mechanical properties of the printed parts. The attacks were launched with varying degrees of severity to assess the finest granularities of anomaly detection.

Four types of anomaly creation attacks were executed in the experiments:

- **Void Insertion:** This type of attack inserts voids in a design file during the designing step. Inserting voids in a part changes how the part is built and affects part strength [4, 25]. Large voids may be detectible via non-destructive testing (e.g., visual inspection or weighing) whereas small voids may not be detectible without destructive testing.

   Two types of voids were inserted in the printed parts. The first type of void had fixed cross sections arising from the exclusion of 2.45% of the sintering area per layer for 12 consecutive layers. The second type of void had cross sections that varied in size due to the exclusion of 0.57% to 2.73% of the sintering area per layer over 40 consecutive layers.

- **Layer Thickness Alteration:** This type of attack modifies the part layer thickness during the slicing step. The layer thickness affects inter-layer adhesion and, thus, part quality [10]. Normal layer thicknesses for a Sintratec Kit printer are in the order of microns (μm). This resolution makes it virtually impossible to distinguish individual layers by visual inspection.

   The layer thickness alteration attacks were executed by adjusting the Sintratec Central slicing parameters. The Sintratec Central software requires all the layers to have the same thickness, typically $100\,\mu m$. The three experimental attacks increased the layer thicknesses to $105\,\mu m$, $110\,\mu m$ and $150\,\mu m$, respectively.

- **Temperature Modification:** This type of attack modifies the print chamber temperature during printing. Printing a part at a lower temperature negatively impacts inter-layer adhesion whereas printing at a higher temperature causes consecutive layers to be melted together or curled, both of which can result in warped parts.

  The temperature modification attacks leveraged the parameter control feature provided by the Sintratec Central slicing software. Specifically, the temperature may be changed while printing any layer and may be returned to the original value at any time during printing. The experimental attacks decreased the temperature by $5\,°C$ and increased the temperature by $5\,°C$ from the recommended temperature of $140\,°C$ for seven to ten layers at two locations during printing (bottom or middle portions of the parts).

- **Scanning Speed Variation:** This type of attack modifies the laser scanning speed during printing. Modifying the scanning speed introduces timing-related defects that negatively impact part properties [10].

  The scanning speed variation attacks leveraged the parameter control feature of the Sintratec Central software. The experimental attacks were executed by modifying the scanning speeds to $575\,mm/s$, $600\,mm/s$ and $625\,mm/s$ from the recommended speed of $550\,mm/s$ for the entire prints.

7.   Experimental Setup and Results

This section presents the experimental setup and discusses the anomaly detection results.

7.1   Experimental Setup

Three sensors were used to collect side-channel data in the experiments. An AS5600 magnetic rotary sensor with a magnet was placed on the stepper motor to collect print bed movement data. An SI1145 ultraviolet light sensor was placed inside the laser casing to determine whether or not the laser fired at a given time. A thermistor was placed at the back of the print chamber to collect print chamber temperature data. All the sensors were fixed at their locations throughout the baseline creation and anomaly detection phases.

An Arduino Uno device was used to collect data from the rotary sensor and thermistor. The Arduino Uno communicated with a Raspberry Pi

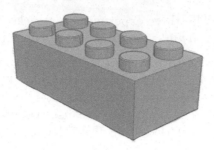

Figure 7.   Printed part sample.

3 computer over a USB serial connection to write timestamped readings to a CSV file. The Raspberry Pi also collected timestamped readings from the ultraviolet light sensor and recorded them in a separate CSV file. Rotary and temperature sensor readings were sampled every 50 ms. The ultraviolet light index in the laser casing was sampled every 3 ms.

Data collection was initiated using a secure shell (SSH) connection to the Raspberry Pi during powder bed preparation, shortly before sintering. Data collection continued until the print was completed and the cooldown phase began. At this point, the data collection was terminated manually via the SSH connection. The data files were transferred to a separate computer via secure copy for processing and analysis. The data collection code was written in Python and Arduino C. The data processing and analysis code was written in Python.

Figure 7 shows a printed part sample used in the experiments. The Lego-brick-shaped sample incorporates basic linear, rectangular and circular features. A print job involved printing ten parts at one time. The ten printed part samples were positioned in exactly the same way on the print bed during each print job.

Additionally, a more complex printed part sample was designed to serve as a challenging test case in the anomaly detection experiments. Figure 8 shows a complex printed part sample. The complex printed part was about the same size as its simpler counterpart, but with twice as many layers and several intricate details.

All the part samples were printed using a mixture of 70% new and 30% used PA 12 powder. No more than two print jobs were executed on a given day to accommodate the time required to heat the powder, sinter the part layers and cool each printed part. As a result, data collection extended over several months – this is not a limitation because the print schedule mirrors typical additive manufacturing operations. Typical printer cleaning and calibration schedules were also followed.

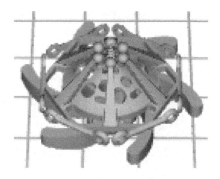

Figure 8. Complex printed part sample.

Four attack thresholds for anomaly determination against the baseline were recorded in the configuration file. The anomaly threshold for layers in a printed part was set to zero (i.e., test and control samples had to have the same numbers of layers). Two anomaly thresholds for laser firing during layer sintering were set – the maximum laser firing time difference was 100 ms and the maximum laser firing pattern difference was 15%. The anomaly threshold for print chamber temperature was set to a maximum difference of 5 °C. The justifications for the threshold settings are described later in this section.

7.2   Anomaly Detection Results

This section presents the results of detecting anomalies in simple and complex printed parts targeted by anomaly creation attacks. The simple parts were targeted by void insertion, layer thickness alteration, temperature modification and scanning speed variation attacks. Void insertion attacks were not executed on the complex printed parts due to their size and shape.

Simple Printed Part Results. Eight control print jobs were executed in the simple printed part experiments. One control print job was used as the baseline for anomaly detection. One control print job was deemed a false positive because it was discovered during the analysis to be anomalous despite creating it in the exact same way as the other control prints. This could be due to timing changes induced by random laser heating variations.

The following results were obtained for the four types of anomaly creation attacks:

- **Void Insertion:** The void insertion attacks introduced two types of voids in the printed parts during the designing step. The first

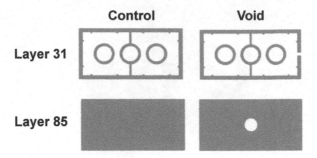

Figure 9.   Screenshot previews of normal layers versus layers with voids.

type of void had fixed cross sections arising from the exclusion of 2.45% of the sintering area per layer for 12 consecutive layers. The second type of void had cross sections that varied in size due to the exclusion of 0.57% to 2.73% of the sintering area per layer over 40 consecutive layers. Seven void attack print jobs were executed with ten printed part copies each. In four of the print jobs, every one of the 40 $(= 4 \times 10)$ total part copies incorporated one consistent void. The remaining three print jobs produced 30 total part copies, each containing one varying void.

The open spaces in the part layers caused by voids induced variations in the laser firing patterns. Figure 9 shows the differences in the laser firing patterns with previews of the layers with open spaces. Parts with consistent and variable voids that excluded more than $44 \, \text{mm}^2$ total area or 1.29% of the layer sintering area were always detected. The $44 \, \text{mm}^2$ total area resulted from a small void of $4.4 \, \text{mm}^2$ in each of the ten parts on the build plate, so the removed area did not have to correspond to one large void in order to be detected. Anomalies were always indicated by the laser timing readings. However, anomalies were not always indicated by the laser firing patterns.

- **Layer Thickness Alteration:** The layer thickness alteration attacks executed during the slicing step modified the individual layer thickness from the recommended setting of $100 \, \mu\text{m}$ to $105 \, \mu\text{m}$, $110 \, \mu\text{m}$ and $150 \, \mu\text{m}$. Five layer thickness alteration print jobs were executed, yielding 50 $(= 5 \times 10)$ total part copies. One print job was executed for each of the $150 \, \mu\text{m}$ and $110 \, \mu\text{m}$ layers, and three print jobs with $105 \, \mu\text{m}$ layers.

  None of the layer thickness modifications were discernible via visual inspection nor did they affect part dimensions and weight. Parts with $150 \, \mu\text{m}$ and $110 \, \mu\text{m}$ layers were observed to have significantly

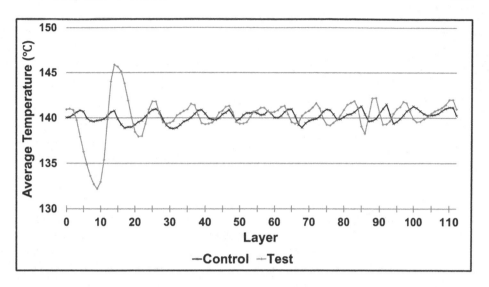

Figure 10. Temperature profiles.

reduced strength; in fact, many of them crumbled during routine post-processing cleaning. Parts with 105 μm layers did not crumble during post-processing.

Anomalies were indicated based on differences in the total numbers of layers, laser timings and laser firing patterns. Parts whose layer thicknesses were increased by 5 μm or more were always detected as anomalous.

- **Temperature Modification:** The temperature modification attacks executed during the printing step either decreased or increased the print chamber temperature by 5 °C from the recommended 140 °C for seven to ten printed layers at the bottom and middle of the printed parts. The error rating for the thermistor at the printing temperature was 5 °C, which is why smaller thresholds were not used. Three print jobs (10 copies each) were executed – one with a 5 °C decrease while printing the bottom portions, one with a 5 °C increase while printing the bottom portions and one with a 5 °C increase while printing the middle portions.

Figure 10 shows the temperature profiles under normal conditions (control) and during an attack (test). Anomalies were indicated based on the laser timing and print chamber temperature. All the temperature attacks were detected for all the print jobs. No changes to the printed parts were discernible by visual inspection.

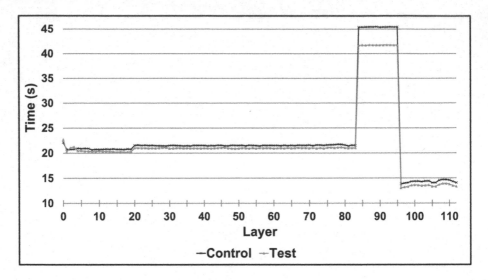

Figure 11.   Laser sintering time profiles.

The locations of the temperature attacks (bottom or middle portions) did not impact anomaly detection.

- **Scanning Speed Variation:** The scanning speed attacks executed during the printing step modified the laser scanning speed from the recommended 550 mm/s to 575 mm/s, 600 mm/s and 625 mm/s. Three print jobs were executed for each of the three scanning speeds for a total of nine print jobs (90 copies).

  Figure 11 shows laser sintering times under normal conditions (control) and during an attack (test). Scanning speed modifications did not induce any discernible changes to the printed parts. Anomalies, which were indicated by laser timing, were detected even when the scanning speed was increased as little as 25 mm/s. As expected, the scanning speed changes on laser timing were more obvious when larger areas were sintered.

Table 2 shows the detection granularities for the four types of anomaly creation attacks. The smallest changes discernible by the anomaly detection method range from just 1.29% to 5%.

Table 3 summarizes the anomaly detection results for the simple printed parts in the experiments. For each print job, the test data was compared against the control data and the entire test print job was assessed as anomalous or normal. The numbers of true positives (anomalies claimed to exist and do exist), true negatives (anomalies claimed not to exist and are non-existent), false positives (anomalies claimed to exist

Table 2. Detection granularities for the anomaly creation attacks.

Attack	Smallest Detected Change	Percentage Change
Void Insertion	$44\,mm^2$	1.29%
Layer Thickness Alteration	$5\,\mu m$	5.00%
Temperature Modification	$5°C$	3.57%
Scanning Speed Variation	$25\,mm/s$	4.55%

Table 3. Anomaly detection results for simple printed parts.

Accuracy	Sensitivity	Specificity	Precision
96.9%	100%	87.5%	96.0%

but are non-existent) and false negatives (anomalies claimed not to exist but do exist) were computed. These values were used to compute the standard accuracy, sensitivity, specificity and precision metrics reported in Table 3. Clearly, the anomaly detection results for the simple printed parts are very good.

Complex Printed Part Results. Two control print jobs and two attack print jobs were executed to evaluate the efficacy of the anomaly detection method on a part with a complex shape with several intricate details. The first attack modified the laser scanning speed from 550 mm/s to 600 mm/s. The second attack modified the layer thickness from the recommended 100 μm to 105 μm and raised the print chamber temperature from the recommended 140°C to 145°C at the bottom of the print. The anomaly detection thresholds used were the same as those used in the simple part experiments.

During the experiment it was determined that the sintering area when building the complex part had to be at least $10\,mm^2$ in order for the ultraviolet light sensor to detect laser firing; otherwise, the laser sintered the layers much too quickly. The method was still able to detect two anomalies in layers with sintering areas larger than the $10\,mm^2$ limit, specifically, anomalies in the total number of layers and print chamber temperature. However, no anomalies were indicated by the laser timing readings during the scanning speed variation attack. This is likely due to the small to very small sintering areas of several complex part layers. The resulting shorter sintering times prevented the scanning speed variation attack from producing detectible differences in laser timing.

8.   Discussion

The proposed anomaly detection method was able to detect anomalies in printed parts targeted by several attacks during various steps of the additive manufacturing process chain. The total cost of the sensors and devices (not including the printer) was under $120.

Positioning parts at different x-axis and y-axis locations on the print bed did not impact anomaly detection. However, varying the z-axis placement induced anomalies due to the differences in the numbers of layers in the print jobs. Additionally, the number of parts in each print job had to be the same or the laser timings would change between print jobs due to variations in the laser sintering area. Recalibration of the laser did not require the creation of a new baseline.

Changing the orientation of the rotary sensor board between print jobs did not affect anomaly detection because all the magnet angle readings were relative to each other. Ultraviolet light sensor placement between print jobs also did not affect anomaly detection as long as the sensor was positioned in the laser casing. However, the thermistor was sensitive to placement – moving it closer or farther away from the heating element vastly affected the readings.

Selective laser sintering is a highly time-dependent process. Laser timing proved to be the most reliable side channel for anomaly detection because all four types of attacks induced timing-related anomalies. However, installing the rotary sensor was essential to performing anomaly detection on a per-layer basis. Using the ultraviolet light sensor without the rotary sensor would have significantly increased the computations required to perform laser-layer correlation while increasing the error rate. Additionally, combining laser timing data with the other two side-channel readings further distinguished the types of anomalies.

An unexpected observation was that the laser firing pattern data was less useful than the print bed movement, laser firing time and print chamber temperature data. In fact, the laser firing data consistently indicated anomalies only when the layer thickness was changed.

Detecting anomalies on a per-layer basis – where each layer is evaluated independently – provides the opportunity for real-time quality control of printed parts. The real-time computations would also be reduced because the retroactive parsing of the collected data into layers is eliminated. Additionally, the detection of significant anomalies in a few layers could result in a print job being terminated immediately, saving time and reducing print material wastage.

A limitation of the anomaly detection method is that the additional sensors and devices increase the attack surface. Physical countermeasures such as access control and anti-tampering mechanisms, and cyber security countermeasures such as access control and authentication would have to be instituted. The Raspberry Pi network should also be isolated and secured.

However, the principal limitation is that, when an anomaly is detected, it is often not possible to identify the specific anomaly creation attack that was responsible. Other side channels such as print bed movement and print chamber temperature could be used to narrow the type of attack and direct mitigation efforts.

The anomaly detection method requires destructive testing to create a baseline for every new part design, but this may not be a large limitation for mission-critical parts where quality control is essential. Indeed, the verification of printed parts is a part of the normal workflow. The proposed method just adds an additional baseline creation step, which is easily integrated in the manufacturing workflow.

With regard to temperature detection, the main limitation is that the thermistor had a high error rating of 5°C at the printing temperature. Since changing the temperature as little as one degree can affect printed part quality, it is important to use a thermistor with a higher rating in anomaly detection.

It was not possible to reliably detect changes in the layer thickness using rotary sensor data. The attacks executed in this research changed the thickness of every part layer by the same amount during the slicing step, which changed the total number of layers. Therefore, it is possible that an attack that dynamically changes the thickness of individual layers while maintaining the layer count would go undetected. However, this attack would require extreme care to ensure that the other printed part measurements are not affected, requiring considerable skill and access on the part of the attacker.

Finally, the proposed anomaly detection method is unable to determine if a new bed of powder was actually laid when required. A solution is to position additional rotary sensors on the powder bed delivery motors and correlate their timing with print bed movements.

9.   Conclusions

Due to the complexity of additive manufacturing systems, cyber attacks that seek to sabotage printed parts and/or print environments are difficult to detect and mitigate, and impossible to eliminate entirely. Therefore, it is imperative to focus on methods that can verify the integrity of printed parts. While quality control using destructive testing is an option, rapid and reliable non-destructive testing methods are needed to detect anomalies in printed parts induced by cyber attacks during the various steps in the additive manufacturing process chain.

The anomaly detection method developed for a selective laser sintering system does not engage computing-intensive machine learning to detect anomalies, relying instead on three side channels, print bed movement, laser firing time and print chamber temperature, that underlie the physics of selective laser sintering. The side channels provide detection coverage while reducing the sensor requirements. Additionally, they are robust to noise, which enhances the detection of printed part anomalies.

Experimental results demonstrate the efficacy of the anomaly detection method under attacks that target the mechanical properties of printed parts. The method yielded 96.9% anomaly detection accuracy. The smallest discernible changes to printed parts were 1.29% for void insertion attacks, 5% for layer thickness alteration attacks, 3.57% for temperature modification attacks and 4.55% for scanning speed variation attacks. The cost of the sensors and peripheral devices is under $120 and anomaly detection for each test part requires less than three seconds, rendering the method inexpensive and efficient for use in industrial environments.

This research can be leveraged to develop reliable anomaly detection methods for more expensive systems, including those employing metal-based selective laser melting. Future research will focus on enhancing anomaly detection by incorporating data from additional side channels and considering other types of attacks that target the mechanical properties of printed parts. Despite promising experimental results, the proposed method merely identifies anomalies in parts after they are printed. Future research will attempt to address this limitation by leveraging side channels to detect anomalies in parts and print environments while parts are being printed, contributing to better attack detection and mitigation capabilities as well as reduced material wastage.

Acknowledgement

This research was supported by the National Science Foundation under Grant no. DGE 1501177 and by UT-Battelle under Contract no. DE-AC05-00OR22725 with the U.S. Department of Energy.

References

[1] M. Al Faruque, S. Chhetri, S. Faezi and A. Canedo, Forensics of Thermal Side Channels in Additive Manufacturing Systems, CECS Technical Report #16-01, Center for Embedded and Cyber-Physical Systems, University of California, Irvine, Irvine, California, 2016.

[2] C. Bayens, T. Le, L. Garcia, R. Beyah, M. Javanmard and S. Zonouz, See no evil, hear no evil, print no evil? Malicious fill pattern detection in additive manufacturing, *Proceedings of the Twenty-Sixth USENIX Security Symposium*, pp. 1181–1198, 2017.

[3] S. Belikovetsky, Y. Solewicz, M. Yampolskiy, J. Toh and Y. Elovici, Digital audio signature for 3D printing integrity, *IEEE Transactions on Information Forensics and Security*, vol. 14(5), pp. 1127–1141, 2018.

[4] S. Belikovetsky, M. Yampolskiy, J. Toh, J. Gatlin and Y. Elovici, dr0wned – Cyber-physical attack with additive manufacturing, presented at the *Eleventh USENIX Workshop on Offensive Technologies*, 2017.

[5] J. Brandman, L. Sturm, J. White and C. Williams, A physical hash for preventing and detecting cyber-physical attacks on additive manufacturing systems, *Journal of Manufacturing Systems*, vol. 56, pp. 202–212, 2020.

[6] S. Chhetri, A. Canedo and M. Al Faruque, KCAD: Kinetic cyberattack detection method for cyber-physical additive manufacturing systems, *Proceedings of the IEEE/ACM International Conference on Computer-Aided Design*, 2016.

[7] J. Ellis, 3D-printed nuclear reactor promises faster, more economical path to nuclear energy, *Oak Ridge National Laboratory News*, Oak Ridge National Laboratory, Oak Ridge, Tennessee (`www.ornl.gov/news/3d-printed-nuclear-reactor-promises-faster-more-economical-path-nuclear-energy`), May 11, 2020.

[8] S. Faaezi, S. Chhetri, A. Malawade, J. Chaput, W. Grover, P. Brisk and M. Al Faruque, Oligo-Snoop: A non-invasive side-channel attack against DNA synthesis machines, *Proceedings of the Twenty-Sixth Annual Network and Distributed Systems Security Symposium*, 2019.

[9] J. Gatlin, S. Belikovetsky, S. Moore, Y. Solewicz, Y. Elovici and M. Yampolskiy, Detecting sabotage attacks in additive manufacturing using actuator power signatures, *IEEE Access*, vol. 7, pp. 133421–133432, 2019.

[10] L. Graves, W. King, P. Carrion, S. Shao, N. Shamsaei and M. Yampolskiy, Sabotaging metal additive manufacturing: Powder delivery system manipulation and material-dependent effects, *Additive Manufacturing*, vol. 46, article no. 10209, 2021.

[11] A. Hojjati, A. Adhikari, K. Struckmann, E. Chou, T. Nguyen, K. Madan, M. Winslett, C. Gunter and W. King, Leave your phone at the door: Side channels that reveal factory floor secrets, *Proceedings of the ACM SIGSAC Conference on Computer and Communications Security*, pp. 883–894, 2016.

[12] Inspector General, U.S. Department of Defense, Audit of the Cybersecurity of Department of Defense Additive Manufacturing Systems, Washington, DC (media.defense.gov/2021/Jul/07/2002757308/-1/-1/1/DODIG-2021-098.PDF), 2021.

[13] T. Kellner, Mind Meld: How GE and a 3D-Printing Visionary Joined Forces, GE Report, General Electric, Boston, Massachusetts (www.ge.com/news/reports/mind-meld-ge-3d-printing-visionary-joined-forces), July 10, 2017.

[14] E. Kurkowski, A. Van Stockum, J. Dawson, C. Taylor, T. Schulz and S. Shenoi, Manipulation of G-code toolpath files in 3D printers: Attacks and mitigations, in *Critical Infrastructure Protection XVI*, J. Staggs and S. Shenoi (Eds.), Springer, Cham, Switzerland, pp. 155–174, 2022.

[15] M. Leary, *Design for Additive Manufacturing*, Elsevier, Amsterdam, The Netherlands, 2020.

[16] Manufactur3D Magazine, The seven types of additive manufacturing technologies, Thane, India (manufactur3dmag.com/7-types-additive-manufacturing-technologies), April 6, 2018.

[17] S. Moore, W. Glisson and M. Yampolskiy, Implications of malicious 3D printer firmware, *Proceedings of the Fiftieth Hawaii International Conference on System Sciences*, 2017.

[18] H. Pearce, K. Yanamandra, N. Gupta and R. Karri, FLAW3D: A Trojan-Based Cyber Attack on the Physical Outcomes of Additive Manufacturing, arXiv: 2104.09562 (arxiv.org/abs/2104.09562), 2021.

[19] B. Post, B. Richardson, P. Lloyd, L. Love, S. Nolet and J. Hannan, Additive Manufacturing of Wind Turbine Molds, Document ORNL/TM-2017/290, Oak Ridge National Laboratory, Oak Ridge, Tennessee, 2017.

[20] M. Rais, Y. Li and I. Ahmed, Spatiotemporal G-code modeling for secure FDM-based 3D printing, *Proceedings of the Twelfth ACM/IEEE International Conference on Cyber-Physical Systems*, pp. 177–186, 2021.

[21] Sintratec, Sintratec Kit: Most innovative product in the Polish market, Press Release, Brugg, Switzerland (`staticcontent.sintratec.com/wp-content/uploads/2018/08/19073627/180412_Press_Release_Sintratec_wins_award_for_most_innovative_product_2018.pdf`), April 12, 2018.

[22] Sintratec, Sintratec Kit, Brugg, Switzerland (`sintratec.com/product/sintratec-kit`), 2022.

[23] C. Song, F. Ling, Z. Ba, K. Ren, C. Zhou and W. Xu, My smartphone knows what you print: Exploring smartphone-based side-channel attacks against 3D printers, *Proceedings of the ACM SIGSAC Conference on Computer and Communications Security*, pp. 895–907, 2016.

[24] L. Sturm, M. Albakri, P. Tarazaga and C. Williams, In situ monitoring of material jetting additive manufacturing process via impedance based measurements, *Additive Manufacturing*, vol. 28, pp. 456–463, 2019.

[25] L. Sturm, C. Williams, J. Camelio, J. White and R. Parker, Cyber-physical vulnerabilities in additive manufacturing systems: A case study attack on the .STL file with human subjects, *Journal of Manufacturing Systems*, vol. 44(1), pp. 154–164, 2017.

[26] H. Vincent, L. Wells, P. Tarazaga and J. Camelio, Trojan detection and side-channel analyses for cyber security in cyber-physical manufacturing systems, *Procedia Manufacturing*, vol. 1, pp. 77–85, 2015.

[27] M. Wu, V. Phoha, Y. Moon and A. Belman, Detecting malicious defects in 3D printing process using machine learning and image classification, *Proceedings of the ASME International Mechanical Engineering Conference and Exposition*, article no. 67641, 2016.

[28] C. Xiao, Security attack on 3D printing, presented at the *xFocus Security Conference* (`www.claudxiao.net/Attack3DPrinting-Claud-en.pdf`), 2013.

[29] S. Yu, A. Malawade, S. Chhetri and M. Al Faruque, Sabotage attack detection for additive manufacturing systems, *IEEE Access*, vol. 8, pp. 27218–27231, 2020.

Chapter 8

LOW-MAGNITUDE INFILL STRUCTURE MANIPULATION ATTACKS ON FUSED FILAMENT FABRICATION 3D PRINTERS

Muhammad Haris Rais, Muhammad Ahsan, Vaibhav Sharma, Radhika Barua, Rob Prins and Irfan Ahmed

Abstract   As 3D printing applications in industry verticals increase, researchers have been developing new attacks on additive manufacturing processes and appropriate defense techniques. A major attack category on additive manufacturing processes is printed object sabotage. If an attack causes obvious deformations, the part will be rejected before it is used. However, the inherent layer-by-layer printing process enables malicious actors to induce hidden defects in the internal layers of finished parts. The stealthiness of an attack increases its chances of evading detection and the printed part being used in an operational environment where it can cause harm. Several detection schemes have been proposed for identifying attacks on external and internal features of printed objects, but all these schemes have detection thresholds that are well above printer accuracy. Reducing the attack magnitude to the order of printer accuracy can evade detection.

This chapter describes two infill structure manipulation attacks that are easy to launch at the cyber-physical boundary and evade conventional cyber security tools by employing subtle printed part variations below the detection horizon. Specifically, the magnitudes of the variations fall within the printer resolution and trueness values, rendering it challenging for detection schemes to differentiate printed part modifications from benign printing errors. Destructive testing demonstrates that the infill structure manipulation attacks consistently reduce the strength of printed parts. This chapter also highlights the need to incorporate the physical characteristics of printed parts in attack detection.

Keywords: 3D printing, fused filament fabrication, localized infill structure attacks

© IFIP International Federation for Information Processing 2022
Published by Springer Nature Switzerland AG 2022
J. Staggs and S. Shenoi (Eds.): Critical Infrastructure Protection XVI, IFIP AICT 666, pp. 205–232, 2022.
https://doi.org/10.1007/978-3-031-20137-0_8

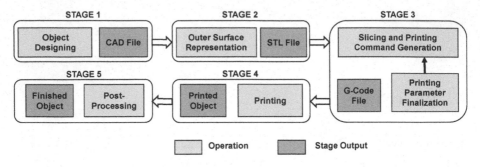

Figure 1.　Additive manufacturing process chain.

1.　Introduction

Additive manufacturing (AM) or 3D printing encompasses manufacturing techniques that create objects by stacking thin layers of material. Additive manufacturing is inherently different from conventional subtractive manufacturing in which a block of material is cut from various sides to create the desired part. Rapid prototyping, customized design, reduced wastage and complex object printing capabilities are some of the distinctive features offered by additive manufacturing. The increased range of printing materials and reduced capital expenditures for printing have significantly expanded the additive manufacturing footprint. In fact, additive manufacturing is forecasted to grow at a sustained compound annual growth rate of 22.5% over the next five years [12]. Additive manufacturing is an essential component of Industry 4.0, which advocates mass customization in the manufacturing industry [6].

Figure 1 shows the five-stage additive manufacturing process chain. During the first stage, a design file is created using computer-aided design (CAD) software. Next, the 3D design is converted to an outer geometry representation, commonly a stereolithography (STL) file. An STL file represents the outer surfaces of an object as a collection of contiguous triangles. The STL file and a set of printing design parameters are then sent to slicer software, which generates the corresponding series of printing commands such as G-code. The commands are executed sequentially by the printer firmware to create the object layer by layer. The printed object finally undergoes post-processing, which involves operations such as curing and surface polishing.

3D printers are increasingly used to print functional components of critical systems [8], rendering them attractive targets for malicious actors. Appreciating the need for cyber security, researchers have examined the attack opportunities in the additive manufacturing process chain. The most obvious attacks are intellectual property (object design) theft, denial of printing service, illegal printing and printed part sabotage.

Additive manufacturing is a cyber-physical process with the first three stages belonging to the cyber domain and the last two stages belonging to the physical domain. Conventional cyber attacks and mitigation schemes are applicable to the cyber portion of the additive manufacturing process chain. The uniqueness of additive manufacturing security primarily lies beyond the cyber domain of the process chain. To mitigate cyber-physical attacks, researchers have proposed approaches that independently examine the printing process in the physical domain using various side channels. Although the attack detection thresholds are improving, they are still well above printer tolerances. The main reason for the current gap is the inability of detection schemes to reliably capture the physical process at high resolution.

If a malicious actor keeps the attack magnitudes within the tolerances of a printing process, the attacks would likely circumvent most detection approaches. To ascertain the exploitation potential of tiny deviations, this research focuses on two low-magnitude attacks that are within the order of magnitude of printing tolerances and well below attack detection thresholds. The new attacks are computed and launched within 150 ms using multiple attack vectors, including a man-in-the-middle (MitM) attack after Stage 3 of the additive manufacturing process chain (Figure 1) or by compromising the printer firmware in Stage 4. The attack vectors have been demonstrated to be feasible for cyber-physical systems [2, 17, 18]

This research has targeted infill connecting segments by modifying the G-code commands at the point of attack. The attacks were executed on ASTM D638 Type IV tensile bars created by a fused filament fabrication (FFF) printer using polylactic acid (PLA) material. Fused filament fabrication is the most common additive manufacturing technique in use today [24] and most additive manufacturing attack detection techniques in the research literature are demonstrated using fused filament fabrication printers. Infill structure manipulation attacks ensure that no visual deformations are observed on the finished objects. Object dimensions, toolpath profiles, printing timing profiles and filament consumption profiles show imperceptible deviations, but destructive tensile strength tests confirm that the attacks significantly reduce the mechanical strength of the printed objects. Micro-computed tomography (Micro-CT) scans also confirm the structural abnormalities in the internal layers of attacked objects.

2.   Related Work

This section discusses research related to sabotage attacks on the fused filament fabrication process and techniques for detecting attacks that bypass pure cyber-domain security mechanisms.

Researchers intending to create hidden defects in printed objects have targeted CAD and STL files during the design stage of the additive manufacturing process chain. Zeltmann et al. [29] introduced tiny defects in the internal layers of printed objects through design file modifications to degrade their strength. Sturm et al. [25] manipulated STL files to create internal voids in printed objects. Belikovetsky et al. [4] demonstrated an attack on the propeller joint of a drone that induced hidden structural weakness, causing it to fail during flight. However, a key limitation of these design file modification attacks is their enlarged footprints during the printing stage.

Rais et al. [22] demonstrated how subtle variations in design file attacks are translated to large, easy-to-detect footprints during the printing stage. They also presented G-code attacks that create internal cavities and filament density and thermodynamic variations that have minimal impacts on the kinetic and thermodynamic profiles of printing operations. Moore et al. [14] identified and exploited a firmware validation vulnerability to install malicious code and demonstrated its harmful effects. Xiao [28] attacked open-source fused filament fabrication printers using an Android device and a computer connected to the USB printer port. Pearce et al. [16] created a bootloader-level Trojan for Marlin-compatible 3D printers. They demonstrated two attacks, implemented via simple code inserted in constrained bootloader space, that manipulated printing operations.

Defensive research has leveraged various side channels to detect sabotage attacks. Chhetri et al. [5] utilized audio signals emitted from 3D printer stepper motors to identify the printing profiles of objects. Belikovetsky et al. [3] employed audio sensors to detect one-second deviations in printing time per layer; attacks were detected by matching the actual printing profiles to a master profile generated in a secure, non-compromised environment. Gao et al. [7] used inertial measurement unit sensors and a camera to detect kinetic attacks on a printing process. Wu et al. [27] utilized static and moving cameras to detect infill pattern attacks; good results were obtained for deviations of 10% or higher. Rais et al. [23] employed optical encoders and thermal sensors to estimate the printing state. They transformed the G-code file and sensor inputs into a compatible format to accurately identify most of the attacks reported in the literature with high accuracy.

A common problem with all these detection methods is that they do not engage printing process knowledge. The low-magnitude infill structure attacks developed in this research exploit knowledge about the fused filament fabrication process to target the mechanical strength of printed objects.

3. Low-Magnitude Infill Structure Attacks

The low-magnitude infill structure attacks degrade the mechanical properties of printed objects in a manner that evades most detection and assurance checks. The degraded objects would fail prematurely during operation.

3.1 Attack Success Criteria

The following criteria are used to assess attack success:

- **Criterion 1:** Feasible to launch the attack after Stage 3 (after the control computer shown in Figure 1).

- **Criterion 2:** No deviations in printhead kinetics above the printing tolerance specifications.

- **Criterion 3:** Detection schemes described in the literature are bypassed.

- **Criterion 4:** Imperceptible visual deformations to the dimensions and shape of the printed object.

- **Criterion 5:** Reduction in the mechanical strength of the printed object.

3.2 Printing Accuracy

Kim et al. [10] evaluated the precision and trueness of 3D printers by printing dental models using four additive manufacturing technologies. The precision and trueness values for fused filament fabrication printers were reported to be $99 \pm 14\,\mu m$ and $188 \pm 14\,\mu m$, respectively. In another study, Msallem et al. [15] reported precision and trueness values of $50 \pm 5\,\mu m$ and $160 \pm 9\,\mu m$, respectively, for an Ultimaker 3 Ext fused filament fabrication printer. Stratasys [9], a renowned 3D printer manufacturer, reported that Fortus 360mc/400mc printers produce two-sigma (95%) parts within a $130\,\mu m$ tolerance of the true value.

These precision and trueness values offer malicious actors windows of opportunity. Without increasing the false positive rate, a detection scheme that relies on the printer toolpath and applies thresholding to

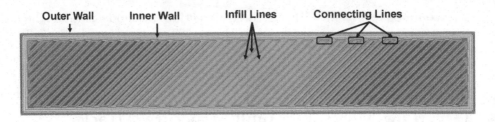

Figure 2. Lines-type infill structure showing infill and connecting lines.

identify anomalies may not work for attacks that produce deviations of the order of 0.1 mm. The low-magnitude infill structure attacks described here exploit the windows of opportunity to maintain stealth, an important success criterion.

3.3   Attacking Infill Structures

Infill refers to the internal printing structure of a printed object. The outer walls and bottom and top layers of a printed object completely hide its infill structure. The infill pattern in each print layer is encapsulated by the inner and outer walls.

Figure 2 shows a cross-section of an intermediate layer of a rectangular bar with a lines-type infill pattern. For 100%-filled parts, slicer software, such as Ultimaker Cura, replaces any selected infill pattern with a lines-type pattern. The strength of a printed object depends on the infill pattern and density of the infill structure.

Figure 3 shows six examples of infill patterns commonly provided by slicer software. If the slicer software is compromised, the infill patterns of printed objects can be modified very easily. However, even a simple design modification triggers much larger modifications to the printer toolpath (nozzle kinetics) and filament kinetics. Almost all the independent-monitoring-based detection schemes discussed in the literature would be able to detect such attacks.

The kinetic process in fused filament fabrication printing constitutes nozzle kinetics, filament kinetics and printbed kinetics. Printing the infill structure of a single layer involves nozzle kinetics and filament kinetics. Most attack detection schemes monitor nozzle kinetics. Previous research has exploited the less-monitored filament kinetics to create cavities and density variations in the internal layers of printed objects [22]. The attacks developed in this research evade these detection schemes by maintaining nozzle kinetics and filament kinetics by employing highly-localized, compensating patterns to minimize the attack footprints. In

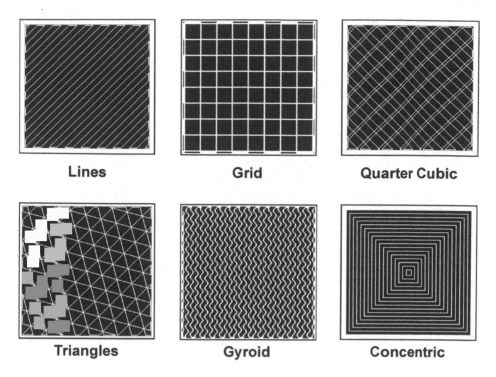

Figure 3. Common infill patterns.

the lines-type infill structure shown in Figure 2, consecutive infill lines are connected by a small line segment called the connecting segment. The attacks manipulate the connecting segments to create a localized asymmetric distribution of material at the target location that results in a weaker structure.

The length of a connecting segment is inversely proportional to the gap between two consecutive infill lines, and is also inversely proportional to the infill density. As the infill percentage is increased, the connecting segment length is reduced and the infill lines get closer. The connecting segments are attractive targets for stealthy attacks due to their small lengths. A fractional change in length of a connecting segment results in a very low absolute deviation, increasing the complexity of attack detection. Moreover, even a small deviation in an infill pattern can induce structural weakness in the printed object.

Infill Lines Spacing Attack. An infill lines spacing attack moves two consecutive infill lines at the target location by a fraction of the length of the connecting segment. This modification is repeated over

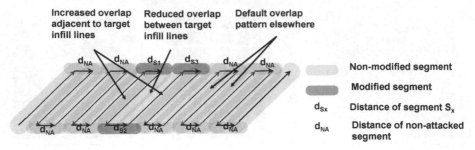

Figure 4. Infill lines spacing attack.

multiple internal layers. The attack is computed and launched within 150 ms from a man-in-the-middle position. It is assumed that a malicious actor leverages knowledge about the targeted object to select the specific locations and layers to be attacked. The malicious actor identifies the infill structure zone in each layer of the G-code file. After identifying the connecting segment linked to the infill lines bordering the targeted location, the malicious actor increases its length in the G-code by a small fraction.

Figure 4 shows an exaggerated view of the attacked and compensatory segments resulting from an infill lines spacing attack. For an object with 100% infill density, the rule of thumb is to maintain the attack magnitude under 50% of the segment length to avoid creating an obvious cavity at the point of attack. Figure 4 shows the attack scheme. The targeted zone is selected in the infill section of the G-code and the following condition is evaluated:

$$0 \; < \; \Delta d_{S_1} = \Delta d_{S_3} \; < \; \Delta d_{S_2}$$

where Δd_{S_2} is the deviation in the length of the connecting segment between the targeted infill lines, Δd_{S_1} and Δd_{S_3} are the deviations in the lengths of the adjacent segments. An appropriate Δd_{S_2} value is selected to compensate for the increase in the length of segment S_2 by distributing Δd_{S_2} equally between the adjacent segments S_1 and S_3 as shown in Figure 4.

Infill Vertices Spacing Attack. An infill vertices spacing attack creates an inverse-wedge-shaped cavity at the targeted location. Figure 5 shows the attack scheme. Instead of moving two consecutive infill lines at both ends, the consecutive lines are only parted at one end. The lengths d_{S_1} and d_{S_3} of the connecting segments S_1 and S_3 are reduced whereas there is no change to d_{S_2}. After confirming that the targeted location is part of the infill structure, the attack magnitude is finalized

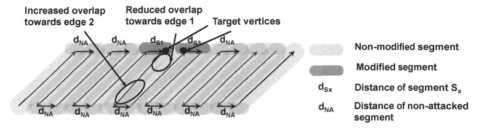

Figure 5. Infill vertices spacing attack.

to ensure that the deviation remains within the printing tolerance and does not create an obvious inverse-wedge-shaped cavity.

The infill vertices spacing attack modifies the lengths and (raster) angles of the infill lines slightly. The modified infill line length $d_{IF_{atk}}$ and angle $\theta_{IF_{atk}}$ are given by:

$$d_{IF_{atk}} = \sqrt{d_{IF_{dft}}^2 + 2 \cdot \Delta d_S \cdot sin(\theta_{dft}) \cdot d_{IF_{dft}} + \Delta d_S^2}$$

$$\theta_{IF_{atk}} = tan^{-1}\{(d_{IF_{dft}} \cdot sin(\theta_{dft}) + \Delta d_S)/d_{IF_{dft}} \cdot cos(\theta_{dft})\}$$

where $d_{IF_{dft}}$ is the original infill line length, Δd_S is the change in the connecting segment length and θ_{dft} is the infill line angle configured during the slicing stage. For example, given a 10 mm infill line configured at an angle of 45°, a 0.1 mm decrease in the connecting segment length changes the infill line length Δd_{IF} by around 0.07 mm. This magnitude is well within the printing tolerance and far from the detection thresholds reported in the literature. Similarly, the change in infill line angle is approximately 0.4^o for an infill angle of 45°. Because the attack modifies two consecutive infill lines, the polarities of the changes are opposite for the pairs of infill line lengths and angles. If infill line 1 IF_1 is larger than $d_{IF_{dft}}$, then infill line 2 IF_2 is smaller than $d_{IF_{dft}}$, and vice versa. This compensation within each instance deceives detection schemes that monitor the accumulated values of performance parameters such as the total nozzle travel and toolpath.

Algorithm 1 specifies the infill lines spacing and infill vertices spacing attacks.

4.   Attack Implementation

The performance of the infill lines spacing and infill vertices spacing attacks at various attack magnitudes was evaluated on objects produced by an Ultimaker-3 fused filament fabrication printer. The printed objects were ASTM D638 Type IV standard tensile bars printed using polylactic

---

Algorithm 1: Infill lines spacing and infill vertices spacing attacks.

Input: G-code$_{Original}$
Input: Layers$_{Attacked}$
Input: Loc$_{Attacked}$
Input: Magnitude (A_m)
Output: G-code$_{Attacked}$
while *Location$_{Attacked}$ $\notin$ Infill-structure* **do**
    Shift_location
end
Compute $A_{m_{max}}$ based on segment length, filament consumption and
        maximum attack magnitude
if $A_m > A_{m_{max}}$ **then**
    $A_m \leftarrow A_{m_{max}}$
end
for $\forall i \in$ *Layers$_{Attacked}$* **do**
    Seg$_1 \leftarrow$ Nearest connecting segment to Loc$_{Attacked}$
    Attack 1: Displace two consecutive infill lines
        Compute new x and y coordinates such that there are
        no changes to the slopes of all the infills and segments
    $|d_{S_1}| \leftarrow |d_{S_1}| - |A_m|$
    $|d_{S_2}| \leftarrow |d_{S_2}| + |A_m|$
    $|d_{S_3}| \leftarrow |d_{S_3}| - |A_m|$
    No changes to $|Infill_1|$ and $|Infill_2|$
    for $\forall i \in$ *Attacked commands* **do**
        modified_G-code $\leftarrow$ compute_new_G-code(i)
    end
    Attack 2: Displace two consecutive infill vertices
        Compute new x and y coordinates such that there are
        no changes to the slopes of the old and new segments
        (Infill line slopes change slightly)
    $|d_{S_1}| \leftarrow |d_{S_1}| - |A_m|$
    No change to $|d_{S_2}|$
    $|d_{S_3}| \leftarrow |d_{S_3}| - |A_m|$
    (Infill lines magnitude changes slightly)
    for $\forall i \in$ *Attacked commands* **do**
        modified_G-code $\leftarrow$ compute_new_G-code(i)
    end
end
G-code$_{Attacked} \leftarrow$ update_G-code(G-code$_{Original}$, modified_G-code)
    return G-code$_{Attacked}$

---

acid polymer. The printer was controlled by Ultimaker Cura software version 4.10, which also served as the slicer software. Table 1 specifies the printing parameters.

Five attacked specimens were printed for each variant of the two types of attacks along with two sets of five reference (non-attacked) specimens. Specimens corresponding to each attack type were printed using a differ-

Table 1. Printing parameters.

Printing Parameter	Value
Layer Thickness	0.2 mm
Nozzle Diameter	0.4 mm
Build Plate Temperature	60°C
Nozzle Temperature – Layer 1	210°C
Nozzle Temperature – Layer 2 Onwards	205°C
Infill Pattern	Lines at 45°
Infill Percentage	100%
Number of Layers	20
Printing Speed – Layer 1	20 mm/s
Printing Speed – Layer 2 Onwards	45 mm/s
Top and Bottom Layers	0
Number of Walls	2

ent polymer spool with a different color primarily to address availability issues. The reference specimens were printed using each spool and their test results were used to gauge the attack impacts. This arrangement did not affect the study results.

Non-destructive tests included measurements, optical microscopy and micro-computed tomography (micro-CT) imaging. Destructive tensile tests performed using MTS Insight 30 equipment enabled the evaluation of the impacts of the attacks on the mechanical strength of the printed parts.

4.1 Attack Overview

The malicious actor is assumed to be an insider with local area network access, but is not authorized to access the printer control computer. Since the printer and control computer employ an unencrypted communications channel, the malicious actor chooses to obtain a man-in-the-middle position using ARP poisoning. Figure 6 shows an attack scenario in which the legitimate communications channel between a client and the printer is interrupted and routed through the malicious actor's machine. When the authorized client sends a print request to the printer, the malicious actor's code receives the original G-code file, computes the attacks, modifies the G-code and sends the modified G-code file to the printer. The sub-second delay introduced by the attack is imperceptible to the authorized client in a practical additive manufacturing environment.

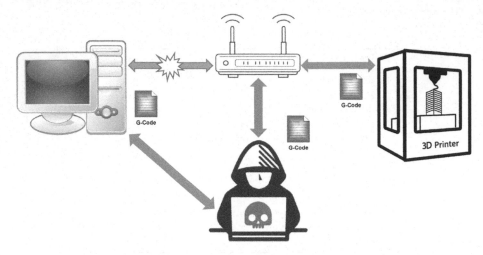

Figure 6. Attack scenario using a MitM position to sabotage a G-code file.

4.2   Attack Plan

The infill attacks were targeted at the central portions of the internal layers of the tensile bar specimens. The unmodified lengths of the infill lines $d_{IF_{dft}}$ and connecting segments $d_{S_{dft}}$ were 6.54 mm and 0.594 mm, respectively. The attacks involved two phases:

- **Phase 1:** The first phase established the maximum attack magnitude that enables an attack to evade detection. Since it was infeasible to implement all the attack detection techniques mentioned in the literature, the Sophos tool that identifies sub-millimeter variations was employed [23]. Infill lines spacing attacks starting with an initial maximum attack magnitude $A_{m_{max}}$ of 0.3 mm infill lines (IFLs) spacing were conducted. The attack magnitude was reduced over several iterations until Sophos was unable to reliably detect the deviations. The stealthiness and impacts of the attacks were evaluated by performing measurements, visual inspections, micro-CT scans and tensile strength tests.

  No measurement changes or visual deformations were observed on the attacked printed parts. The tensile tests showed consistent and significant reductions in part strength and all the attacked specimens broke at the point of attack. However, Sophos successfully detected the infill lines spacing attack with a 0.3 mm magnitude at every attacked layer. Figure 7 shows the attacked specimens and the Sophos verdict about a specimen.

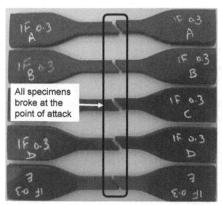

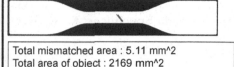

Sophos Detection Scheme Results
Attack Presentation and Report Excerpt

Total mismatched area : 5.11 mm^2
Total area of object : 2169 mm^2
Largest mismatched contiguous region
size : 2.58 mm^2
Percentage error out of total pixels : 0.2355%
SOPHOS VERDICT : FAIL

Figure 7. Phase 1 attacked specimens and detection results.

Table 2. Phase 1 measurements and tensile test results for the attacked specimens.

	Average of Five Specimens	Standard Deviation	Difference from Normal Specimen	Percentage Difference
Width (mm)	6.576	0.013	0.022	0.33%
Thickness (mm)	4.090	0.025	0.026	0.64%
Peak Load (N)	606.540	42.371	−311.180	−51.30%
Peak Stress (MPa)	22.540	1.705	−12.140	−53.86%
Strain at Break (mm/mm)	0.027	0.007	−0.002	−5.88%
Young's Modulus (MPa)	1,246.074	136.373	−418.399	−33.58%

Table 2 presents the measurements and tensile test results for the attacked specimens, including a greater than 50% reduction in tensile strength. The micro-CT scan identified an anomaly (slit) in the affected layers. Because the 0.3 mm attack magnitude could not evade detection by Sophos, the attack does not satisfy the third success criterion and is, therefore, considered unsuccessful. However, reducing the attack magnitude to 0.2 mm enabled the attack to evade detection by Sophos. Therefore, the maximum attack magnitude $A_{m_{max}}$ was set to 0.2 mm in the experiments.

- **Phase 2:** The second phase executed attacks with magnitudes ranging from 0.2 mm to 0.015 mm in five steps. Although all the attacks evaded detection, the stealthiness of the attacks increased as their magnitudes reduced. Six types of specimens were printed for each of the two infill spacing attacks, making a total of 60 specimens. Dimensional verification and visual inspection were

Table 3. Phase 2 infill structure manipulation attack details.

Attack Magnitude	Infill Lines Specimens	Spacing Attacks Attack Location	Infill Vertices Specimens	Spacing Attacks Attack Location
No Attack	5	NA	5	NA
0.015 mm	5	6 IFLs from center	5	Center
0.025 mm	5	6 IFLs from center	5	Center
0.050 mm	5	Center	5	4 IFLs from center
0.100 mm	5	Center	5	4 IFLs from center
0.200 mm	5	4 IFLs from center	5	4 IFLs from center

performed on all the specimens, but micro-CT scans were performed only for certain specimens. Table 3 presents the attack details.

5.   Evaluation Results

This section analyzes the experimental data in accordance with the five attack success criteria. All the attacks were launched after Stage 3 of the additive manufacturing process chain and none of the attacks created perceptible deformations to the final printed objects. Thus, the first and fourth attack success criteria were met by all the attacks. The footprints produced by the attacks in Phase 2 were small enough to bypass detection schemes, although the micro-CT scans revealed the presence of structural anomalies. As the attack magnitude was reduced, the impact on the mechanical strength was also reduced, providing a minimum effective deviation threshold value for successful attacks. The experimental data was examined in terms of stealthiness and effectiveness (mechanical strength impacts).

5.1   Stealthiness Performance

Attacks on the additive manufacturing process chain can be detected by a broad spectrum of methods, including visual inspection, dimension measurement, microscopic surface analysis, computer tomography, toolpath verification and others. Bulk parameters, such as the total printing time, total filament consumption and outer part dimensions, provide cumulative insights into the additive manufacturing process. Localized parameters, such as toolpath deviations, G-code command execution time and printing speed profile, offer instantaneous estimates of an additive manufacturing process.

Bulk Parameters. Table 4 presents the stealthiness performance of the attacks assessed using bulk parameters. The bulk parameters include the printing time per attacked layer, printed part dimensions and visual deformations. The maximum printing time variation for the attacks was within 14 ms of the mean value of the non-attacked specimens. The dimensions of the printed parts did not change – the maximum mean difference along each dimension of the attacked specimens was less than 0.036 mm, well within the printer accuracy tolerance. The dimension measurements of the attacked specimens fell on both sides of the mean values of the non-attacked specimens and were all within one standard deviation. No deformations were observed on the objects during naked eye inspections and optical microscope examinations.

Localized Parameters. Since some of the attack detection schemes monitor additive manufacturing processes continuously in the time and space domains to identify anomalies, it was important to assess the attack footprints with respect to localized or instantaneous process deviations.

Table 5 shows the performance with respect to the localized parameters. The parameters include the attack launch time delay, toolpath distance and direction (angle) deviations, and execution time and filament consumption per G-code command. The attack launch time delay is a key stealthiness performance parameter because a large delay in receiving an acknowledgement to a printing request could raise an attack alert. Detailed manual analyses of micro-CT scans were also conducted to identify the attacked areas in the printed parts.

The results reveal that the attack launch time delays were under 150 ms for all the attacks. The largest toolpath deviation per G-code command was just 0.2 mm for the infill lines spacing attacks. For the infill vertices spacing attacks, the largest toolpath deviation was 0.2 mm for the connecting segment and 0.143 mm for the corresponding infill line. The angular deviation was zero for the infill lines spacing attacks and a maximum of 1.21° for the infill vertices spacing attacks. The maximum G-code execution time deviation was less than 5 ms. For the selected sampling rate of 200 samples/s, the time deviation resolution of the measurements was 5 ms. Although the attacks had different time variations within the 5 ms interval, the values were below existing attack detection thresholds. None of the attacks produced deviations in the filament consumption per command values.

The microstructures of the 3D printed specimens were evaluated using x-ray micro-computed tomography. A Skyscan 1173 machine was employed to recreate the 3D models. Micro-CT analysis was performed

Table 4. Stealthiness performance (bulk parameters).

Attack Magnitude	Printing Time per Attacked Layer (s)		Printed Part Dimensions (Complete Printed Parts)				Visual Deformations
	Ave.	Std. Dev.	Width (mm) Ave.	Std. Dev.	Thickness (mm) Ave.	Std. Dev.	
Infill Lines Spacing Attacks							
No Attack	61.513	0.000	6.582	0	4.088	0	None
0.015 mm	61.518	0.005	6.580	0.002	4.080	0.008	None
0.025 mm	61.520	0.008	6.568	0.014	4.090	−0.002	None
0.050 mm	61.523	0.010	6.568	0.014	4.083	0.005	None
0.100 mm	61.521	0.009	6.570	0.012	4.090	−0.002	None
0.200 mm	61.526	0.014	6.563	0.019	4.085	−0.003	None
Infill Vertices Spacing Attacks							
No Attack	61.513	0.000	6.582	0	4.088	0	None
0.015 mm	61.525	0.012	6.562	0.020	4.086	0.002	None
0.025 mm	61.525	0.012	6.592	−0.010	4.084	0.004	None
0.050 mm	61.521	0.009	6.546	0.036	4.064	0.024	None
0.100 mm	61.523	0.010	6.580	0.002	4.078	0.010	None
0.200 mm	61.520	0.008	6.584	−0.002	4.086	0.002	None

Table 5. Stealthiness performance (localized parameters).

Attack Magnitude	Launch Time Delay (s)	Toolpath Deviation per IF Line Distance (mm)	Cmd Max Angle (deg)	Max Time Deviation per Command (ms)	Filament Deviation per Command (mm)	Micro-CT Scan Manual Detection
Infill Lines Spacing Attacks						
0.015 mm	0.15	0.015	0	< 5	None	Negative
0.025 mm	0.15	0.025	0	< 5	None	Negative
0.050 mm	0.15	0.050	0	< 5	None	Positive
0.100 mm	0.15	0.100	0	< 5	None	Positive
0.200 mm	0.15	0.200	0	< 5	None	Positive
Infill Vertices Spacing Attacks						
0.015 mm	0.15	0.011	0.093	< 5	None	Negative
0.025 mm	0.15	0.018	0.154	< 5	None	Negative
0.050 mm	0.15	0.035	0.308	< 5	None	Negative
0.100 mm	0.15	0.071	0.612	< 5	None	Probable
0.200 mm	0.15	0.143	1.211	< 5	None	Positive

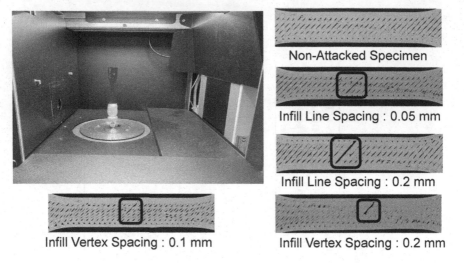

Figure 8.   Micro-CT scan results for selected attack specimens.

at 40 kV, 200 µA, 1,800 ms exposure, 0.5 rotational step and 20 µm pixel size. The scanned raw data was reconstructed using N-Recon software version 1.7.4.4. Volumes of interest were defined in the 3D reconstructed coronal image views and the images were subsequently analyzed using data viewing software.

Micro-CT analysis detected infill lines spacing attacks with magnitudes of 0.05 mm and higher. However, it did not reveal any signs of infill vertices attacks at a magnitude of 0.05 mm and only a hint of a probable attack at a magnitude of 0.1 mm. At the 0.2 mm magnitude, the infill vertices spacing attack was clearly visible in the micro-CT scan. As the attack magnitude increased, micro-CT analysis identified the attacked area with higher confidence. Figure 8 shows the micro-CT equipment employed along with selected attack specimens.

5.2   Mechanical Strength Impacts

Tensile tests were employed to evaluate the impacts of attacks on the mechanical strength of printed specimens. The tests were conducted using an MTS-Insight 30 tensile testing machine. Not all the attacks were consistently effective at reducing the tensile strength or load-extension profiles. All the attacked specimens broke at the point of attack for attack magnitudes above 0.05 mm. Figure 9 shows sample attacked specimens after the tensile tests.

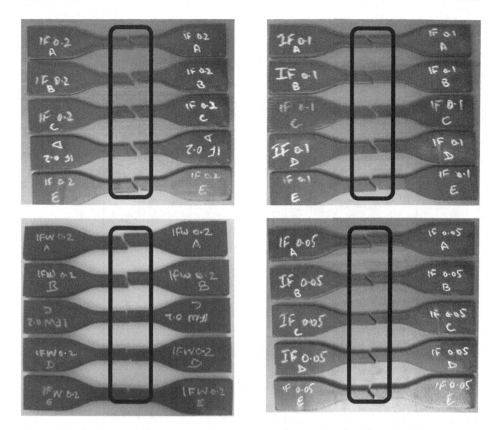

Figure 9. Broken tensile test specimens at attack magnitudes above 0.05 mm.

Tables 6 and 7 show the tensile test results for non-attacked specimens and specimens exposed to infill lines spacing and infill vertices spacing attacks, respectively. The maximum reductions in the peak loads of the attacked specimens were 33.55% for infill lines spacing attacks and 11.57% for infill vertices spacing attacks.

Figures 10 and 11 show the stress-strain curves for infill lines spacing and infill vertices spacing attack specimens, respectively. Most of the infill lines spacing and infill vertices spacing attack specimens broke earlier in the load versus time (stress-strain) curves compared with the non-attacked specimens. The Young's modulus decreased for the infill lines spacing attack specimens. However, the variations were not as consistent and pronounced for the infill vertices spacing attacks.

Table 6. Tensile test results for infill lines spacing attacks.

Attack Magnitude	Peak Load (N)			Peak Stress (MPa)			Young's Modulus (MPa)		
	Ave.	Std. Dev.	Diff.	Ave.	Std. Dev.	Diff.	Ave.	Std. Dev.	Diff.
No Attack	936.94	98.78	0.00%	35.45	3.45	0.00%	1,730.22	167.85	0.00%
0.015 mm	938.09	40.86	0.12%	35.49	1.65	0.12%	1,708.45	75.17	-1.26%
0.025 mm	919.89	35.68	-1.82%	34.37	1.55	-3.06%	1,756.83	42.87	1.54%
0.050 mm	694.75	18.01	-25.85%	25.93	0.68	-26.87%	1,267.56	106.84	-26.74%
0.100 mm	622.57	34.66	-33.55%	23.17	1.39	-34.65%	1,498.47	147.25	-13.39%
0.200 mm	624.32	32.57	-33.37%	23.28	1.29	-34.34%	1,323.59	107.12	-23.50%

Table 7. Tensile test results for infill vertices spacing attacks.

Attack Magnitude	Peak Load (N)			Peak Stress (MPa)			Young's Modulus (MPa)		
	Ave.	Std. Dev.	Diff.	Ave.	Std. Dev.	Diff.	Ave.	Std. Dev.	Diff.
No Attack	1,036.11	42.45	0.00%	38.60	1.54	0.00%	1,771.42	129.52	0.00%
0.015 mm	1,054.48	30.37	1.77%	39.33	1.35	1.88%	1,850.70	168.24	4.48%
0.025 mm	1,041.91	59.80	0.56%	38.70	2.41	0.26%	2,052.87	116.97	15.89%
0.050 mm	1,008.68	39.05	-2.65%	37.92	1.28	-1.76%	1,901.28	44.97	7.33%
0.100 mm	953.37	44.39	-7.99%	35.52	1.76	-7.98%	1,726.44	163.31	-2.54%
0.200 mm	916.28	36.46	-11.57%	34.06	1.19	-11.76%	1,796.00	261.93	1.39%

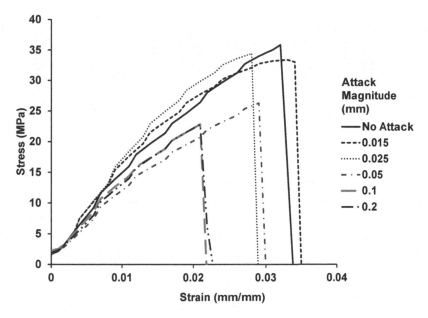

Figure 10. Stress-strain curves for infill lines spacing attack specimens.

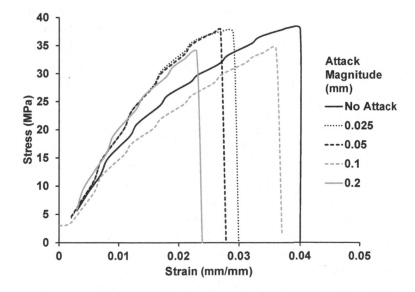

Figure 11. Stress-strain curves for infill vertices spacing attack specimens.

6. Analysis and Discussion

Conducting an attack on a design file is a pure cyber-domain modification that can be detected by conventional cyber security methods such

Figure 12.   Detection of a 0.2 mm magnitude infill vertices spacing attack.

as file hashing and operating system audit logs. However, the infill modification attacks launched between the control computer (excluded) and printer (included) bypassed cyber-domain operating systems and standard security tools. A recent study by McCormack et al. [13] revealed that 12 out of 13 surveyed printing environments did not use encrypted communications between the control computers and printers, exposing them to man-in-the-middle attacks.

The low-magnitude infill modification attacks created footprints smaller than the reported resolutions of attack detection schemes that monitor printing processes. The attack magnitudes were also within the order of fused filament fabrication printer accuracy, which would pose challenges to threshold-based detection methodologies. Although, all the infill modification attacks were concealed in the final printed objects, the effects of higher magnitude attacks were somewhat visible during printing. As shown in Figure 12, a continuous imaging technique can detect the anomalies induced by attacks. Specifically, the image taken after pausing the process when printing an attacked layer revealed the inverse-wedge-shaped cavity. Very low magnitude attacks – up to 0.025 mm for infill lines spacing attacks and up to 0.05 mm for infill vertices spacing attacks – had limited impacts on the physical strength of attacked parts.

For identical attack magnitudes, infill lines spacing attacks were more damaging than infill vertices spacing attacks. Figures 13 and 14 show the strength vs. attack magnitude plots for infill lines spacing and infill vertices spacing attacks, respectively. The two types of attacks exhibit different strength-reduction profiles based on the attack magnitudes. Infill lines spacing attacks have a peak impact zone between attack magnitudes of 0.35 mm and 0.1 mm. In contrast, the peak impact zone for infill vertices spacing attacks is between 0.05 mm to about 0.1 mm and has a gradual reduction thereafter. In an infill lines spacing attack, the separation of two adjacent infill lines is increased from end to end. In an infill vertices spacing attack, the separation between two adjacent infill lines is increased only at one end, resulting in increased bonding and overlap between the two lines as they progress from the point of attack

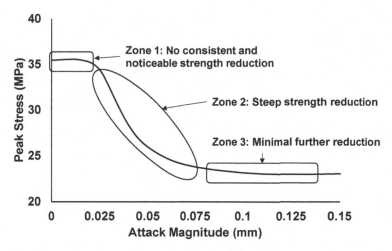

Figure 13. Strength vs. attack magnitude plot for infill lines spacing attacks.

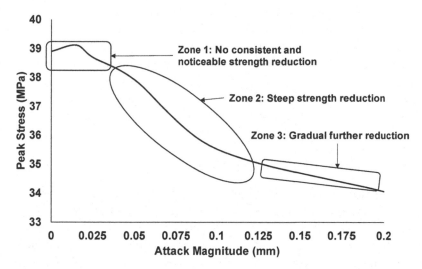

Figure 14. Strength vs. attack magnitude plot for infill vertices spacing attacks.

towards the other vertex. This explains the lower strength reduction and shifted impact zone in the case of infill vertices spacing attacks.

The micro-CT analysis revealed that non-attacked printed objects with 100% infill density also contained tiny gaps between the infill structure and surrounding walls, and within the infill structure. Optimizing the printing parameters could remove these gaps and also increase the overlaps of infill lines. In such cases, the attacks would be more interesting and more pronounced. Although the optimization of printing parameters is not considered in this work, it is important to note that this finding impacts the choices made by a malicious actor. Interestingly, when micro-CT analysis confirmed the presence and location of an attack, destructive tests also showed reductions in part strength. For a 20-layer object with around 200 cross-sectional images, a micro-CT scan can capture the structural weakness due to a single attacked layer, making it an important tool for detecting microstructural attacks.

A limitation of the infill lines spacing and infill vertices spacing attacks is that they effectively target only solid-filled objects. In a variation of these attacks, the infill connecting segments may be made to drift slightly in order to weaken the bonds between the infill and walls. These weaknesses would reduce the compression strength and shear strength of a part with a minimal attack footprint.

In a low-magnitude sabotage attack, a malicious actor would target one or more physical properties of the printed object. Since most detection techniques compare actual process behavior against true or expected behavior, a low-magnitude attack can evade detection. Instead of mapping the space, thermal and timing profiles of a printer to the expected state, a different detection approach is to estimate the potential targeted physical properties. For example, a small variation at one location may be safely ignored, but it could induce high residual stress at another location. A detection scheme that considers this phenomenon can be more effective at distinguishing between damaging low-magnitude attacks and benign printing errors.

7.   Attack Countermeasures

This section discusses two categories of countermeasures for the low-magnitude infill spacing attacks described in this chapter.

The first category of countermeasures focuses on attack avoidance. Controlling physical access to a printing facility reduces the probability that malicious code would make its way through physical printer ports. Implementing authenticated and encrypted communications between the control computer and printer would significantly hinder man-in-the-middle attacks. Techniques such as DHCP snooping and ARP inspection would help prevent ARP table manipulation. Researchers have proposed several techniques for countering network layer attacks in cyber-physical environments [1, 11]. Reverse engineering application layer transactions in network traffic is also helpful in detecting anomalies [19]. To avoid attacks from compromised printer firmware, the firmware should be verified periodically. Instead of inline firmware acquisition, researchers have proposed out-of-band methods for securely acquiring memory content for embedded systems [20] and extracting running firmware [21, 26].

The second category of countermeasures focuses on attack detection. If a malicious actor succeeds in launching an attack, micro-CT scans can identify a potent structural abnormality caused by the attack. However, the time and manual effort required to perform micro-CT scans and analyze them do not render this a scalable solution. Although some implementation challenges exist, in-printing scanning with an automated anomaly detection function is more feasible in a busy printing facility. While micro-CT scans are far more detailed, high-speed in-printing optical imaging may still be useful for detecting structural non-conformity.

8.   Conclusions

This research has developed two low-magnitude infill structure manipulation attacks on objects created by fused filament fabrication printers. An infill lines spacing attack reduces the overlap between two consecutive infill lines at the target location whereas an infill vertices spacing attack creates an inverse-wedge-shaped low-density zone at the target location. The magnitudes of the infill structure manipulation attacks are maintained below the horizon of existing detection methods as well as within the resolution and trueness tolerances of fused filament fabrication printers. The attacks were executed on solid-filled ASTM D638 type-IV tensile bars by manipulating G-code commands corresponding to attack locations in selected internal layers. Tensile tests conducted on the attacked specimens demonstrate that attacks with magnitudes of just 0.05 mm can reduce the mechanical strength of printed parts. Such attack magnitudes are within the confusion zones of detection schemes that only monitor printer actions against printing commands. However, if an attack detection scheme can obtain adequate physical property estimates for current process states, attacked specimens can be distinguished from random printing errors. Another scheme for detecting low-magnitude attacks is to incorporate automated real-time analysis of micro-CT scans to identify structural abnormalities in attacked parts.

Acknowledgement

This research was partially supported by the Virginia Commonwealth Cyber Initiative.

References

[1] H. Adjei, T. Shunhua, G. Agordzo, Y. Li, G. Peprah and E. Gyarteng, SSL stripping technique (DHCP snooping and ARP spoofing inspection), *Proceedings of the Twenty-Third International Conference on Advanced Communication Technology*, pp. 187–193, 2021.

[2] A. Ayub, H. Yoo and I. Ahmed, Empirical study of PLC authentication protocols in industrial control systems, *Proceedings of the IEEE Security and Privacy Workshops*, pp. 383–397, 2021.

[3] S. Belikovetsky, Y. Solewicz, M. Yampolskiy, J. Toh and Y. Elovici, Digital audio signature for 3D printing integrity, *IEEE Transactions on Information Forensics and Security*, vol. 14(5), pp. 1127–1141, 2018.

[4] S. Belikovetsky, M. Yampolskiy, J. Toh, J. Gatlin and Y. Elovici, dr0wned – Cyber-physical attack with additive manufacturing, presented at the *Eleventh USENIX Workshop on Offensive Technologies*, 2017.

[5] S. Chhetri, A. Canedo and M. Al Faruque, KCAD: Kinetic cyber-attack detection method for cyber-physical additive manufacturing systems, *Proceedings of the IEEE/ACM International Conference on Computer-Aided Design*, 2016.

[6] U. Dilberoglu, B. Gharehpapagh, U. Yaman and M. Dolen, The role of additive manufacturing in the era of Industry 4.0, *Procedia Manufacturing*, vol. 11, pp. 545–554, 2017.

[7] Y. Gao, B. Li, W. Wang, W. Xu, C. Zhou and Z. Jin, Watching and safeguarding your 3D printer: Online process monitoring against cyber-physical attacks, *Proceedings of the ACM on Interactive, Mobile, Wearable and Ubiquitous Technologies*, vol. 2(3), article no. 108, 2018.

[8] G. Goh, S. Sing and W. Yeong, A review of machine learning in 3D printing: Applications, potential and challenges, *Artificial Intelligence Review*, vol. 54(1), pp. 63–94, 2021.

[9] J. Hanssen, Fortus 360mc/400mc Accuracy Study, Stratasys, Eden Prairie, Minnesota (nanopdf.com/download/fortus-360mc-400mc-accuracy-study_pdf), 2013.

[10] S. Kim, Y. Shin, H. Jung, C. Hwang, H. Baik and J. Cha, Precision and trueness of dental models manufactured with different 3-dimensional printing techniques, *American Journal of Orthodontics and Dentofacial Orthopedics*, vol. 153(1), pp. 144–153, 2018.

[11] Y. Li, L. Zhu, H. Wang, F. Yu and S. Liu, A cross-layer defense scheme for edge-intelligence-enabled CBTC systems against MitM attacks, *IEEE Transactions on Intelligent Transportation Systems*, vol. 22(4), pp. 2286–2298, 2021.

[12] Markets and Markets, 3D Printing Market by Offering (Printer, Material, Software, Service), Process (Binder Jetting, Direct Energy Deposition, Material Extrusion, Material Jetting, Powder Bed Fusion), Application, Vertical, Technology and Geography (2021–2026), Market Research Report SE 2936, Northbrook, Illinois (`www.marketsandmarkets.com/Market-Reports/3d-printing-market-1276.html`), 2021.

[13] M. McCormack, S. Chandrasekaran, G. Liu, T. Yu, S. DeVincent Wolf and V. Sekar, Security analysis of networked 3D printers, *Proceedings of the IEEE Security and Privacy Workshops*, pp. 118–125, 2020.

[14] S. Moore, W. Glisson and M. Yampolskiy, Implications of malicious 3D printer firmware, *Proceedings of the Fiftieth Hawaii International Conference on System Sciences*, 2017.

[15] B. Msallem, N. Sharma, S. Cao, F. Halbeisen, H. Zeilhofer and F. Thieringer, Evaluation of the dimensional accuracy of 3D-printed anatomical mandibular models using FFF, SLA, SLS, MJ and BJ printing technology, *Journal of Clinical Medicine*, vol. 9(3), article no. 817, 2020.

[16] H. Pearce, K. Yanamandra, N. Gupta and R. Karri, FLAW3D: A Trojan-Based Cyber Attack on the Physical Outcomes of Additive Manufacturing, arXiv: 2104.09562 (`arxiv.org/abs/2104.09562`), 2021.

[17] S. Qasim, A. Ayub, J. Johnson and I. Ahmed, Attacking the IEC-61131 logic engine in programmable logic controllers, in *Critical Infrastrucure Protection XV*, J. Staggs and S. Shenoi (Eds.), Springer, Cham, Switzerland, pp. 73–95, 2022.

[18] S. Qasim, J. Lopez and I. Ahmed, Automated reconstruction of control logic for programmable logic controller forensics, in *Information Security*, Z. Lin, C. Papamanthou and M. Polychronakis (Eds.), Springer, Cham, Switzerland, pp. 402–422, 2019.

[19] S. Qasim, J. Smith and I. Ahmed, Control logic forensics framework using a built-in decompiler of engineering software in industrial control systems, *Forensic Science International: Digital Investigation*, vol. 33(S), article no. 301013, 2020.

[20] M. Rais, R. Awad, J. Lopez and I. Ahmed, JTAG-based PLC memory acquisition framework for industrial control systems, *Forensic Science International: Digital Investigation*, vol. 37(S), article no. 301196, 2021.

[21] M. Rais, R. Awad, J. Lopez and I. Ahmed, Memory forensic analysis of a programmable logic controller in industrial control systems, *Forensic Science International: Digital Investigation*, vol. 40(S), article no. 301339, 2022.

[22] M. Rais, Y. Li and I. Ahmed, Dynamic thermal and localized filament kinetic attacks on a fused-filament-fabrication-based 3D printing process, *Additive Manufacturing*, vol. 46, article no. 102200, 2021.

[23] M. Rais, Y. Li and I. Ahmed, Spatiotemporal G-code modeling for secure FDM-based 3D printing, *Proceedings of the Twelfth ACM/IEEE International Conference on Cyber-Physical Systems*, pp. 177–186, 2021.

[24] D. Roach, C. Roberts, J. Wong, X. Kuang, J. Kovitz, Q. Zhang, T. Spence and H. Qi, Surface modification of fused filament fabrication (FFF) 3D printed substrates by inkjet printing polyimide for printed electronics, *Additive Manufacturing*, vol. 36, article no. 101544, 2020.

[25] L. Sturm, C. Williams, J. Camelio, J. White and R. Parker, Cyber-physical vulnerabilities in additive manufacturing systems, *Proceedings of the International Solid Freeform Fabrication Symposium*, pp. 951–963, 2014.

[26] S. Vasile, D. Oswald and T. Chothia, Breaking all the things – A systematic survey of firmware extraction techniques for IoT devices, in *Smart Card Research and Advanced Applications*, B. Bilgin and J. Fischer (Eds.), Springer, Cham, Switzerland, pp. 171–185, 2019.

[27] M. Wu, H. Zhou, L. Lin, B. Silva, Z. Song, J. Cheung and Y. Moon, Detecting attacks in cyber manufacturing systems: Additive manufacturing example, *Proceedings of the International Conference on Mechanical, Aeronautical and Automotive Engineering*, 2017.

[28] C. Xiao, Security attack on 3D printing, presented at the *xFocus Security Conference* (`www.claudxiao.net/Attack3DPrinting-Claud-en.pdf`), 2013.

[29] S. Zeltmann, N. Gupta, N. Tsoutsos, M. Maniatakos, J. Rajendran and R. Karri, Manufacturing and security challenges in 3D printing, *Journal of the Minerals, Metals and Manufacturing Society*, vol. 68(7), pp. 1872–1881, 2016.

IV

INFRASTRUCTURE DEVICE SECURITY

Chapter 9

LEVERAGING CONFIDENTIAL COMPUTING TO ENABLE SECURE INFORMATION SHARING

Samuel Chadwick, Scott Graham, James Dean and Matthew Dallmeyer

Abstract   The emergence of the RISC-V Instruction Set Architecture incentivizes the critical infrastructure protection community to consider the use of emerging open-source security mechanisms to facilitate secure information sharing. An exemplar is Keystone, a Confidential Computing Consortium project, that offers an accessible open-source framework for building trustworthy secure hardware enclaves based on the RISC-V Instruction Set Architecture.

This chapter describes an attempt at extending Keystone to the Hi-Five Unmatched development platform and proposes enclave application development to effectively and affordably supplement deployed supervisory control and data acquisition devices with secure information sharing capabilities. Since the implementation of confidential computing principles axiomatically degrades real-time performance, the performance of supervisory control and data acquisition devices must be characterized to ensure that the devices enhanced with trusted execution environments meet operational requirements while supporting critical infrastructure operations with secure information sharing capabilities.

Keywords: Secure information sharing, confidential computing, Keystone enclave

1.   Introduction

The persistent desire to securely share information drives the continuing evolution of mechanisms for enforcing information security that keeps pace with and responds to technological advancements. This research proposes the application of confidential computing principles to implement secure information sharing across a wide range of supervisory control and data acquisition used in critical infrastructure assets. Expressly, the research establishes the plausibility of building trusted

© IFIP International Federation for Information Processing 2022
Published by Springer Nature Switzerland AG 2022
J. Staggs and S. Shenoi (Eds.): Critical Infrastructure Protection XVI, IFIP AICT 666, pp. 235–252, 2022.
https://doi.org/10.1007/978-3-031-20137-0_9

execution environments using commodity RISC-V personal computer hardware to supplement deployed SCADA devices with improved communication and operational security at reasonable, or even low, cost.

Keystone, a project of the Confidential Computing Consortium [2], is the first open-source framework for building customized trustworthy secure hardware enclaves based on the RISC-V Instruction Set Architecture [3]. The ability to port Keystone security monitor to new RISC-V hardware enables Linux distribution support and enclave application development. The use cases would exploit trusted execution environment primitives by equipping deployed SCADA devices with secure, isolated enclaves that appropriately segregate control mechanisms from data collection and sharing protocols.

This chapter describes an attempt at extending Keystone to the Hi-Five Unmatched development platform, the only commercially-available RISC-V development platform that satisfies the criteria of form factor standardization, commodity personal computer hardware compatibility, Linux operating system support and enhanced system-on-chip monitoring capabilities. This would support enclave application development to provide deployed supervisory control and data acquisition devices with secure information sharing capabilities effectively and affordably.

Since the implementation of confidential computing principles axiomatically degrades real-time performance, it is imperative to determine the performance overhead imposed by trusted execution environment implementations. This chapter describes synthetic benchmarking conducted for the HiFive Unmatched system that executed 20 compatible benchmarks from the Stress-NG benchmarking suite. At a price point of $655, the HiFive Unmatched underperformed competitively-priced x86-64 commodity workstations. Nevertheless, as a Linux-capable, native RISC-V development platform that supports open-source trusted execution environment implementations, HiFive Unmatched sets the bar in the emerging RISC-V market.

2.   Background and Related Work

This section discusses confidential computing and provides details about the RISC-V Instruction Set Architecture and Keystone enclave used in this work. Also, it discusses related work in the area.

2.1   Confidential Computing

The Confidential Computing Consortium is a Linux Foundation initiative that seeks to secure data in use through open collaboration. Commonly-deployed encryption techniques enforce confidentiality, in-

Figure 1. Security mechanisms applied to classical computing data states.

tegrity and availability for data at rest in storage media and for data in transit across public and private networks. However, these techniques are limited by the conventional computing infrastructure. To adequately secure data in use, specifically during execution, computations must be performed in a hardware-based trusted execution environment (TEE) [2] or properly manipulate encrypted data without decrypting it first, as in the case of homomorphic computing, which is outside the scope of this work. Figure 1 illustrates the security mechanisms that apply to classical computing data states.

While a formal definition of a trusted execution environment has not been arbitrated, the Confidential Computing Consortium defines it as an environment that provides a level of assurance of data confidentiality, data integrity and code integrity [1, 5]. This work uses the definition of trusted execution environment interchangeably with variations commonly used by industry.

Many trusted execution environment implementations are proprietary, including the Intel Software Guard Extensions, ARM TrustZone and AMD Secure Encrypted Virtualization. Vendor-specific trusted execution environment implementations have two distinct disadvantages. The first is that intellectual property ties new features and bug fixes directly to vendors. The second is that different threat models have been ascribed to specific instruction set architectures. For example, Intel Software Guard Extensions focus on server and desktop application isolation, ARM TrustZone addresses vendor-provisioned mobile application isolation and AMD Secure Encrypted Virtualization focuses on virtual machine isolation.

In the context of critical infrastructure protection, the disadvantages of vendor-specific trusted execution environment implementations must be weighed against emerging open-source alternatives. A Keystone enclave provides an extensible open-source trusted execution environment implementation for the RISC-V Instruction Set Architecture. This research asserts that Keystone and supporting hardware offer an avenue for extending deployed SCADA devices with secure information sharing functionality while avoiding the deficiencies found in proprietary trusted execution environments.

2.2   RISC-V Instruction Set Architecture

The free and open RISC-V Instruction Set Architecture is intended to enable a new era of processor innovation through open standard collaboration [8]. The RISC-V Instruction Set Architecture is organized into an unprivileged instruction set architecture and a privileged instruction set architecture.

Unprivileged Instruction Set Architecture. The unprivileged instruction set architecture comprises the base integer architecture I and additional optional instruction set extensions. The set of standard extensions currently includes multiply/divide operations M, atomic operations A, single- and double-precision floating-point arithmetic operations F and D, respectively, and compressed 16-bit instructions C [8]. The M, A, F and D identifiers are standard extensions that are collectively referred to as G. This research employs 64-bit integer registers with all the standard and compressed extensions. Thus, the instruction set architecture descriptor used in the research is designated as RV64GC, where RV denotes RISC-V, 64 denotes the register width, G denotes the base instruction set architecture with standard extensions and C denotes support for compressed operations.

Privileged Instruction Set Architecture. The privileged instruction set architecture covers all aspects of RISC-V systems beyond the unprivileged instruction set architecture [9]. The features pertinent to this research are physical memory protection and three of the four specified privilege levels, user mode (u-mode), supervisor mode (s-mode) and machine mode (m-mode). The fourth mode, hypervisor mode (h-mode), is not employed in this research. Keystone makes appropriate use of these features to enforce isolated execution in trusted execution environments. These memory-isolated environments are often referred to as "secure enclaves." Because Keystone is employed throughout the creation, execution and destruction lifecycles of the enclaves, they are named Keystone enclaves.

2.3   Keystone Enclave

As a current project of the Confidential Computing Consortium, Keystone offers an accessible open-source framework that provides academia and industry with resources for building trustworthy secure hardware

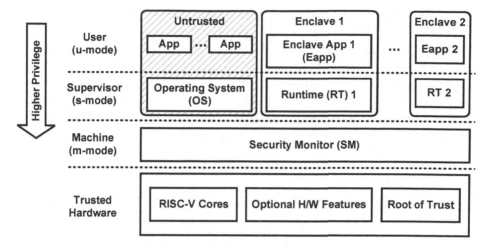

Figure 2. Compute system operations with Keystone [3].

enclaves. Keystone is the first open-source framework for building customized trusted execution environments [3]. It is designed for and built on the RISC-V privileged instruction set architecture. By leveraging trusted hardware, Keystone enables software-defined, hardware-enforced, isolated, memory-mapped execution beneath an untrusted operating system [3]. Currently, Keystone supports three standard trusted execution environment primitives, secure boot, secure randomness source and remote attestation [3]. Figure 2 shows the distinct Keystone components as they operate within the RISC-V Instruction Set Architecture privilege levels alongside an untrusted operating system.

Keystone Security Monitor. The Keystone security monitor, a core component of a Keystone enclave, relies entirely on the RISC-V standards for operation. This intentional design constraint promotes portability across RISC-V hardware platforms. This design principle is leveraged to port Keystone security monitor to SiFive's HiFive Unmatched development platform, a multi-core, native RISC-V, application-specific integrated circuit (ASIC) computer. The Keystone security monitor achieves memory isolation for enclave runtimes and enclave applications by utilizing physical memory protection hardware built directly into each hardware application core [6]. The development platform features and specifications are provided later in this chapter. This research focuses on extending the Keystone security monitor to the HiFive Unmatched platform.

Keystone Root-of-Trust. Although the root-of-trust is typically depicted as a hardware component, Keystone also supports tamperproof software implementations. The research described in this chapter leverages this feature by employing modified first- and second-stage bootloaders to simulate the secure boot primitive. The research does not attempt to verify, validate or otherwise assess the cryptographic techniques employed by Keystone to realize trusted execution environment primitives. Instead, it supports Keystone's portability claims by extending its use to previously-unsupported hardware.

Keystone Enclave Applications. With successful modifications to hardware-specific (m-mode) software (firmware), a HiFive Unmatched development platform equipped with Keystone could be configured to execute Keystone enclave applications. Application development would support any statically-compiled RISC-V binary as long as all the supporting libraries are included in Eyrie, the Keystone runtime environment. Specifically, secure enclave applications are envisioned that enable secure information sharing between SCADA devices across internal and external networks. Thus, sensitive SCADA operations could be appropriately decoupled from data collection tasks to shield critical infrastructure assets from untrusted actors and devices.

2.4   Related Work

Porting the Keystone security monitor to new hardware platforms is just an initial step on the path towards critical infrastructure device integration. To fully implement Keystone on contemporary RISC-V hardware, additional Linux kernel modifications will have to be baselined to support Linux distributions. Moreover, to encourage confidential computing practices, Linux distributions will likely need to provide flexible tools to facilitate the porting of Keystone enclaves to more devices. To justify the incorporation of trusted execution environments in deployed SCADA devices, strict performance requirements must also be maintained. The addition of secure enclave computing unavoidably impacts system performance. Therefore, characterization studies must be conducted to effectively evaluate trusted execution environment performance.

Tullos [7] has conducted performance characterizations of embedded RISC-V devices configured with Keystone implemented on field-programmable gate array (FPGA) hardware. As the RISC-V landscape matures, future performance characterizations must include ASIC hardware implementations with representative system evaluations for workstation-focused systems such as the HiFive Unmatched platform.

3.   Experimental Configuration

The HiFive Unmatched development platform was selected due to its form factor standardization, commodity personal computer hardware compatibility, Linux operating system support and enhanced system-on-chip monitoring capabilities. HiFive Unmatched is currently the only commercially-available RISC-V development platform that satisfies the four desired criteria. In particular, it has the Mini-ITX form factor used by many AMD/Intel x86-64 systems. This standard personal computer form factor enables straightforward hardware extensions via PCIe and NVMe interconnects. Moreover, HiFive Unmatched is advertised as the world's fastest native RISC-V development platform, which sets it apart from other platforms by positioning it as an independent, Linux-capable, RISC-V workstation as opposed to an embedded system.

Importantly, the HiFive Unmatched is manufactured by SiFive, an industry leader in the RISC-V technology space. The SiFive leadership includes three co-founders of the RISC-V Instruction Set Architecture. Their involvement inspires confidence that SiFive will continue to support its products as the RISC-V specifications evolve.

Development Board Specifications and Features.   The HiFive Unmatched platform is powered by a SiFive Freedom U740 system-on-chip, a multi-core, 64-bit dual-issue, superscalar RISC-V processor whose advertised performance is comparable to the ARM Cortex-A55. The Freedom U740 system-on-chip contains four Linux-capable U74 application cores that support RV64GC operations and includes a fifth S7 monitor core that supports RV64IMAC operations. All the cores have dual-issue in-order execution pipelines that support peak sustained execution rates of two instructions per cycle and maintain a fully-coherent 2 MB shared L2 cache. Additional board specifications include 16 GB DDR4 SDRAM, 32 MB Quad-SPI flash memory, MicroSD card expansion, Gigabit Ethernet, four USB 3.2 Gen 1 Type A ports, a microUSB JTAG console port, x16 PCIe Gen 3 expansion slot, M.2 M-Key slot for NVMe 2280 SSD modules and M.2 E-Key slot for Wi-Fi and Bluetooth modules.

Figure 3 shows the test platform configuration. The test configuration utilized the M.2 M-Key NVMe slot to leverage a 500 GB Samsung 980 PRO PCIe 4.0 SSD. Additional components were not strictly required in the research, but they enhanced performance by providing faster memory technology for testing in environments without wired Internet access. The PCIe expansion slot was not used in the research; the graphical capabilities are left for future investigations.

Figure 3. HiFive Unmatched Mini-ITX development platform configuration.

Boot Flow Modifications. The SiFive FU740-C000 manual details the boot process of the HiFive Unmatched platform [6]. Figure 4 shows the unmodified (standard) boot flow for the test HiFive Unmatched platform configuration. The boot operations proceed in the following order of precedence: power on reset (PoR) (0), zeroth stage bootloader (ZSBL) stored in on-chip mask read-only memory (1), first stage bootloader (U-Boot secondary program loader (SPL)) (2), secondary bootloader (SBL) containing the U-Boot image tree blob (ITB), device tree blob (DTB) and OpenSBI (3), EXTLINUX (4) and Linux kernel (5). In order to per-

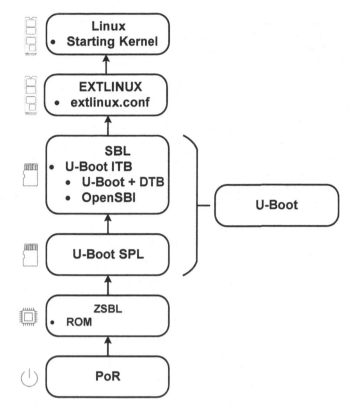

Figure 4. Standard boot flow.

form baseline performance characterizations of the HiFive Unmatched system without the Keystone security monitor, a preinstalled Ubuntu server image was employed. The bootable image was flashed to a microSD card, which was used to boot the HiFive Unmatched platform successfully with Ubuntu.

In order to implement the Keystone security monitor on the Hi-Five Unmatched platform, OpenSBI was used as the interface between the bootloader and platform-specific firmware executing in m-mode. OpenSBI is an independent RISC-V Foundation project that provides an open-source reference implementation of a platform-independent static library to implement a serial binary interface [4]. OpenSBI also provides platform-specific support, including Freedom-U740-specific libraries required to modify the HiFive Unmatched development kit.

To construct the modified bootable microSD card image, the Keystone security monitor was built in OpenSBI using an out-of-tree plat-

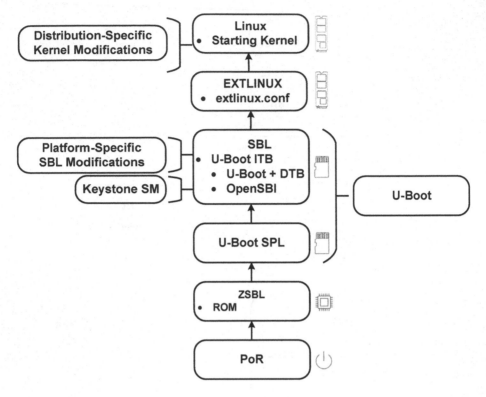

Figure 5. Modified boot flow with the Keystone security monitor.

form build configuration supported by the OpenSBI toolchain. All the development work was conducted on an external x86-64 Kubuntu Linux workstation, although the Linux distribution used for development was arbitrary. Because Keystone does not officially support the HiFive Unmatched development platform, several Keystone components required the manual application of patch files provided by SiFive; the modifications included platform-specific changes to OpenSBI, U-Boot and the Linux kernel. Figure 5 highlights the boot flow modifications required to implement the Keystone security monitor on the test platform.

After the Keystone security monitor was configured in the OpenSBI platform build, the fw_dynamic.bin platform configuration binary used by U-Boot was created. Next, the u-boot.itb image tree blob and u-boot-spl.bin binary files required to build the U-Boot bootloader were created. These two files, which comprise the U-Boot bootloader, were flashed to the microSD card image.

Kernel Modifications. After successfully building the modified bootloader with the Keystone security monitor, the next step was to build the Linux kernel in order to apply the Keystone security monitor and SiFive patches and cross-compile the build for the RV64GC target. The Keystone kernel build process produced the `Image.gz` Linux kernel for the OpenEmbedded distribution; this is an artifact of hardware support for the discontinued HiFive Unleashed development platform. The build used a `makefile` script to generate the `hifive-unmatched-a00.dtb` device tree blob containing the specific board hardware descriptor. The Linux kernel for the Ubuntu distribution was employed for unmodified device performance characterization. These Linux kernels, created by Canonical, are provided in pre-built server images for HiFive Unmatched. Performance characterizations of the modified Linux kernel for the OpenEmbedded distribution are available for future testing efforts.

Root Filesystem and Distribution. Since the research did not require building a root filesystem from scratch, pre-built server images provided by Canonical were employed. The research used various daily builds of Ubuntu distributions, including 21.04 (Hirsute Hippo), 21.10 (Impish Indri) and 22.04 LTS (Jammy Jellyfish).

Bootable Image. The development concluded by creating a bootable image file and flashing it to a microSD card. The modified Ubuntu image was built by flashing the desired pre-built server image to the microSD card to create a default bootable medium. The `dd` tool was then used to overwrite the image tree blob and device tree blob boot partitions with the modified U-Boot bootloader and the included Keystone security monitor.

The OpenEmbedded distribution was built by creating an empty image file, which was partitioned with the appropriate disk identifiers. The bootloader partitions were written, following which the root filesystem was created and mounted. Next, the root filesystem was unpacked and the Linux kernel packages were copied to the root filesystem. Following this, the Linux kernel was installed, the image tree blob and device tree blob were copied to the correct partitions and the `extlinux.conf` file for EXTLINUX was created. Finally, the newly-created image file was flashed to the microSD card and the root partition was resized.

Upon inserting the microSD card into the HiFive Unmatched platform and booting the device, the serial console shown in Figure 6 was displayed. The `U_BOOT_ROOT` environment variable was then set to use

```
U-Boot SPL 2022.01-rc2-00024-g3144ba23bf (Nov 18 2021 - 00:26:34 -0500)
Trying to boot from MMC1


U-Boot 2022.01-rc2-00024-g3144ba23bf (Nov 18 2021 - 00:26:34 -0500)

CPU:   rv64imafdc
Model: SiFive HiFive Unmatched A00
DRAM:  16 GiB
MMC:   spi@10050000:mmc@0: 0
Loading Environment from nowhere... OK
EEPROM: SiFive PCB EEPROM format v1
Product ID: 0002 (HiFive Unmatched)
PCB revision: 3
BOM revision: B
BOM variant: 0
Serial number: SF105SZ212000130
Ethernet MAC address: 70:b3:d5:92:f6:40
CRC: 23109999
In:    serial@10010000
Out:   serial@10010000
Err:   serial@10010000
Model: SiFive HiFive Unmatched A00
Net:   eth0: ethernet@10090000
Hit any key to stop autoboot:  0
PCIE-0: Link up (Gen1-x8, Bus0)

Device 0: unknown device
starting USB...
Bus xhci_pci: Register 4000840 NbrPorts 4
Starting the controller
USB XHCI 1.00
scanning bus xhci_pci for devices... 3 USB Device(s) found
       scanning usb for storage devices... 0 Storage Device(s) found

Device 0: unknown device
switch to partitions #0, OK
mmc0 is current device
scanning bus for devices...
```

Figure 6.   U-Boot serial console output.

the preconfigured NVMe drive with the Ubuntu operating system. Figure 7 shows the Ubuntu terminal after system login.

4.   Proposed Development

The ability to port Keystone security monitor to new RISC-V hardware enables Linux distribution support and enclave application develop-

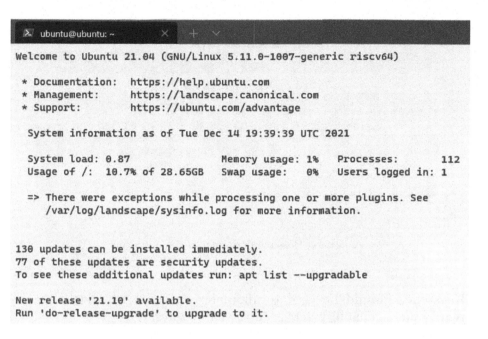

```
ubuntu@ubuntu: ~                    ×    +  ⌄

Welcome to Ubuntu 21.04 (GNU/Linux 5.11.0-1007-generic riscv64)

 * Documentation:   https://help.ubuntu.com
 * Management:      https://landscape.canonical.com
 * Support:         https://ubuntu.com/advantage

 System information as of Tue Dec 14 19:39:39 UTC 2021

 System load: 0.87              Memory usage: 1%   Processes:       112
 Usage of /: 10.7% of 28.65GB   Swap usage:   0%   Users logged in: 1

 => There were exceptions while processing one or more plugins. See
    /var/log/landscape/sysinfo.log for more information.


130 updates can be installed immediately.
77 of these updates are security updates.
To see these additional updates run: apt list --upgradable

New release '21.10' available.
Run 'do-release-upgrade' to upgrade to it.
```

Figure 7. Ubuntu 21.04 (Hirsute Hippo) terminal.

ment, especially for critical infrastructure protection applications. These use cases would exploit trusted execution environment primitives by equipping SCADA devices with secure, isolated enclaves that segregate control mechanisms from data collection and sharing protocols.

Supplementing deployed SCADA devices with open-source trusted execution environments would be a practical secure information sharing solution that avoids the large-scale replacement of proprietary implementations. By leveraging Keystone, the RISC-V Instruction Set Architecture and a growing list of compatible commodity personal computer hardware components, legacy SCADA devices can be made extensible by augmenting information sharing responsibilities with emerging native RISC-V devices. Promising scenarios would employ capable RISC-V platforms such as HiFive Unmatched to empower decision makers by operating as intermediary confidential computing networks that securely obtain relevant data from SCADA devices, process the data in secure enclaves and transmit encrypted information for secure collection.

As the RISC-V landscape evolves, it is anticipated that confidential computing practices will be adopted widely. In particular, low-cost native RISC-V platforms with commodity personal computing hardware augmented with open-source trusted execution environments – such as

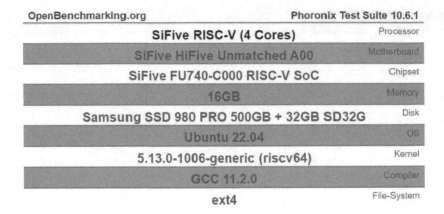

OpenBenchmarking.org	Phoronix Test Suite 10.6.1	
SiFive RISC-V (4 Cores)	Processor	
SiFive HiFive Unmatched A00	Motherboard	
SiFive FU740-C000 RISC-V SoC	Chipset	
16GB	Memory	
Samsung SSD 980 PRO 500GB + 32GB SD32G	Disk	
Ubuntu 22.04	OS	
5.13.0-1006-generic (riscv64)	Kernel	
GCC 11.2.0	Compiler	
ext4	File-System	

Figure 8. Baseline performance configuration.

Keystone – would be used to affordably facilitate confidentiality, integrity and availability across all the data states.

5. Experimental Results and Analysis

Before endowing deployed SCADA devices with trusted execution environments and secure information sharing features, it is important to obtain a thorough understanding of system performance requirements. Specifically, it is imperative to determine the performance overhead imposed by a trusted execution environment implementation. In the case of Keystone and the HiFive Unmatched system, synthetic benchmarking can yield insights for evaluating system performance.

Baseline benchmarking was conducted to evaluate SiFive's performance claims about the HiFive Unmatched system. Figure 8 specifies the baseline performance configuration.

The Phoronix Test Suite, an open-source, comprehensive testing and benchmarking tool, was employed to run 20 compatible benchmarks from the Stress-NG benchmarking suite (version 1.4.0). Table 1 describes the benchmarks used in the baseline performance evaluation.

Table 2 shows the baseline performance for the benchmark stress tests in bogo-ops/s, where higher scores indicate better performance. Each benchmark test was trialed three times or trialed repeatedly until a standard deviation of less than one was obtained.

The results establish an upper threshold for typical HiFive Unmatched system performance. With the inclusion of trusted execution environments via Keystone, subsequent benchmark scores are expected to decline. At a price point of $655, the HiFive Unmatched dramatically

Table 1. Selected benchmarks from Stress-NG 1.4.0.

Benchmark	Description
MMAP	Memory map
NUMA	Non-uniform memory access
MEMFD	Anonymous kernel memory management
Atomic	Atomic operations
Crypto	MD5, SHA-256, SHA-512, scrypt, NT, yescrypt
malloc	Memory allocation
Forking	CPU forking
io_uring	Asynchronous input/output
SENDFILE	Read/write
CPU Cache	Cache thrashing
CPU Stress	Integer, multiplication, floating point, double precision
Semaphores	Shared resources
Matrix Math	Two- and three-dimensional matrix operations
Vector Math	128-bit vector operations
Memory Copying	memcpy method operation
Socket Activity	IPv4, TCP congestion control
Context Switching	Memory clobbering
glibc C String Functions	glibc C string functions
glibc Qsort Functions	glibc Qsort functions
System V Message Passing	System V message passing

underperformed competitively-priced x86_64 PC workstations. For the CPU stress test, the average time required to complete the benchmark for all publicly-listed systems at openbenchmarking.org was only 1.8 minutes whereas it exceeded 16 minutes for HiFive Unmatched. Compared against a quad-core ARM Cortex-A55 system-on-chip, the HiFive Unmatched system recorded an average of 208.20 bogo-ops/s that outperformed the average 156.28 bogo-ops/s recorded by the ARM Cortex-A55 system-on-chip; this meets the advertised HiFive Unmatched performance claims for CPU operations. Substantially cheaper ARM alternatives, such as the Raspberry Pi 400, which does not fully support ARM TrustZone and hardware-enforced trusted execution environments, handily doubled the CPU stress performance achieved by HiFive Unmatched. Nevertheless, as a Linux-capable, native RISC-V development platform that supports open-source trusted execution environment implementations, HiFive Unmatched sets the bar in the emerging RISC-V market.

Table 2.   Baseline performance.

Benchmark	Score (bogo-ops/s)
MMAP	1.55
NUMA	12.66
MEMFD	7.49
Atomic	55,245.91
Crypto	91.75
malloc	1,572,568.61
Forking	3,163.54
io_uring	2,440.31
SENDFILE	7,338.63
CPU Cache	16.52
CPU Stress	208.20
Semaphores	119,929.34
Matrix Math	617.00
Vector Math	440.98
Memory Copying	34.48
Socket Activity	177.85
Context Switching	144,396.00
glibc C String Functions	18,746.18
glibc Qsort Functions	5.68
System V Message Passing	375,212.46

6.   Conclusions

Supplementing deployed SCADA devices with open-source trusted execution environments is a practical secure information sharing solution that eliminates the large-scale replacement of proprietary implementations. By leveraging Keystone, the RISC-V Instruction Set Architecture and a growing list of compatible commodity personal computer hardware components, legacy SCADA devices can be made extensible by augmenting information sharing responsibilities with emerging native RISC-V devices. Promising scenarios would employ capable RISC-V platforms such as HiFive Unmatched to empower decision makers by operating as intermediary confidential computing networks that securely obtain relevant data from operational SCADA devices, process the data in secure enclaves and transmit encrypted information for secure collection.

The RISC-V Instruction Set Architecture is new and does not yet rival the market share of AMD/Intel x86_64 and ARM instruction set architectures. It was only in December 2021 that the RISC-V privileged instruction set was officially ratified for a few compatible hardware-optimized applications and devices. Nevertheless, the experimentation with RISC-V hardware and software demonstrates a renewed interest in instruction set architecture development. Clearly, proprietary computer architectures with undisclosed security mechanisms will not suffice for future data security applications. Therefore, it is important to advocate open technologies that offer innovative solutions for securing data in use. As the RISC-V landscape evolves, it is anticipated that confidential computing practices will be adopted widely. In particular, low-cost native RISC-V platforms with commodity personal computing hardware augmented with open-source trusted execution environments like Keystone would be attractive because they can affordably facilitate information confidentiality, integrity and availability across all the data states.

Future research will focus on Keystone enclave application development for comparative benchmarking as well as on Keystone enclave development.

The views expressed in this chapter are those of the authors, and do not reflect the official policy or position of the U.S. Air Force, U.S. Space Force, U.S. Department of Defense or U.S. Government. This document has been approved for public release; distribution unlimited (Case #88ABW-2021-1035).

References

[1] Confidential Computing Consortium, A Technical Analysis of Confidential Computing (v1.1), The Linux Foundation, San Francisco, California (`confidentialcomputing.io/wp-content/uploads/sites/85/2021/03/CCC-Tech-Analysis-Confidential-Computing-V1.pdf`), 2021.

[2] Confidential Computing Consortium, What is the Confidential Computing Consortium? The Linux Foundation, San Francisco, California (`confidentialcomputing.io`), 2022.

[3] D. Lee, D. Kohlbrenner, S. Shinde, K. Asanovic and D. Song, Keystone: An open framework for architecting trusted execution environments, *Proceedings of the Fifteenth European Conference on Computer Systems*, article no. 38, 2020.

[4] opensbi Contributors, RISC-C Open Source Supervisor Binary Interface, GitHub (`github.com/riscv-software-src/opensbi`), 2021.

[5] M. Sabt, M. Achemlal and A. Bouabdallah, Trusted execution environment: What it is and what it is not, *Proceedings of the IEEE International Conference on Trust, Security and Privacy in Computing and Communications*, pp. 57–64, 2015.

[6] SiFive, SiFive FU740-C000 Manual (v1p6), San Mateo, California (`sifive.cdn.prismic.io/sifive/1a82e600-1f93-4f41-b2d8-8 6ed8b16acba_fu740-c000-manual-v1p6.pdf`), 2021.

[7] J. Tullos, Characterizing Security Monitor and Embedded System Performance Across Distinct RISC-V IP-Cores, M.S. Thesis, Department of Electrical and Computer Engineering, Air Force Institute of Technology, Wright-Patterson Air Force Base, Ohio, 2021.

[8] A. Waterman and K. Asanovic (Eds.), The RISC-V Instruction Set Manual Volume I: Unprivileged ISA, Document Version 20191213, RISC-V Foundation, Department of Electrical Engineering and Computer Sciences, University of California Berkeley, Berkeley, California, 2019.

[9] A. Waterman, K. Asanovic and J. Hauser (Eds.), The RISC-V Instruction Set Manual Volume II: Privileged Architecture, Document Version 20211203, RISC-V Foundation, Department of Electrical Engineering and Computer Sciences, University of California Berkeley, Berkeley, California, 2021.

Chapter 10

EVALUATING THE USE OF BOOT IMAGE ENCRYPTION ON THE TALOS II ARCHITECTURE

Calvin Muramoto, Scott Graham and Stephen Dunlap

Abstract   Critical infrastructure devices operating in unprotected end-node environments are vulnerable to malicious actors who conduct hardware attacks such as reverse engineering and side-channel analysis. Boot data is rarely encrypted and typically travels across an accessible bus, enabling the data to be easily intercepted during system start-up. Encrypting the firmware would make reverse engineering extremely difficult for malicious actors and competitors. It would improve the effectiveness of tamper detection methods and deter zero-day vulnerability discovery. Increasing boot security could be a fundamental part of decreasing attack surfaces across the critical infrastructure sectors.

This chapter describes a Talos II architecture implementation that encrypts a section of the boot image and decrypts it during initial program load. During power-on, the encrypted image travels across the Low Pin Count bus into a POWER9 module Level 3 cache and is decrypted in the processor. Boot image encryption is implemented using ciphers of different strengths. An analysis of their efficiency is conducted to determine the optimal algorithm.

Keywords: Secure boot, hardware security, firmware encryption, Talos II system

1.   Introduction

As the demand for critical infrastructure grows, the systems required to maintain consistent and reliable operation increase in complexity. This opens up attack surfaces for malicious actors and competitors because the systems are often placed in unprotected environments [3].

Electric power grids use phasor measurement units as sensors to measure voltages and current phasors in the power system. The data collected by each unit is sent to a phasor data collector that may contain

J. Staggs and S. Shenoi (Eds.): Critical Infrastructure Protection XVI, IFIP AICT 666, pp. 253–273, 2022.
https://doi.org/10.1007/978-3-031-20137-0_10

sensitive information. The phasor measurement units must be able to measure the power grid at system end-points, resulting in their placement in relatively-insecure environments [10]. Manipulating the data collected at these locations can cause problems, including power grid disruptions. Similar problems are also encountered in water management systems where water pressure sensors and data collection systems are placed at unprotected end-nodes. Protecting the boot process of devices such as phasor measurement units and water pressure sensors would require the addition of a layer of hardware security to industrial control systems.

Encrypting boot firmware can help prevent unauthorized entities from discovering vulnerabilities in infrastructure computer systems. Tamper detection checks should be executed during system boot sequences to detect intruders before the operating systems execute. However, an unauthorized entity who can observe the boot instructions executed during start-up may be able to avoid tamper detection to manipulate and gain access to the system. Boot firmware is rarely encrypted under the assumption that an unauthorized entity does not have physical access to the hardware. As the complexity and frequency of cyber attacks increase, implementing hardware security becomes a priority. Absent hardware security, adequate security can be achieved by encrypting boot firmware when it is stored in memory and decrypting it in the processor when the instructions are to be executed.

Secure boot has become a standard for improving hardware security – it works by ensuring that only signed firmware is executed on a system. Although it can prevent unauthorized firmware from executing on a system processor, it cannot protect against physical hardware attacks such as chip substitution and bus traffic recording [5]. This research attempts to prevent these types of attacks via boot image encryption. Efforts have also been made to encrypt bootloader firmware that is decrypted during start-up in microcontroller platforms [8]. However, microcontroller bootloaders are very simple and typically employ only two start-up stages. This research focuses on expanding the encrypted microcontroller boot firmware concept to a workstation incorporating a powerful POWER9 module.

Although this research implements boot image encryption on the Talos II architecture, it could also be applied to any system that utilizes a multi-stage bootloader. For example, Intel and Advanced Micro Devices include bootloaders in BIOS chips that function similarly to the Talos II firmware. Expanding the implementation of boot firmware encryption from Talos II to other architectures should be straightforward as long as their initial program load flows are similar.

Previous research has detailed the notional process of encrypting a section of a boot image along with the requirements to decrypt it during initial program load [9]. The research employed a simple XOR cipher to demonstrate a minimalist encryption approach as a proof of concept. This research extends the previous work by incorporating real encryption algorithms that require more processing and storage for boot images and processors. SPECK [1] was selected as the lightweight cipher and Advanced Encryption Standard (AES) as the heavyweight cipher to compare runtime performance. An analysis of the three boot firmware encryption methods is presented to provide a comprehensive comparison.

2. Background

This section describes the Talos II architecture, processor-based NOR (PNOR) image structure, initial program load, ciphers employed and secure key management.

2.1 Talos II Architecture

A Talos II workstation was selected as the platform to develop and test the boot encryption implementation. Designed by Raptor Computing Systems, Talos II is the world's first owner-controllable workstation-class motherboard that is compatible with open-source firmware. The Talos II architecture supports dual POWER9 central processing units (CPUs) and trusted boot, and is compatible with OpenBMC. The OpenBMC compatibility enables Talos II to boot from custom firmware, which is essential to this research.

A baseboard management controller (BMC) is a specialized service processor residing on a motherboard that monitors all physical and network data. It is primarily used in server environments to control and monitor multiple systems to ensure normal operation. The baseboard management controller provides an avenue for a system administrator to communicate with the server, specifically to enable remote power cycling and rebooting. Having full control of the baseboard management controller firmware enables the instructions executed during initial program load to be modified [4].

Initial program load refers to the operations that the Talos II system executes from power-on until the operating system starts up. During the initial start-up, several interfaces are used to transfer data between the PNOR flash memory, random access memory and POWER9 module. The Intelligent Platform Management Interface and Fast Serial Interface are two important communications interfaces that are used later during the initial program load. Since this research focuses on the early portions of the boot flow, Intelligent Platform Management Interface and Fast Serial Interface are not covered. However, the Low Pin Count (LPC) and Pervasive Interconnect Bus (PIB) interfaces are essential to the boot process. The Low Pin Count bus connects the POWER9 module to external systems such as the baseboard management controller. If trusted boot is enabled, the Low Pin Count bus is used to communicate with the trusted platform module [5]. The Pervasive Interconnect bus located inside each POWER9 CPU provides read/write access to the various attached components such as the on-chip controller (OCC), self boot engine (SBE) and serial electrically-erasable programmable read-only memory (SEEPROM). All data transfers within the processor travel across the Pervasive Interconnect Bus and are considered to be secure because they are contained within the POWER9 module.

The Pervasive Interconnect Bus connects several components essential to starting the boot flow, including the self boot engine and SEEP-ROM [4]. The self boot engine is an auxiliary microprocessor in a POWER9 CPU that initializes the first core to begin the initial program load process. It executes from a Programmable PowerPC-lite Engine and its firmware is stored in the SEEPROM. Two redundant copies of the initial boot stage as a backup in the event that the system fails to reach the second stage bootloader. The SEEPROM also stores the root of trust hash when secure boot is enabled.

2.2   PNOR Image Structure

Memory space limitations imposed by the Level 3 (L3) cache of the POWER9 module are significant concerns in this research. The beginning portion of the initial program load executes code retrieved from the processor cache, which is limited to 10 MB. This could cause boot problems if the firmware requires more space than in available in the L3 cache. Another problem is posed by the limited amount of space for a PNOR image. Each partition in a PNOR image is allocated a specific amount of space so that the entire image can fit on the flash chip. Although a PNOR image has built-in buffer space for each partition, problems could occur if the compiled firmware overflows the space. This concern was addressed by ensuring that space requirement checks are performed during the firmware compilation stage.

The PNOR flash image contains all the instructions needed to boot the Talos II system. The image split into several sections defined in the table of contents (Figure 1). The table of contents contains essential data, including the partition name, physical offset and physical size. It is located at the beginning and end of the PNOR image and is queried

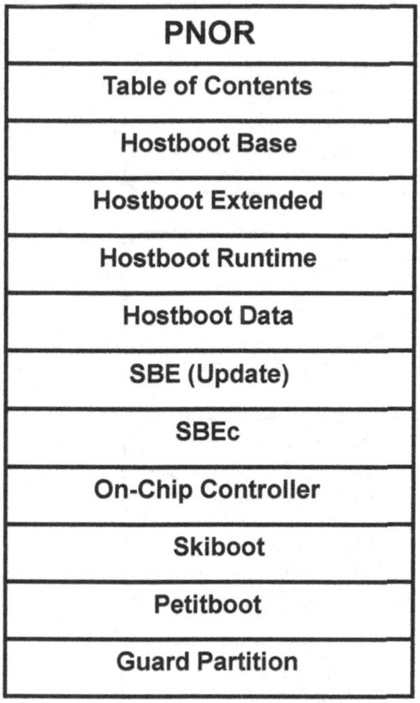

PNOR
Table of Contents
Hostboot Base
Hostboot Extended
Hostboot Runtime
Hostboot Data
SBE (Update)
SBEc
On-Chip Controller
Skiboot
Petitboot
Guard Partition

Figure 1. High-level PNOR flash image layout [4].

multiple times by the POWER9 module during the initial program load. The PNOR version specific to booting the Talos II system has a capacity of 4 MB and contains 31 sections ranging from 28 KB of memory configuration to 1.8 MB of boot kernel firmware data [11]. Each section of the PNOR image contains a firmware module that is used during initial program load. The most important sections relevant to this research are the Hostboot and Skiboot partitions.

2.3   Initial Program Load

Initial program load is a term used in OpenPOWER systems that refers to the operations executed by the systems from power-on until their operating systems start up. Figure 2 shows the five main sections of the initial program load, two self boot engine stages, Hostboot, Skiboot and Petitboot. This research focuses on the stages of the initial program load up to Skiboot because the earlier sectors are easier to alter and contain important details about start-up. The initial program load is started when the baseboard management controller sends the system start signal to the SEEPROM through the Pervasive Interconnect Bus, which initiates the first stage bootloader.

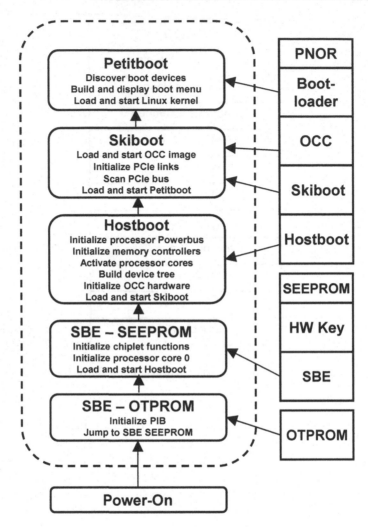

Figure 2.   Firmware boot flow [4].

First Stage Bootloader.   When altering the self boot engine firmware, it is important to consider that a first stage bootloader faces tight memory constraints. This is because the boot sector has to work with limited flash memory and a dedicated boot processor. Any additional code in the firmware must not exceed the flash memory space and can only contain instructions that the self boot engine can execute.

The first stage bootloader in a Talos II system has two sections. The first section is permanently written to one-time programmable read-only memory (OTPROM) using e-fuses on the POWER9 silicon. The self boot engine firmware in one-time programmable read-only memory contains the first instructions executed by the engine. These instructions load the second section, self boot engine firmware from the SEEPROM into the self boot engine core [4]. The self boot engine firmware from the SEEPROM is responsible for initializing the first CPU core on which the Hostboot bootloader (HBBL) executes. The firmware also loads the Hostboot bootloader into the L3 cache.

Hostboot. Hostboot is a major portion of the initial program load because it configures all the interfaces needed by Skiboot and the operating system kernel. It acts as a cache-contained operating system for self-hosting chip initialization in POWER9 platforms. Virtual memory and a virtual filesystem layer are used for demand paging to bring code out of the flash chip as necessary [6]. This is because the code and data required for Hostboot do not fit in the 10 MB of available L3 cache. Hostboot is split into three main sections comprising the Hostboot bootloader, Hostboot base (HBB) and Hostboot extended image (HBI). These sections function differently and have unique purposes related to the initial program load.

The Hostboot bootloader, which is stored in the SEEPROM, contains the first instructions executed by the CPU core initiated by the self boot engine. It cryptographically verifies Hostboot if secure boot is enabled [6] and loads the Hostboot base binary from the PNOR image into the POWER9 L3 cache and start execution on the first CPU core.

The Hostboot bootloader partition has a base initialization service task list that starts all the services needed by the Hostboot extended image. The Hostboot bootloader contains the hostboot kernel and services necessary to read and write to the PNOR image. It also initializes the DRAM, processor bus and memory buffers, acting as the foundation for the Hostboot extended image [12].

The Hostboot extended image stage is executed via an extended initialization service task list in the form of ISTEPs [6]. Each task in the service task list serves to move the initialization of the chip. The Hostboot extended image contains Hostboot sub-component code with the Hostboot extended table of contents. The last two ISTEPs in the Hostboot extended image are to load and start Skiboot. After the final ISTEPs are complete, Hostboot releases control of the CPU to Skiboot.

Skiboot. Skiboot is late-stage boot firmware that provides the Open-POWER abstraction layer runtime services used later by Skiroot. Skiboot provides wider platform initialization compared with Hostboot and initializes the Peripheral Component Interconnect Express (PCIe) controllers, device trees, real-time clock and several sensors [12]. The sensors are integral to the on-chip controller, which is also started in the Skiboot boot stage. When working with the compiled PNOR image, it is important to note that Skiboot is compressed to fit 16 MB of instructions into 1 MB of space. The decompression of the Skiboot image is executed at the end of the Hostboot stage in ISTEP 20.1. After Skiboot is complete, Skiroot and Petitboot are chain-loaded.

2.4   Ciphers

Two ciphers were selected to encrypt sections of the boot firmware, the lightweight SPECK [1] cipher and heavyweight AES cipher. In addition, the XOR cipher used in previous work [9] was employed due its simplicity as a proof of concept and possible use as a one-time pad. These three cyphers provide good benchmarks for comparing the encryption performance during the initial program load process.

XOR.   An XOR cipher is an encryption algorithm that essentially uses a one-time pad. The one-time pad is an encryption technique that cannot be cracked because it requires a key that is as long as the plaintext and the key can only be used once. In the implementation, the key was set to 16 bits because the key has to be as long as Skiboot to be deemed a one-time pad. This is because it would take up an additional 1 MB of valuable memory just to store the decryption key. Instead, an XOR operation was employed evaluate the capabilities of POWER9 during initial program load.

SPECK.   SPECK is a lightweight block cipher that is optimized for software implementation. It was developed by the National Security Agency alongside SIMON, which is also a lightweight block cipher, but is optimized for hardware implementation [1]. The SPECK and SIMON ciphers offer several options for block size and key size. The two cyphers are designed for use in Internet of Things devices due to minimal performance impacts while providing an added layer of security. SPECK was selected in this research because it is one of the best-performing lightweight ciphers and does not use lookup tables. This reduces the size of the compiled code because the tables do not have to be stored in the Hostboot source code.

Advanced Encryption Standard.   AES was selected because it is a widely-used block cipher and an encryption standard. Although AES supports a range of block sizes, this research opted to use AES-256 because it is the most secure configuration. The block size was a concern because the limited memory space poses potential problems during run-time.

2.5   Secure Key Management

Secure key management must be investigated when attempting to use an encrypted PNOR image. The principal challenge to using encrypted boot firmware is that a boot stage must exist in source code within the hardware capable of decrypting the subsequent firmware section. If the decryption boot stage is stored on the PNOR flash chip, the plaintext code must travel across the Low Pin Count bus from the PNOR to the POWER9 module, which is vulnerable to attackers. The data contained in the POWER9 module is secure because it is assumed that adversaries do not have the ability to sniff the interfaces in the processor. This implies that data and keys are secure if they are stored in the POWER9 module, provided no methods are available for retrieving them using external interfaces. Under these assumptions, three candidate methods can address secure key management.

The first candidate method requires a one-time pad storage chip to be incorporated in the POWER9 module, which is how manufacturers typically manage keys in computer systems. The one-time pad storage chip is connected to the Pervasive Interconnect Bus and transmits the decryption key to the POWER9 L3 cache when the firmware decryption code executes. Although this implementation enables secure key management for boot firmware encryption, it requires additional hardware to be added to the POWER9 module. Since this research focuses on firmware-only solutions for booting subsequent firmware that is encrypted, this method is not feasible.

The second candidate method requires a storage chip to be incorporated in the POWER9 module to utilize the existing SEEPROM memory space on the self boot engine. The SEEPROM memory stores the self boot engine firmware along with verification keys for the secure boot. During secure boot, the verification keys are compared against the hash of the boot image. The key management system can be used to securely transport keys to the image decryption firmware as needed. However, a significant constraint is that the SEEPROM memory space is extremely limited in size. In fact, the verification keys have to be stored as hashes because they require too much space as raw keys. This limitation imposed by the SEEPROM memory renders this method infeasible.

The third candidate method for secure key management can be implemented in firmware by utilizing the structure of the initial program load with boot firmware encryption. The Hostboot bootloader stage is integral to this method because it is stored and runs in the self boot engine. This means that it is isolated in the POWER9 module and secured from unauthorized entities. In the next stage, the Hostboot base image travels from the PNOR, across the Low Pin Count bus and into the POWER9 L3 cache. The Hostboot base section can be secured by implementing a decryption function in the bootloader and encrypting the base section.

This option also enables a user to update the decryption firmware via the PNOR image because the boot image contains a Hostboot bootloader section, meaning that the bootloader firmware can be altered and recompiled into a new PNOR image. After the first successful Talos II system boot with an altered Hostboot bootloader image, the self boot engine detects a firmware difference and proceeds to update the SEEP-ROM side 0 memory at the start of the initial program load. The system then reboots from side 0 and, if the system successfully reaches ISTEP 10.5, the SEEPROM side 1 is also updated. This is important because it enables a user to safely update the self boot engine and Hostboot bootloader firmware.

After the final bootloader firmware is updated on both sides of the SEEPROM, several steps are executed to ensure that the bootloader remains protected. The first step is to ensure that SEEPROM-side updates are disabled. This is required because the self boot engine automatically updates the Hostboot bootloader firmware if it detects a firmware change. The step enables Hostboot bootloader encryption or the removal of the Hostboot bootloader section in the PNOR image while still using the unencrypted Hostboot bootloader stored in the self boot engine, thereby protecting the key stored in the firmware.

To implement this method, a PNOR image containing the decryption code in the Hostboot bootloader with an unencrypted Hostboot base has to be flashed to the system. This is required because, on the initial boot, the self boot engine does not have the decryption code in the Hostboot bootloader to decrypt the Hostboot base. After reaching ISTEP 10.5, the system flashes the new Hostboot bootloader to the self boot engine. This endows the system with the ability to boot with an encrypted Hostboot base section in subsequent system start-ups.

To eliminate secure key management, the method is executed in reverse. A PNOR image with the Hostboot bootloader firmware without the decryption code and encrypted Hostboot base firmware must be compiled and flashed. After the SEEPROM side update, the self boot engine has the Hostboot bootloader firmware without the decryption code, meaning it can boot an unencrypted Hostboot base. SEEPROM side 2 is updated in ISTEP 10.5, enabling the system to boot with an unencrypted Hostboot base. A PNOR image without decryption firmware and an unencrypted Hostboot base is then flashed to enable normal PNOR updates.

3. Related Work

Before implementing the ciphers for boot firmware encryption, background research was conducted to understand previous work in this field. Three examples of successful boot firmware encryption were used as a foundation in this research. Although the implementations were intended for secure firmware updates, the structures for decrypting encrypted firmware updates are similar to the structure for boot firmware encryption.

3.1 Secure Firmware Updates Using AES

The process that encrypts sections of a bootloader before being loaded on a system is important in this research. A guide by Silicon Labs [13] introduced the idea of encrypting boot firmware and decrypting it in secure storage space. The goal was to provide a secure distribution system for firmware updates to microcontrollers. This is required because application-sensitive information stored in firmware updates could be accessed by malicious actors to develop zero-day vulnerabilities. The Silicon Labs implementation enables a microcontroller system to receive encrypted firmware and decrypt it after it is stored in its internal flash chip. This structure is applicable to boot firmware encryption in a Talos II system by applying the encryption and decryption portions to the initial program load flow.

Microchip Technology [8] has implemented an encrypted bootloader that functions similar to the AES-encrypted bootloader from Silicon Labs [13]. A vulnerable firmware update process for embedded systems deployed in the field would enable malicious actors to compromise system security and possibly gain complete control of the deployed systems. The purpose of the encrypted bootloader was to safely update ultra-low-power microprocessor firmware using encryption.

3.2 Image Encryption

Digi International [2] developed a method for encrypting signed firmware to obscure image data from unauthorized users. It was applied to U-Boot, an open-source bootloader used in embedded devices, and compiles the instructions necessary to boot embedded system operating system kernels, just like PNOR images in OpenPOWER systems. The processes for encrypting and decrypting firmware during the boot sequence are identical to those employed in this research. In fact, the implementation of encrypted U-boot firmware can be applied in specific stages to a PNOR image.

4.   Experimental Setup

Boot firmware encryption is applicable to a wide range of systems, each with varying performance impacts due to the specific implementations. An experiment was designed to analyze various types of encryption to assess the impacts on performance. It was important that the experiment would provide adequate data to understand the boot firmware encryption options and their security-performance trade-offs.

Consistent test runs are required to gather reliable boot time data because artifacts from previous boot images could affect the boot times of future trials. To address this problem, the PNOR images were randomized to minimize the influence of noise and other anomalies. During a new PNOR image boot sequence, an error correction check was executed that updated the boot image. This was done during the first few boots of a new image so that each PNOR image had to be booted multiple times until it stabilized. The final images were downloaded after they booted without requiring a reboot during the initial program load.

4.1   Microcontroller Setup

Figure 3 shows the microcontroller setup with the Talos II system for collecting experimental data in an efficient manner. Instead of booting from the Talos-supplied ASPEED 2400 baseboard management controller, an ARM Cortex microcontroller was employed to accomplish the task. A field-programmable gate array was also used as the Low Pin Count bridge between the microcontroller and POWER9 module. This setup enabled the modification of how PNOR images were transferred to the Talos II system using custom OpenBMC firmware. Note that the Serial Peripheral Interface (SPI), External Peripheral Interface (EPI), Flexible Service Interface (FSI) and Inter-Integrated Circuit (I2C) are specialized buses supported by the POWER9 module and used as part of the boot process.

The PNOR images were supplied to the Talos II system through Ethernet via a User Datagram Protocol (UDP) server. The system was set up such that the microcontroller serving as the baseboard management controller would wait for a PNOR image over Ethernet during a boot. A laptop with all the PNOR images would select one image to send via UDP, saving three minutes per boot over the File Transfer Protocol (FTP). The ability to boot without flashing the PNOR chip also saved

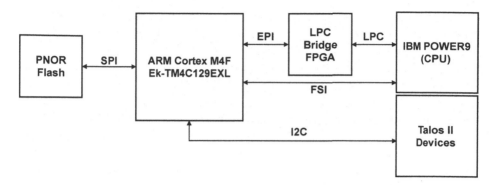

Figure 3. Microcontroller setup.

five minutes per boot. Although the PNOR images were supplied to the Talos II system over Ethernet, the performance of boot time decryption, which is dependent on the POWER9 module, was not impacted.

The microcontroller also executed a UDP logger that was set up to collect data from the boot process. All the boot and error logs were transferred to a laptop for straightforward data collection on repeated runs. The logger recorded the Low Pin Count data transfers, PNOR access messages, warning logs and POWER9 messages. The data of interest was stored in the POWER9 message log file.

5. Experimental Methodology

This section provides key experimental details, such as the experimental factors and data collection approach, to replicate the experiment and analyze the data. It also describes the application scenarios and assumptions.

5.1 Experimental Factors

Several factors must be considered when designing an experiment to capture boot image encryption performance. The effort focused on two experimental factors that directly answer the research questions. The main research objective was to understand the performance impacts of various types of encryption on boot firmware encryption. Therefore, the first experimental factor was the encryption type, which covered no encryption and the XOR, SPECK and AES ciphers. The second experimental factor was the size of the encrypted section, which is referred to as the encryption ratio. The Skiboot firmware was originally encrypted entirely, but was subsequently altered to measure the encryption overhead per byte. In addition to collecting metrics for 100%-encrypted Skiboot, two more boot images were created to measure the 50%-encrypted and 25%-encrypted boot performance.

A full factorial design was employed when narrowing down the experimental factors. Since the experiment involved two factors, with each factor having three to four levels, an analysis would require at least 16 trials. However, it was decided to run 100 trials per factor level, resulting in 1,000 total runs. This helped determine the main effects and interactions on the boot time metrics. The full factor analysis was expected to reveal the optimal encryption type and encryption ratio for security and boot performance.

5.2 Data Collection

Data collection was accomplished using a Python script that ran boot encryption trials of the 10 PNOR images. The list of encrypted PNOR images was randomized, resulting in 1,000 total trials with 100 trials per PNOR image. The Python script looped through the randomized list of PNOR images and coordinated the boot over Ethernet and the UDP logger. The code also checked for a string that prints at the end of the boot sequence that signaled a complete boot, and proceeded to restart the data collection script for the next trial. The data collection script helped provide consistent boot time metrics for the complete analysis of boot firmware encryption.

The POWER9 module log data extracted for each trial enabled the characterization of each boot image based on its boot time performance. A Python script was created to process the log file and save the boot time data to a comma-separated value (CSV) file. This data represents the PNOR image file through boot time metrics. The log file contains the start and end timestamps for Hostboot, loading Skiboot, transferring data to the buffer, decrypting and decompressing the encrypted sector. These timestamps were used to compute the times taken for the various stages employed in the security-performance analysis.

5.3 Application Scenarios

Boot firmware encryption can be applied to devices used in a number of critical infrastructure sectors, including electric power and water distribution. In the power grid, phasor measurement units record phasor data at various points in the grid [10]. The collected data is aggregated at phasor data collectors. The data collectors may be vulnerable to hardware attacks that enable malicious actors to gain access to systems in the infrastructure. Manipulating the sensor systems could cause power grid failures and damage power plant systems. The water distribution system faces similar threats due to pressure and water flow sensors positioned in vulnerable end-node environments. The data collectors for sensors used in electric power and water distribution could be protected via boot firmware encryption, preventing hardware attacks.

5.4 Assumptions

The experiment assumed that the system already supports secure key management. This assumption is necessary in a finalized boot image encryption system because the decryption key is currently stored in unencrypted code. In fact, it would defeat the purpose of boot image encryption because the attacks described above would enable malicious actors to observe details of initial program loads. The development of a secure key management solution is a topic for future research.

Another assumption is that a malicious actor is unable to remove the CPU from the motherboard and examine the L3 cache contents. Since the encrypted firmware is decrypted in the processor, the plaintext would be observable in the cache. It would be extremely difficult to pause the boot process at the right time and remove volatile memory from the POWER9 module, but it could be possible for a malicious actor with substantial hardware expertise.

6. Experimental Results and Analysis

After conducting the 1,000 boot data collection trials, a Python script was used to process the experimental data. The timestamps corresponding to the boot stages important to the research were extracted using regular expressions and inserted into data frames. The data was exported to a CSV file that was processed using RStudio.

6.1 Boot Image Encryption Performance Impact

The first research objective was to observe performance differences when implementing boot image encryption. Figure 4 shows the times required to complete the Hostboot phase of the initial program load. This was measured from ISTEP3 until the start of Skiboot, which helps place the performance impacts of the various boot image encryption methods in perspective. The median Hostboot time for AES was 25.51 s whereas the time for a normal boot was 24.69 s. This means that it took Hostboot 0.86 s longer to run by protecting the entire Skiboot firmware section with AES-256. The SPECK implementation had a median Hostboot execution time of 24.99 s whereas XOR had a median time of 25.06 s.

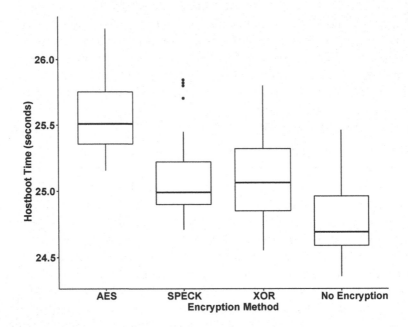

Figure 4.   Hostboot execution times.

Figure 5, which shows the times for loading Skiboot in ISTEP 20.1 for the encryption methods, clarifies the differences in performance overhead. The differences in Hostboot execution times are caused by the execution of the load Skiboot step, which contains the decryption function.

The median times were 1.0443 s for AES, 0.5923 s for SPECK, 0.5193 s for XOR and 0.2796 s for unencrypted firmware. The variation in Skiboot loading times are much smaller than the Hostboot execution times in Figure 5, which may be due to the earlier ISTEPs in Hostboot introducing variability.

One-way analysis of variance (ANOVA) tests were performed on the boot time data to see if significant differences exist between the encryption methods. The first ANOVA test on the Hostboot execution times revealed that the boot times had significant differences between the different factors. The second ANOVA test on the execution times for loading Skiboot also revealed significant differences between the encryption methods. These two tests answer the research question in that performance differences do exist between each encryption method and the unencrypted Skiboot implementation.

Figure 6 shows an interesting pattern related to image encryption implementations. In the case of a PNOR image without Skiboot en-

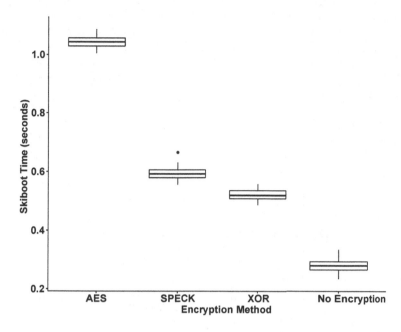

Figure 5. Skiboot loading times.

cryption, the decompression code must wait for the compressed Skiboot section to be transferred into working memory, which took 0.2654 s on average. In the case of the decryption code for the encrypted Skiboot firmware, memory was allocated for the decryption to execute before decompression. The average decompression time for encrypted firmware was 0.1281 s, 0.1373 s faster than the stock boot image. This helps offset the decryption time by frontloading the effort to transfer PNOR image data.

6.2   Comparison of Encryption Methods

The implementations of the three ciphers demonstrate the range of encryption overhead that a POWER9 module can handle during initial program load. Figure 7 shows the Skiboot decryption times for the encryption methods. The XOR cipher takes an average of 0.0103 s, which demonstrates its efficiency. The XOR implementation would be efficient in systems that require minimal boot firmware execution delays while providing several megabytes of free memory to store the one-time pad key. The SPECK cipher also ran efficiently with decryption requiring 0.0875 s. Although the SPECK cipher is not as secure as the AES cipher, it provides a layer of protection while decrypting Skiboot around six

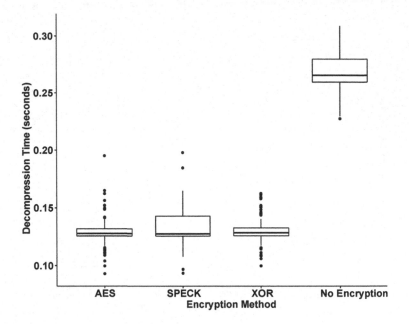

Figure 6.   Skiboot decompression times.

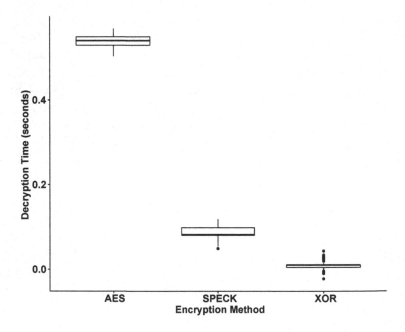

Figure 7.   Skiboot decryption times.

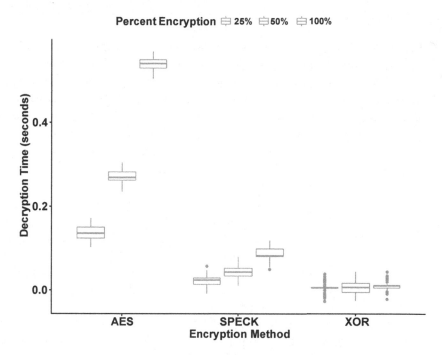

Figure 8. Skiboot decryption times for different encryption methods and ratios.

times faster. As expected, the AES cipher, which is the most secure encryption implementation, had the largest decryption time of 0.5397 s.

6.3   Encryption Ratio

The encryption ratio expresses the amount of Skiboot that is subject to encryption. Figure 8 shows the Skiboot decryption times for different encryption methods and ratios. The XOR cipher performance for each encryption ratio shows that the percentage of Skiboot that is encrypted does not affect the overall performance by a significant amount. The increase from 25% to 100% only increased the Skiboot decryption time by 0.00471 s. In contrast, the SPECK and AES implementations show linear increases in decryption time as the encryption ratio increases. AES takes longer to decrypt per byte compared with SPECK. Specifically, AES takes 0.00543 s for each percentage of Skiboot encrypted whereas SPECK takes 0.00089 seconds. A two-way ANOVA test revealed that significant differences exist for the encryption methods and encryption ratios.

7.   Conclusions

This research demonstrates that the Talos II system is capable of decrypting firmware during initial program loads. The firmware comprises the decryption function and is encrypted before being flashed on the system. The experimental results reveal that AES encryption of a portion of the boot image is cost-efficient when considering the increase in hardware security. SPECK encryption would work effectively in an implementation where one second of boot time is significant. Since a system only needs to boot once in most implementations, a 0.86 s delay when using AES-256 to the boot firmware is acceptable.

A useful avenue for future research is to expand boot image encryption to Intel and AMD systems. Since both systems use BIOS or Unified Extensible Firmware Interface bootloaders, their initial program structures should be similar. With access to detailed documentation and source code of the boot firmware, implementing the decryption code should be straightforward. Accomplishing this goal would enable boot image encryption to be applied to consumer workstations.

The views expressed in this chapter are those of the authors, and do not reflect the official policy or position of the U.S. Air Force, U.S. Department of Defense or U.S. Government. This document has been approved for public release; distribution unlimited (Case #88ABW-2021-1005).

References

[1] R. Beaulieu, D. Shors, J. Smith, S. Treatman-Clark, B. Weeks and L. Wingers, SIMON and SPECK: Block ciphers for the Internet of Things, presented at the *NIST Lightweight Cryptography Workshop*, 2015.

[2] Digi International, Image Encryption, Hopkins, Minnesota (`www.digi.com/resources/documentation/digidocs/embedded/dey/2.6/cc8x/yocto-trustfence_t_image-encryption.html`), 2019.

[3] A. Fournaris, Using Hardware Means to Secure Critical Infrastructure Devices, CIPSEC Project, University of Patras, Patras, Greece (`www.cipsec.eu/content/using-hardware-means-secure-critical-infrastructure-devices`), 2020.

[4] D. Heller and N. Sastry, OpenPower secure and trusted boot, Part 2: Protecting system firmware with OpenPOWER secure boot, *IBM Developer*, IBM, Armonk, New York (`developer.ibm.com/articles/protect-system-firmware-openpower`), 2019.

[5] IBM, Secure Initial Program Load (IPL) Process, Armonk, New York (`www.ibm.com/docs/en/power9/9009-42A?topic=9009-42A/p9ia9/p9ia9_secure_ipl_proc_concept.htm`), 2021.

[6] A. Jeffery, General Architecture of Hostboot (`amboar.github.io/notes/2018/08/19/hostboot-architecture.html`), 2018.

[7] A. Jeffery, Hacking Hostboot (`amboar.github.io/notes/2018/08/19/hacking-hostboot.html`), 2018.

[8] Microchip Technology, AVR231: AES Bootloader, Application Note AN2462, DS00002462A, Chandler, Arizona (`ww1.microchip.com/downloads/en/AppNotes/00002462A.pdf`), 2017.

[9] C. Muramoto, S. Dunlap and S. Graham, Improving hardware security on the Talos II architecture through boot image encryption, *Proceedings of the Seventeenth International Conference on Cyber Warfare and Security*, pp. 489–496, 2022.

[10] R. Nuqui and A. Phadke, Phasor measurement unit placement techniques for complete and incomplete observability, *IEEE Transactions on Power Delivery*, vol. 20(4), pp. 2381–2388, 2005.

[11] Raptor Computing Systems, Default PNOR Layout, Belvidere, Illinois (`git.raptorcs.com/git/pnor/tree/p9Layouts/defaultPnorLayout_64.xml`), 2019.

[12] Raptor Computing Systems, OpenPOWER Firmware, Belvidere, Illinois (`wiki.raptorcs.com/wiki/OpenPOWER_Firmware`), 2021.

[13] Silicon Labs, AN0060: Booloader with AES Encryption, Revision 1.05, Austin, Texas (`www.silabs.com/documents/public/application-notes/an0060-bootloader-with-aes-encryption.pdf`), 2016.

V

TELECOMMUNICATIONS SYSTEMS SECURITY

Chapter 11

SECURING INFINIBAND TRAFFIC WITH BLUEFIELD-2 DATA PROCESSING UNITS

Noah Diamond, Scott Graham and Gilbert Clark

Abstract   InfiniBand is employed in applications outside of high performance computing, including in critical infrastructure assets. This requires efforts at securing InfiniBand networks with encryption and packet inspection. Unfortunately, the performance benefits realized via the use of remote direct memory access by InfiniBand are at odds with many kernel-stack-based IP datagram encryption and network monitoring technologies. As a result, it is necessary to offload these tasks to other hardware. A promising candidate is the NVIDIA Mellanox Bluefield-2 data processing unit, which combines high-performance processors, network interfaces and flexible hardware accelerators, and runs a tailored version of Linux that provides several network management applications.

    This chapter characterizes the ability of Bluefield-2 data processing units to encrypt and monitor remote direct memory access traffic. The results demonstrate that the hardware accelerators of Bluefield-2 data processing units can support throughputs of nearly 86 Gbps when encrypting remote direct memory access over Converged Ethernet Version 2 traffic with Internet Protocol security (IPsec) encryption. Offloading IPsec encryption to the hardware accelerators on Bluefield-2 data processing units is a promising method for achieving confidentiality, integrity and authentication in InfiniBand networks with minimal interaction from host processors.

Keywords: InfiniBand, Bluefield-2 data processing unit, encryption

1.   Introduction

InfiniBand (IB) is an industry-leading high-bandwidth, low-latency interconnect for hyperscale data centers and high performance computing clusters. Previous research has identified that native InfiniBand

© IFIP International Federation for Information Processing 2022
Published by Springer Nature Switzerland AG 2022
J. Staggs and S. Shenoi (Eds.): Critical Infrastructure Protection XVI, IFIP AICT 666, pp. 277–300, 2022.
https://doi.org/10.1007/978-3-031-20137-0_11

plaintext key exchange is vulnerable to man-in-the-middle, denial-of-service and replay attacks [8]. Concerns about these vulnerabilities were minimal during the development of InfiniBand because data centers were assumed to be physically secure. However, interest in securing Infini-Band with encryption is growing because it is increasingly employed in applications outside high performance computing, including in critical infrastructure assets.

Encryption supports data confidentiality, integrity and authentication, but it is computationally expensive and increases the compute load on central processing units (CPUs). Data processing units (DPUs) are new programmable processors designed to assist CPUs in meeting the workloads of large data centers. Data processing units are systems on chips that incorporate a high-performance programmable processor, network interface card (NIC) and flexible hardware accelerators. They are designed to support data-center-specific tasks such as virtualization, networking, storage and security. Data processing units have the potential to join central processing units and graphics processing units as a pillar of networked computing.

Preliminary experiments have demonstrated that Bluefield-2 data processing units can encrypt Ethernet traffic by offloading Internet Protocol security (IPsec) operations to hardware accelerators. This chapter characterizes the ability of the hardware accelerators in Bluefield-2 data processing units to encrypt remote direct memory access (RDMA) traffic without placing a burden on their host CPUs.

2.   Background and Related Work

This section provides an overview of InfiniBand networks, convergent technologies and related security issues.

2.1   InfiniBand Network Overview

The switched-fabric InfiniBand architecture (IBA) provides reliability, availability, performance and scalability far beyond bus-oriented input/output architectures for server input/output and inter-server communications [16]. The InfiniBand architecture is maintained by the InfiniBand Trade Association (IBTA), which is led by a steering committee that includes Broadcom, HPE, IBM, Intel, Marvell Technology, Mellanox Technologies and Microsoft [6]. As of 2022, six of the top ten supercomputers in the world use InfiniBand as their core interconnect and InfiniBand is used in thousands of data centers, high performance computing clusters and embedded applications [18]. Figure 1 provides an overview of the InfiniBand fabric.

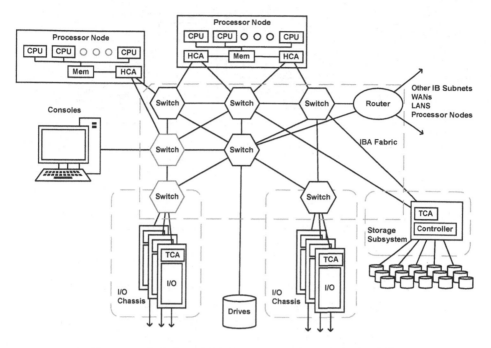

Figure 1. InfiniBand fabric overview (adapted from [5]).

Bus topologies enable multiple devices to connect to a shared physical medium, with all the devices in the same collision domain. This requires the end devices to implement collision detection and collision avoidance protocols. The requirement to support shared access and recover from collisions limits Ethernet bus network throughput to around 1 Gbps [15]. To improve performance, many networks employ star topologies that eliminate collisions via dedicated physical connections to end nodes. Dedicated links also provide flexibility in the choice of protocols implemented at each node [7].

Networks are limited by the speed of processors, input/output interfaces and network protocols. Fortunately, network device performance has steadily improved as manufacturers create chip sets with smaller feature sizes, more efficient computer architectures and faster clock speeds. As these improvements materialize, the governing bodies of network protocols must make careful decisions with respect to future protocols, considering the effects of compatibility with established network protocols. The growing demand for improved network performance and frustrations with the limitations of legacy technologies in the high performance computing domain led to the formation of the InfiniBand Trade Association to promote the use of the InfiniBand architecture.

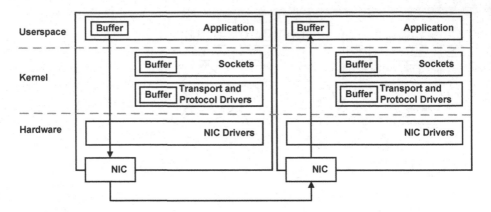

Figure 2. Remote direct memory access traffic flow (adapted from [5]).

Host processors are often responsible for virtualization, networking, storage and security applications. The computational power of the processors limits the performance of traditional data centers and high performance computing clusters. Remote direct memory access is a technology that enables data to be transferred with minimal host processor involvement. InfiniBand implements remote direct memory access in hardware to minimize intervention by host processors.

Figure 2 shows how remote direct memory access traffic moves between applications and avoids latencies incurred by buffers in the operating system kernel. Although the host processor may be responsible to authorize the transfer, the hardware-based remote direct memory access implementation bypasses the host kernel for execution.

Figure 3 shows a side-by-side comparison of the Ethernet and Infini-Band network stacks using the five-layer TCP/IP stack as a reference. Between the application and transport layers, InfiniBand uses verbs in place of Ethernet sockets. InfiniBand verbs are the basis for specifying application programming interfaces [2]. Additionally, InfiniBand has a number of transport services. The two primary types are reliable and unreliable connections, which are analogous to TCP and UDP, respectively. At the network layer, native InfiniBand employs local identifiers, global identifiers and globally unique identifiers that are analogous to and used in place of IP and MAC addresses. InfiniBand uses a subnet manager to configure local subnets. At least one subnet manager must be present in a subnet to manage all the switch and router setups, and reconfigure the subnet when a link drops or a new link appears [10].

InfiniBand is an interconnect for end nodes that includes processors, memory subsystems and input/output devices. At a minimum, subnets

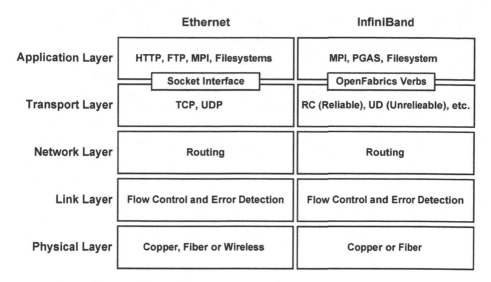

Figure 3. Ethernet and InfiniBand network stacks (adapted from [15]).

comprise two or more end nodes connected via channel adapters and managed by a subnet manager running on at least one device. InfiniBand subnets may also include a switch to take full advantage of the star topology. End nodes can be connected to multiple switches to create a switched fabric network [16].

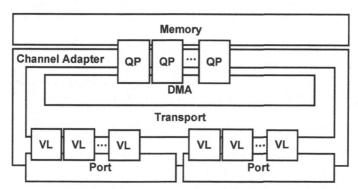

Figure 4. High-level design of a channel adapter (adapted from [15]).

Every end node in an InfiniBand network must have a channel adapter to generate and consume InfiniBand traffic. Figure 4 shows the high-level design of a channel adapter. A channel adapter typically has a few physical links that are multiplexed into independent data streams called virtual lanes (VLs). Each virtual lane is assigned a quality of service on a packet-boundary basis. Most channel adapters support up to 16 virtual lanes per physical link [10].

InfiniBand offloads traffic control from a software client using execution queues [10]. Figure 5 illustrates the InfiniBand communications stack in which control is offloaded from a software client to a work queue (WQ) managed by InfiniBand. Each communications channel has a queue pair (QP) comprising a send queue and receive queue assigned at the corresponding end node. A client places transactions in the work queue in the form of a work queue entry (WQE) that is processed by the channel adapter. When the transaction is completed, the channel adapter notifies the client by placing an entry in the completion queue (CQ) [10]. Complete hardware implementations of the InfiniBand network stack streamline InfiniBand communications models. They also enable applications to interface with InfiniBand solely using InfiniBand verbs.

Remote direct memory access in InfiniBand requires memory partitions to be protected and registered. Memory registration involves four steps:

- **Registration Request:** The client application sends a virtual address and length to the operating system kernel.

- **Virtual to Physical Mapping:** The operating system kernel handles memory mapping and reserves regions of physical memory for remote direct memory access transactions. This adds a level of security because a process cannot map memory that it does not own.

- **Channel Adapter Cache Mapping:** The channel adapter caches the virtual to physical mapping and issues an alphanumeric handle that includes a local key and remote key.

- **Handle Return:** The handle is returned to the client application.

It is important to note that all InfiniBand keys, namely, partition-level and queue-pair-level keys, are sent in plaintext across a network when remote direct memory access transactions are initiated. This presents an inherent security risk in that an adversary can gain access to the physical memory used by the end nodes in the network [15].

2.2 Convergent Technologies

The layered abstraction of the Open Systems Interconnection network model enables new network protocols to be integrated with legacy systems. The InfiniBand architecture was developed with this in mind –

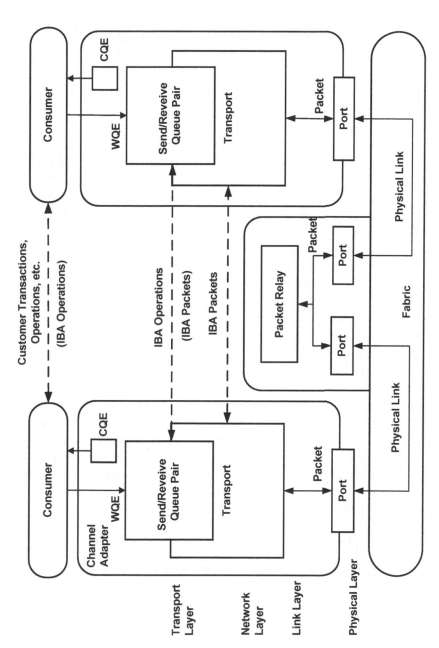

Figure 5. InfiniBand architecture transactions (adapted from [5]).

it is very flexible and backward-compatible with the conventional five-layer network stack. In fact, most channel adapters are compatible with InfiniBand and Ethernet.

Virtual Protocol Interconnect is a distributed messaging technology that supports InfiniBand and Ethernet. It enables the auto-sensing of Layer 2 protocols and may be configured to work with InfiniBand or Ethernet. This enables multi-port channel adapters to use one port for InfiniBand and the other for Ethernet. The integration of Virtual Protocol Interconnect in data centers and clusters allows InfiniBand and Ethernet networks to be hosted on the same hardware [10].

Remote direct memory access over Ethernet (RoE), remote direct memory access over Converged Ethernet (RoCE) and RoCE Version 2 (RoCEv2) are products of the convergence of the InfiniBand network and transport layers with the Ethernet link layer. RoE, which encapsulates InfiniBand packets in Ethernet frames, works natively in Ethernet environments and provides all the benefits of InfiniBand verbs. Congestion control, multicast, prioritization and fixed-bandwidth quality of service are optional in (regular) Ethernet, but are required in the native InfiniBand link layer. RoE, RoCE and RoCEv2 are often used interchangeably, but Converged Ethernet is a lossless link layer. Converged Ethernet uses all the features of the link layer of native InfiniBand [15].

RoCE does not carry an IP header so it cannot be routed across the boundaries of Ethernet Layer 2 subnets using regular IP routers. RoCEv2 is a straightforward extension of the RoCE protocol that replaces InfiniBand global route headers with IP and UDP headers. This enables RoCEv2 packets to traverse IP Level-3 routers [4]. The UDP transport header serves as a stateless encapsulation layer for the RDMA over IP protocol. These convergent communications approaches only affect packet format on the wire because remote direct memory access packets are generated and consumed below the application programming interface. Therefore, applications can operate over any form of remote direct memory access service in a completely transparent manner [4].

2.3   Security Concepts

This section briefly discusses IPsec encryption and security issues related to InfiniBand.

IPsec.   Figure 6 shows the format of an IPsec datagram using an encapsulating security payload (ESP) and the tunnel mode. The IPsec datagram meets the requirements of an IPv4 datagram. In the IPsec datagram, the payload comprises an encapsulating security payload header,

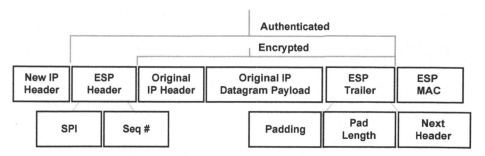

Figure 6. IPsec datagram format (adapted from [7]).

original IP datagram, encapsulating security payload trailer and authentication field.

IPsec headers and trailers create additional overhead that must be considered when configuring the maximum transfer unit (MTU) of a network interface. In total, the protocol suite can add more than 100 bytes of overhead to IP datagrams. Therefore, care must be taken to ensure that a payload combined with the IPsec headers does not exceed the maximum transfer unit of the network link. If the maximum transfer unit is exceeded, packets could be fragmented or dropped.

InfiniBand Security. Demand for high-performance, scalable and reliable networks for diverse applications has attracted considerable interest in InfiniBand networks. During the rapid development of the Infini-Band architecture, developers paid more attention to performance and cost efficiency than to security. For this reason, numerous security loopholes in the InfiniBand architecture have been identified. In fact, the design of secure clusters has recently emerged as a critical issue [17].

The confidentiality, integrity and availability triad covers the key security requirements for secure transmission across networks, and authentication is commonly added to the security triad to provide additional security:

- **Confidentiality:** Only the sender and intended recipient(s) may correctly decode or decrypt message contents.

- **Integrity:** A received message is correct and not altered.

- **Availability:** Services are accessible and available to authorized users.

- **Authentication:** The sender and recipient(s) are able to confirm the identities of each other.

Lee et al. [8, 9] have identified security vulnerabilities in the Infini-Band architecture that stem from its plaintext key management scheme. These vulnerabilities can be exploited with modest effort. Two major vulnerabilities are related to authentication.

As mentioned above, InfiniBand partitioning keys are sent in plaintext. An adversary who compromises partitioning keys would be able to transmit unauthorized InfiniBand remote direct memory access traffic. To address the problem, Lee et al. [8, 9] proposed a partition-level and queue-pair-level symmetric key management/distribution scheme. The partition-level key management scheme ensures that all communications in a partition use the same shared secret key. The queue-pair-level key management scheme guarantees confidentiality and integrity in a partition using temporary session keys between queue pairs. Simulation results have verified that the secret key management schemes harden the InfiniBand architecture with only marginal performance degradation induced by the encryption and authentication algorithms.

Several communications models such as RoCEv2 combine features of InfiniBand and high-speed Ethernet. As a result, most channel adapters and data processing units support InfiniBand as well as high-speed Ethernet. RoCEv2, unlike native InfiniBand, uses IP addresses at the network layer and is compatible with IPsec encryption. Mireles et al. [12] characterized the abilities of the NVIDIA Mellanox Innova Flex Smart-NIC and Innova IPsec Ethernet Adapter to offload and encrypt RoCEv2 traffic with IPsec-enabled hardware. Mireles and colleagues found that the Innova Flex SmartNIC and Innova IPsec Ethernet Adapter were unable to offload RoCEv2 traffic to the IPsec-enabled hardware.

Hintze et al. [3] investigated the offloading and encryption of RoCEv2 traffic using the NVIDIA Mellanox Bluefield-1 data processing unit suite of IPsec-enabled hardware accelerators. They found that the Bluefield-1 data processing unit was also unable to encrypt RoCEv2 traffic in hardware.

3.   Testbed Design

This research has sought to characterize the ability of Bluefield-2 data processing units to encrypt RoCEv2 traffic in hardware and to demonstrate methods for monitoring remote direct memory access traffic. To achieve these goals, a number of throughput tests were performed using NVIDIA Mellanox InfiniBand fabric utilities and network topologies.

Figure 7 shows the network topology used to characterize the performance of Bluefield-2 data processing unit hardware accelerators. The Bluefield-2 devices in the two workstations ride on sixteen lanes of pe-

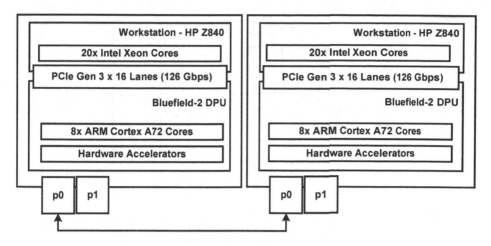

Figure 7. Performance measurement topology.

ripheral component interconnect express (PCIe) Gen 3. Each host has one data processing unit. The two Bluefield-2 data processing units are connected in tandem by a 100 Gbps fiber optic cable.

Figure 8 shows the network topology used to monitor remote direct memory access traffic and verify encryption. The network incorporates an intermediate workstation with a Bluefield-1 data processing unit. The Bluefield-1 device rides on sixteen lanes of PCIe Gen 3 and the data processing unit ports are connected by 100 Gbps fiber optic cables.

An NVIDIA Mellanox Bluefield-1 data processing unit combines a ConnectX-5 DX network adapter with an array of advanced reduced instruction set computer machines (ARM) cores and hardware accelerators. A Bluefield-1 device operates as an independent system that communicates with its host over 16 lanes of third or fourth generation PCIe, offering theoretical transfer rates of 128 Gbps or 256 Gbps, respectively. The card incorporates two multi-function 100 Gbps ports, 16 GB local DDR4 RAM, 16 Cortex A72 ARM cores and local persistent storage. Each core has a 48 KB I-cache and 32 KB D-cache. The ARM CPU also features a 1 MB L2 cache per two cores and two banks of 6 MB L3 cache with sophisticated eviction policies. The card has a tailored version of Ubuntu 18.04 provided by NVIDIA Mellanox that supports the development of new applications and the deployment of existing applications directly on the card. The applications can process and modify traffic before it is seen on the host. Thus, Bluefield-1 devices can host a variety of applications and services for networking, storage and security [11].

An NVIDIA Mellanox Bluefield-2 data processing unit employs a ConnectX-6 DX network adapter. The Bluefield-2 device communicates

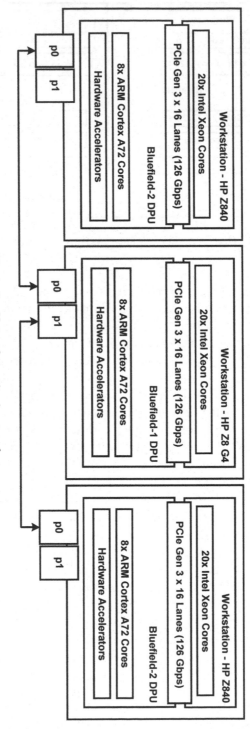

Figure 8.   Network monitoring topology.

with its host over 16 lanes of third/fourth generation PCIe. The card incorporates two multi-function 100 Gbps ports, 16 GB local DDR4 RAM, eight ARM Cortex A72 pipeline processors and local persistent storage. Each core has a 48 KB I-cache and 32 KB D-cache. The ARM CPU also features a 1 MB L2 cache per two cores and a 6 MB L3 cache with multiple eviction policies. The transfer rate of the Bluefield-2 DDR4 RAM is 3,200 Tbps. The card has a tailored version of Ubuntu 20.04 provided by NVIDIA Mellanox [14].

Although desirable, the high data throughput supported by the card can quickly overwhelm its processors and memory if all the traffic is directed through the Linux kernel. To address this problem, the card offers several hardware offload and acceleration features that operate directly on network traffic without routine involvement by the ARM CPU. This enables the ARM multi-core CPU to orchestrate the hardware to perform operations on traffic at high rates instead of processing all the traffic directly.

The Bluefield-1 device was installed on an HP Z8 G4 workstation and the Bluefield-2 devices were installed on two identical HP Z840 workstations. The HP Z8 G4 and HP Z840 workstations have up to PCIe Gen 3, which is capable of supporting 128 Gbps using 16 lanes. The PCIe Gen 3 provided sufficient throughput for the research although the Bluefield-1 and Bluefield-2 devices are compatible with PCIe Gen 4. Additionally, the HP Z8 G4 and HP Z840s each have 20 Intel Xeon Cores, 256 GB RAM and a 1 TB hard drive.

The ARM subsystem of a Bluefield data processing unit must have control of the ConnectX network adapter in order to interact with the hardware accelerators. This mode of operation is called SMARTNIC (embedded) mode. In this mode, a virtual bridge is required to forward packets through the Bluefield devices correctly. The Open Virtual Switch (OVS) and Data Plane Development Kit (DPDK) `testpmd` virtual bridges were evaluated in this research.

The Ubuntu Bluefield images provided by NVIDIA Mellanox are preloaded with OVS and DPDK. OVS interfaces with the operating system kernel and DPDK sits directly above the hardware. OVS tends to be straightforward because a user can rely on the kernel to manage application resources. On the other hand, DPDK requires a user to specify and reserve resources for DPDK applications manually. DPDK provides a platform for developing lightweight, custom userspace applications that interface closely with the hardware. This research compares the abilities of OVS and `testpmd` to provide virtual bridges for monitoring remote direct memory access in man-in-the-middle positions.

Table 1. Data gathering and analysis tools.

Tool	Description
top	Linux command-line tool that presents a real-time system summary, including CPU utilization and Linux processes
numactl	Linux command-line tool that runs processes with specific non-uniform memory access scheduling and memory placement policies
InfiniBand Fabric Utilities	NVIDIA Mellanox application bundle that includes several diagnostic and performance utilities
tcpdump	Free command-line packet analyzer
Wireshark	Free packet analyzer that provides useful decryption features

Table 1 describes the tools used to verify network configurations and conduct throughput tests.

4.   Experimental Scenarios

The research has sought to evaluate whether Bluefield-2 data processing units may be harnessed to add layers of security to the InfiniBand architecture. The experiments specifically investigated the ability of Bluefield-2 data processing units to encrypt RoCEv2 traffic and compared the performance of OVS and DPDK in forwarding RoCEv2 traffic.

NVIDIA Mellanox provides a tuning tool for Bluefield data processing units that optimizes network performance for a variety of use cases. However, this research did not employ the tuning tool because reverting the system to its original state would have required the reinstallation of the operating systems and software on the workstations and Bluefield data processing units. Although performance improvements were likely given incremental configuration changes, the results can be assumed to be representative of the impacts that encryption and hardware acceleration could have on system performance.

Throughput was employed as the response variable throughout the research. Message size was the primary independent variable for creating performance curves that characterize the performance of Bluefield-2 hardware accelerators and virtual switches.

Two experiments were conducted. The first experiment characterized the ability of Bluefield-2 data processing units to accelerate IPsec encryption of RoCEv2 traffic in hardware and the second experiment characterized the performance of OVS and DPDK when used as virtual bridges for TCP and RoCEv2 traffic:

- **Hardware Accelerator Characterization:** Previous work has determined that the hardware accelerators on a Bluefield-2 data processing unit significantly mitigate the performance degradation incurred when Ethernet/TCP frame packets are encrypted with IPsec. In fact, the performance for encrypted traffic was identical to the performance for plaintext traffic [1]. This experiment sought to build on the results of the previous research by investigating the ability of Bluefield-2 hardware accelerators to encrypt RoCEv2 traffic.

  The experiment involved two steps. Plaintext RoCEv2 throughput tests were conducted to provide a baseline for Bluefield-2 data processing unit performance. Next, the IPsec transport mode was configured and verified on the Bluefield-2 data processing units before an additional set of RoCEv2 throughput tests was performed.

- **Virtual Bridge Performance:** The Bluefield data processing unit in the middle of the monitoring network design in Figure 8 caused significant performance degradation to RoCEv2 traffic when OVS served as the virtual bridge on the card. This experiment compared the performance of OVS and DPDK when serving as virtual bridges in the monitoring network design. Additionally, the experiment sought to demonstrate the ability of each platform to sniff traffic by running `tcpdump` with OVS and `testpmd` with DPDK. Unlike `tcpdump`, `testpmd` is a lightweight virtual bridge DPDK application, not a packet analyzer. However, it was reasonable to expect that a DPDK traffic analyzer would have similar performance to `testpmd` when sniffing traffic. The experiment was only conducted with plaintext traffic because the virtual bridges merely forwarded packets.

  The experiment involved two steps. A series of throughput tests were conducted using iPerf3 to compare network performance when OVS and DPDK `testpmd` were used with Ethernet and TCP at the link and transport layers, respectively. Next, an additional set of throughput tests was conducted to compare the network performance of RoCEv2 traffic. The drop rates of the virtual bridges were recorded during all the throughput tests.

Performance Evaluation. The Kruskal-Wallis test is a non-parametric alternative for analyzing variance in situations where the normality assumption does not hold [13]. It employs an F-test analysis of variance that does not require normal residuals. Preliminary throughput tests revealed that network performance using the two designs in Figures 7 and 8 was non-normal. Therefore, the Kruskal-Wallis test is appropriate for analyzing the statistical significance of the data collected in the experiments.

Verification.   As noted in previous research [3], Ethernet traffic analyzers cannot sniff remote direct memory access traffic because kernel bypass packets never traverse the TCP/IP stack. The man-in-the-middle network topology shown in Figure 8 addresses this issue. Bridging the network with OVS on a Bluefield-1 forced traffic through the TCP/IP kernel stack on the card. Forwarding remote direct memory access traffic with this method significantly degraded network performance, but it enabled Ethernet traffic analyzers to sniff network traffic. This helped verify that the Bluefield-2 data processing units were configured properly and actually encrypted the packets.

Verifying IPsec encryption involved the following steps:

- Configuration of the Bluefield-2 data processing units with Ethernet at the link layer and configuration of the desired encryption settings.

- Configuration of the network in the monitoring topology (Figure 8).

- Sniffing of traffic sent across the network by running `tcpdump` and saving the sniffed traffic to a PCAP file.

- Verification of IPsec encryption by uploading the PCAP file to Wireshark to decrypt the captured packets using the known encryption key.

- Configuration of the network in the performance measurement topology by connecting the Bluefield-2 data processing units in tandem (Figure 7).

- Execution of the throughput tests with the verified network configuration.

Validation.   Confounding variables and uncontrolled factors can introduce noise in the experiment results. The Kruskal-Wallis analysis of variance test was applied to a full factorial design to identify the factors that have significant effects on throughput, the response variable.

Table 2. Full factorial design.

Number	Maximum Transfer Unit	RDMA Operation	Transport	Iterations
1	256	Read	DC	1,000
2	256	Read	DC	100,000
3	256	Read	RC	1,000
⋮	⋮	⋮	⋮	⋮
16	4,096	Write	RC	100,000

Table 2 shows how the factor levels were set during each trial of the full factorial design. Sixteen treatments were tested in a full factorial test of four, two level factors (2^4). Three replications of each treatment were performed to further reduce noise. In total, 48 RoCEv2 throughput tests (16 treatments × 3 replications) were performed in the screening test using the InfiniBand fabric utilities.

Only two factor levels were required for the screening test. Screening tests often work best when the factor levels have large differences. The maximum transfer units were set to 256 and 4,096 bytes because they corresponded to the minimum and maximum values supported by a Bluefield-2 data processing unit when handling RoCEv2 traffic. The maximum transfer units were evaluated because network performance is often dependent on packet size. Remote direct memory access read and write are foundational operations. Reliable connection and dynamically-connected transports, which operate similarly to TCP and UDP, respectively, were tested for the connection types. Additionally, 1,000 and 100,000 iterations were tested. Increased throughput test duration may improve the experimental results because longer tests can dilute the noise caused by systems throttling CPU clocks; many end nodes dynamically throttle clock rates to reduce power consumption. Each of these factors was configured using the command-line arguments of the InfiniBand fabric utility applications.

Applying the Kruskal-Wallis test to the results of the full factorial design determined that the maximum transfer unit, remote direct memory access operation type and iterations significantly affected the average RoCEv2 throughput. The effect of the maximum transfer unit was deemed to be significant at a 99.9% ($p = 2.2 \times 10^{-16}$) confidence interval, remote direct memory access operation type at a 99% ($p = 0.0077$) confidence interval and iterations at a 95% ($p = 0.0275$) confidence interval.

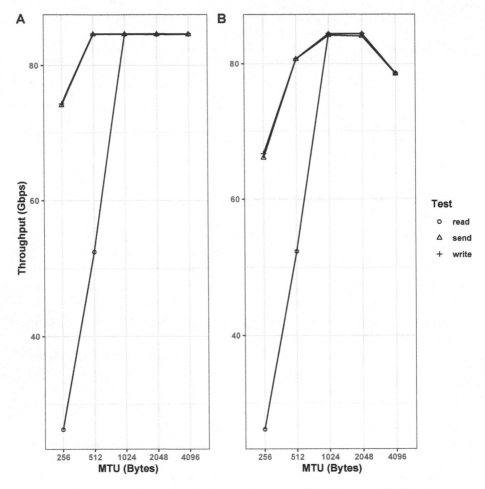

Figure 9. Hardware accelerator performance (A: plaintext, B: IPsec).

The Kruskal-Wallis test assumes that the data is independent of the run order. The experiments ensured independence from run order by randomizing the factor levels.

5. Experimental Results

This section presents the hardware accelerator characterization and virtual bridge performance results.

Hardware Accelerator Characterization.   Figure 9 shows the performance curves of the Bluefield-2 hardware accelerators for plaintext and IPsec-encrypted traffic. A total of 45 throughput tests were con-

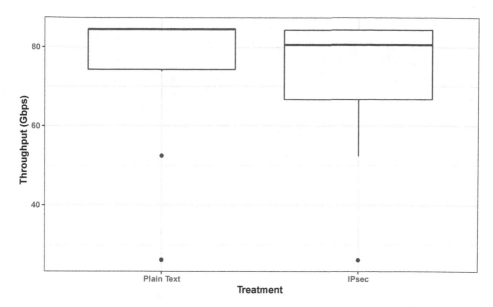

Figure 10. Comparison of plaintext and IPsec RoCEv2 performance.

ducted for each configuration. The Bluefield-2 hardware accelerators encrypted RoCEv2 traffic at a rate of nearly 86 Gbps.

Figure 10 shows that the Bluefield-2 hardware accelerators perform slightly better on average with plaintext traffic at a 99.9% ($p = 2.3 \times 10^{-9}$) confidence interval.

Virtual Bridge Performance. Virtual bridge performance was evaluated for Ethernet and RoCEv2 traffic; the monitoring capability was also evaluated:

- **Ethernet:** Figure 11 shows the performance curves of the OVS and DPDK `testpmd` virtual bridges with the network configured for Ethernet and TCP. The performance of OVS and DPDK `testpmd` reaches a maximum under 10 Gbps, but OVS performs slightly better than DPDK `testpmd` on average at a 99.9% ($p = 2.053 \times 10^{-6}$) confidence interval (Figure 12).

- **RoCEv2:** Figure 13 shows the performance curves of the OVS and DPDK `testpmd` virtual bridges with the network configured for RoCEv2. DPDK `testpmd` performs better than OVS at a 99.9% ($p = 2.2 \times 10^{-16}$) confidence interval (Figure 14). The performance of DPDK peaks around 70 Gbps. Interestingly, the performance of the remote direct memory access read operations across the DPDK

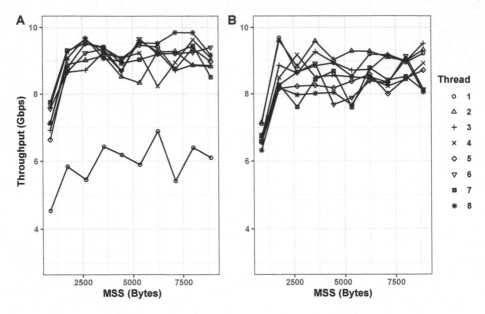

Figure 11. Qualitative Ethernet comparison (A: OVS, B: DPDK).

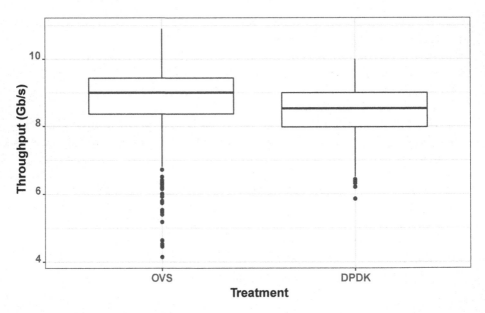

Figure 12. Statistical Ethernet comparison.

`testpmd` virtual bridge are significantly slower than the remote direct memory access write and send operations.

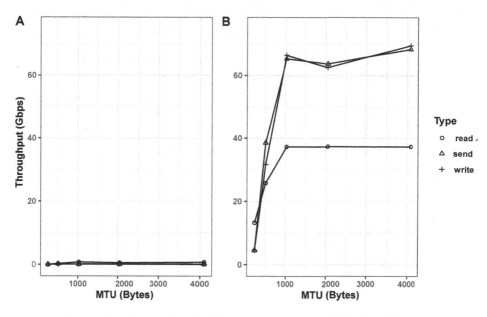

Figure 13. Qualitative RoCEv2 comparison (A: OVS, B: DPDK).

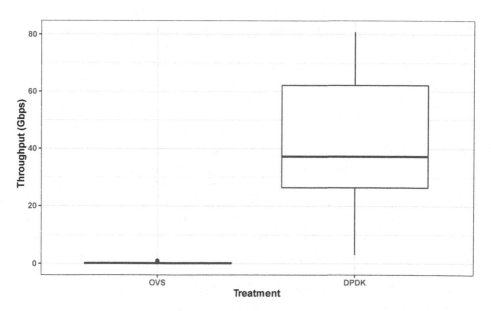

Figure 14. Statistical RoCEv2 comparison.

■ **Monitoring Capability:** Table 3 shows the `tcpdump` and `test-pmd` capture rates. Note that `testpmd` hardly dropped any TCP

Table 3.   Bridge capture capability.

Experimental Treatment	Total Packets Transmitted	Total Packets Received	Capture Rate
tcpdump Ethernet	526,628,133	152,672,846	28.99%
tcpdump RoCEv2	24,479,800	8,775.338	35.85%
testpmd Ethernet	2,055,767,590	2,055,672,563	99.99%
testpmd RoCEv2	923,504,628	920,113,923	99.81%

and RoCEv2 packets whereas tcpdump dropped a significant majority of the packets sent across the network. Also, tcpdump performed the same when forwarding TCP and RoCEv2 traffic.

6.   Conclusions

Convergent InfiniBand and Ethernet communications models such as RoCEv2 leverage the superior performance of remote direct memory access and existing TCP/IP network infrastructure. Direct memory access is a kernel bypass technology that prevents many conventional security applications from being able to sniff network traffic. However, it is imperative that this issue is addressed because these hybrid communications models are being deployed in critical infrastructure assets. Encryption and monitoring techniques such as deep packet inspection are mature and commonly-adopted practices in TCP/IP networks. The Bluefield-2 data processing unit provides a configurable platform capable of supporting a variety of security and network management applications. The Bluefield-2 data processing unit stands out from among other InfiniBand channel adapters because of its high performance, programmable ARM CPU and suite of crypto-enabled hardware accelerators. This research has investigated practical methods for securing the InfiniBand architecture by combining the computational capabilities of Bluefield-2 data processing units with conventional encryption and monitoring technologies.

The first experiment demonstrates that Bluefield-2 data processing units can support confidentiality, integrity and authentication in Infini-Band networks with minimal interaction from host CPUs. The performance of Bluefield-2 devices when encrypting RoCEv2 traffic is nearly identical to when it sends plaintext traffic, peaking at nearly 86 Gbps. This is an impressive level of performance given the computational demands of the AES-GCM cypher used by IPsec.

The second experiment demonstrates the performance benefits gained by using DPDK applications. The DPDK `testpmd` application bridges RoCEv2 traffic at nearly 70 Gbps. This is a significant improvement over the performance of OVS, which struggles to forward RoCEv2 traffic, only achieving a few Mbps of throughput.

Clearly, DPDK is able to support the high data rates created by RoCEv2. Future work will further investigate the abilities of Bluefield-2 data processing units and DPDK to encrypt and monitor network traffic. IPsec is incompatible with native InfiniBand because it does not use IP addresses. Encrypting native InfiniBand at the link layer has the potential to provide secure end-to-end communications. MACsec traditionally provides link layer encryption in Ethernet. Perhaps a similar protocol could be developed in a DPDK bare-metal application and implemented on Bluefield-2 data processing units.

The views expressed in this chapter are those of the authors, and do not reflect the official policy or position of the U.S. Air Force, U.S. Department of Defense or U.S. Government. This document has been approved for public release; distribution unlimited (Case #88ABW-2021-1014).

References

[1] N. Diamond, S. Graham and G. Clark, Securing InfiniBand networks with the Bluefield-2 data processing unit, *Proceedings of the Seventeenth International Conference on Cyber Warfare and Security*, pp. 459–468, 2022.

[2] P. Grun, Introduction to InfiniBand for End Users – Industry-Standard Value and Performance for High Performance Computing and the Enterprise, InfiniBand Trade Association, Beaverton, Oregon (`network.nvidia.com/pdf/whitepapers/Intro_to_IB_for_End_Users.pdf`), 2010.

[3] K. Hintze, S. Graham, S. Dunlap and P. Sweeney, InfiniBand network monitoring: Challenges and possibilities, in *Critical Infrastructure Protection XV*, J. Staggs and S. Shenoi (Eds.), Springer, Cham, Switzerland, pp. 187–208, 2022.

[4] InfiniBand Trade Association, Supplement to InfiniBand Architecture Specification, Volume 1, Release 1.2.1, Annex A17: RoCEv2, Beaverton, Oregon (`cw.infinibandta.org/document/dl/7781`), 2014.

[5] InfiniBand Trade Association, InfiniBand Architecture Specification, Volume 1, Release 1.6, Beaverton, Oregon (`www.infinibandta.org/ibta-specification`), 2022.

[6] InfiniBand Trade Association, InfiniBand Trade Association, Beaverton, Oregon (`www.infinibandta.org`, 2022.

[7] J. Kurose and K. Ross, *Computer Networking – A Top-Down Approach*, Pearson, Hoboken, New Jersey, 2017.

[8] M. Lee and E. Kim, A comprehensive framework for enhancing security in the InfiniBand architecture, *IEEE Transactions on Parallel and Distributed Systems*, vol. 18(10), pp. 1393–1406, 2007.

[9] M. Lee, E. Kim, K. Yum and M. Yousif, Instant attack stopper in the InfiniBand architecture, *Proceedings of the IEEE International Symposium on Cluster Computing and the Grid*, pp. 105–110, 2005.

[10] Mellanox Technologies, Introduction to InfiniBand, White Paper, Document No. 2003WP, Santa Clara, California (`www.mellanox.com/pdf/whitepapers/IB_Intro_WP_190.pdf`), 2003.

[11] Mellanox Technologies, NVIDIA Mellanox BlueField Data Processing Unit (DPU), Data Processor Product Brief, Sunnyvale, California, 2020.

[12] L. Mireles, Implications and Limitations of Securing an InfiniBand Network, M.S. Thesis, Department of Electrical and Computer Engineering, Air Force Institute of Technology, Wright-Patterson Air Force Base, Ohio, 2020.

[13] D. Montgomery, *Design and Analysis of Experiments*, John Wiley and Sons, Hoboken, New Jersey, 2019.

[14] NVIDIA Corporation, NVIDIA Bluefield-2 DPU Data Center Infrastructure on a Chip, Datasheet, Santa Clara, California (`www.nvidia.com/content/dam/en-zz/Solutions/Data-Center/documents/datasheet-nvidia-bluefield-2-dpu.pdf`), 2022.

[15] D. Panda and S. Sur, Designing Cloud and Grid Computing Systems with InfiniBand and High-Speed Ethernet: A Tutorial, presented at the *Cluster, Cloud and Grid Workshops* (`www.ics.uci.edu/~ccgrid11/files/ccgrid11-ib-hse_last.pdf`), 2011.

[16] G. Pfister, An introduction to the InfiniBand architecture, in *High Performance Mass Storage and Parallel I/O: Technologies and Applications*, H. Jin, T. Cortes and R. Buyya (Eds.), John Wiley and Sons, New York, pp. 617–632, 2001.

[17] B. Rothenberger, K. Taranov, A. Perrig and T. Hoefler, ReDMArk: Bypassing RDMA security mechanisms, *Proceedings of the Thirtieth USENIX Security Symposium*, pp. 4277–4292, 2021.

[18] E. Strohmaier, J. Dongarra, H. Simon and M. Meuer, TOP 500 The List, Prometeus, Sinsheim, Germany (`www.top500.org/statistics/list`), 2022.

Printed in the United States
by Baker & Taylor Publisher Services